Water 4.0

Water 4.0

The Past, Present, and Future of
the World's Most Vital Resource

David Sedlak

Yale UNIVERSITY PRESS/NEW HAVEN & LONDON

Yale University Press books may be purchased in quantity for educational,
business, or promotional use. For information, please e-mail
sales.press@yale.edu (U.S. office) or sales@yaleup.co.uk (U.K. office).

Designed by Mary Valencia.
Set in Minion and Futura types by Westchester Book Group.
Printed in the United States of America.

Library of Congress Catalogin-in-Publication Data

Sedlak, David L.
    Water 4.0 : the past, present, and future of the world's most vital
resource / David Sedlak.
        pages cm
    Includes bibliographical references and index.
    ISBN 978-0-300-17649-0 (hardback)
    1. Water—History   2. Water and civilization—History.   3. Water
resources development—History.   4. Water-supply engineering—
History.   I. Title.
    GB659.6.S44 2014
    333.91—dc23
                                                            2013025433

A catalogue record for this book is available from the British Library.

This paper meets the requirements of ANSI/NISO Z39.48–1992
(Permanence of Paper).

10 9 8 7 6 5 4

Contents

Preface

Most of the time we can go about our daily lives without knowing anything about the hidden world of water. The miles of pipes that bring water into our homes from distant locations, the treatment plants that ensure the wastes we pour into the sink and flush down the toilet don't pollute the local river, and the network of storm drains that keep the rain from flooding our homes continue to operate silently, day and night, whether or not we are aware of their existence. These unsung heroes of modern urban life and the people who run them are happy to stay out of the limelight. Except for periods when major investments are required, there really isn't much need to understand how water travels in and out of our cities. Unfortunately, it looks like we are approaching one of those periods.

The need for change bombards us through the media. How many times in recent years have you read about a city squabbling with farmers and environmental groups over water rights? Another article connecting climate change and the increasing frequency of severe droughts or exceptional floods? Or perhaps it's a government report about a familiar pharmaceutical compound showing up in drinking water? These seemingly disparate problems are all signs that water systems built in the nineteenth century and later retrofit with twentieth-century technologies may not be up to the challenges of the twenty-first century.

In response to the growing inadequacies evident in our existing approach to water, politicians, entrepreneurs, multinational corporations, and environmentalists have stepped up to advocate for their vision of a better way of handling water. Some claim that water shortages can be solved by investing in the next generation of treatment plants capable of purifying sewage to a point where it can be piped back into reservoirs or in desalination plants that can turn seawater into drinking water. Those inclined toward minimizing our impact on the environment advocate for water conservation, expanded use of local water sources, and integration of natural processes into the system designed to collect and treat water. And still others tell us that the crisis is one of our own making and that the answers to all of our water problems can be found in commonsense reform of the inefficient institutions that are responsible for allocating and regulating urban water.

How can someone who is not already an expert make informed judgments about the hidden world of urban water? About twenty years ago, when I started getting interested in these issues, I encountered a problem: the books on water intended for a general audience were too general, with large sections dedicated to disparate issues like wasteful agricultural water use, destruction of aquatic habitat, and the water and sanitation needs in the developing world. The more specialized books, reports, and scientific papers on urban water systems I eventually found, along with my own experiences working with people who were trying to overcome some of these problems, filled in many of the gaps in my knowledge, but that's not a path most of us have the time and inclination to follow.

After I learned my way around the topic, I continued to meet members of the public who craved more information about urban water issues, but it was not until 2009, when I was asked to give a talk to several thousand students and community members at Gustavus Adolphus College, that I thought I might have a way to help fill this gap. For my talk, I decided that the most effective way to make the science of potable water reuse more accessible to a general audience was to begin with an explanation of how drinking water systems have evolved over the centuries. Preparing a few slides on the history of drinking water and sewage treatment at the start of my presentation turned out to be a great way to put the problem into perspective, and it didn't require a lot of research on my part to put together a broad overview. At the time, I didn't realize that I had started a much larger project. The success I had in explaining current water problems by providing the historical background sent me on a four-year journey to fill the gaps in my knowledge about the origins of the problems that we currently face and about the wide range of solutions that are being debated by people on the front lines of our current water challenges.

For me, the greatest surprise has been the degree to which the urban water story goes beyond science and technology. As I studied the past, I came to appreciate the ways in which the water systems that we are struggling to maintain and improve are an integral part of the success of our great cities. The world of urban water has been populated by people who were trained in the practices of their times but had to invent new approaches for overcoming the problems that arose as their cities expanded. Whatever the era, when it came time to think about obtaining water, draining streets, and disposing of wastes, the engineers responsible for urban water systems first turned to the strategies that had succeeded in the past, adding incremental improvements as they increased the size of their systems to accommodate an expanding population. Eventually, they reached a point where the old ways were no longer viable. Facing the inertia that frequently accompanies calls for new spending on infrastructure, they struggled with failing water systems for decades until society finally reached a consensus about the need for change. Even after the need for a new approach was recognized, the path was not always clear. Some innovative, new ideas faded away as their shortcomings became evident. Others only improved over time as operating experience made them more efficient. After a while, the cities where the problems had been particularly acute pioneered new ways of handling water that became the norm throughout the developed world.

Viewed as just another stage in the evolution of urban water systems, our current situation does not seem so intractable. Water shortages, flooded streets, and a growing list of water pollutants, coupled with a lack of willingness to pay for upkeep and improvements, certainly feel like a crisis to the people who are struggling to keep the water moving. But our current challenges are not all that different from those that were solved by previous generations. Urban water systems will always need an occasional upgrade. Perhaps this time the added complication of climate change, along with the challenges associated with providing water to tens of millions of people living in the same watershed, is making the problem more complex. But it is difficult to imagine that the rapid advances in electronics, materials science, and biotechnology of recent decades cannot help us to solve these problems.

The repeated cycle of growth, failure, and reinvention that has occurred over the past 2,500 years of urban water systems can be likened to a series of revolutions. The first revolution, Water 1.0, occurred as the piped water systems and sewers first built by the ancient Romans were replicated in European cities that were growing very quickly during the first wave of global industrialization. As these cities continued to expand, public health suffered because the massive volumes of wastes flowing out of sewers transmitted waterborne diseases such as cholera and typhoid. Drinking water treatment, or Water 2.0, was the next revolution—stemming the spread of waterborne disease and leading to unimagined health benefits. Jump ahead half a century to a world in which modern technology and continued economic progress had caused cities to expand until the wastes pouring out of their sewers were causing more than a little bit of trouble immediately downstream. Following decades of decline in the rivers, lakes, and estuaries surrounding cities, a third revolution—Water 3.0—occurred as sewage treatment plants became a standard feature of urban water systems.

Another half century later and all signs point to the approach of a fourth revolution, Water 4.0, as continued population growth and climate change stretch the ability of urban water systems to meet our needs. At this stage of the cycle, the nature of the challenge is poorly understood by the people who will eventually have to make the big decisions. In the cities where water systems are showing the greatest signs of stress, the problems manifest themselves in different ways. In some places, it's too much water, while others struggle with chronic shortages and still others are struggling to maintain pipe networks and treatment plants that are falling apart under the pressure of esca-lating maintenance costs. The components of the fourth revolution are still a work in progress, with multiple paths leading to better water systems, provided that we are willing to invest the resources, energy, and political will needed to make them a reality. Decisions about the future of urban water systems are best made by an informed public. I hope that this book and the associated website (www.water4point0 .com) will not only contribute to a broader, deeper understanding of the issues, but also motivate readers to become personally involved in efforts to improve their community's water system.

Acknowledgments

When I started researching and writing this book, I had no idea how much dedication it takes to create one. It would have never been written without a lot of help from people who share my passion for a better water future.

I am deeply appreciative to Naomi Lubeck for her encouragement and critical reviews of my writing. She helped me to make the transition from dull technical writing to a text that might hold the interest of someone other than an ambitious graduate student. Any lapses back into jargon and passive voice are entirely my fault.

I am also very grateful to my agent, Andy Ross, who stuck with me as I learned my way around the art and inexact science of putting together a book. When the world lost its best bookstore, it gained a fantastic literary agent. Thanks also to my acquisitions editor Jean Thomson Black at Yale University Press for editorial comments on the manuscript; to Sara Hoover for guiding me through all of the tiny but important details that go into a book; to my manuscript editor, Julie Carlson, for her thoughtful copyediting; and to Bill Nelson for his fantastic maps.

I appreciate the help of the people who shared their opinions about water or read and commented on various chapters. Peter David, Mike Kavanaugh, Sasha Harris-Lovett, and members of my research group all provided useful suggestions. Urs von Gunten, Janet Hering, and many other Swiss colleagues provided thought-provoking discussions during my sabbatical in Zurich. And I owe a special thanks to Jürg Hoigné for convincing me that the Middle Ages were a lot more than a bunch of cathedrals and crusaders. I am also grateful to Ronald Linsky, founding executive director of the National Water Research Institute, for his initial faith in my abilities. He had a big impact on the contents of the book even if he never had a chance to read the drafts.

Through the many hours of research that went into writing this book I have come to appreciate the efforts of the great scholars who plowed through the primary literature to reconstruct often forgotten moments in water history. Without them we would not understand how our water systems reached their current stage of development. I learned a lot from the works of scholars such as Martin Melosi, Joel Tarr, A. Trevor Hodge, Roberta Magnusson, and Donald Reid. Likewise, the many engineers, scientists, and policy experts whose works I relied on for my research were indispensable. I also gained a better understanding of the current state of urban water systems and efforts to create Water 4.0 through my interactions with leading practitioners like Mike Wehner, Harry Seah, Alan Plummer, and Rhodes Trussell. I apologize in advance for the errors that I have made as I tried to translate your teachings into a coherent narrative.

I cannot fully express my gratitude to my family. Meg, Jane, and Adam, I appreciate all of your patience in listening to early drafts of chapters, bearing with me during my moments of complete distraction, and maintaining a good sense of humor while touring the sewers of Paris, seeking the outlet of the Cloaca Maxima, and being dragged through various wetlands, recycling plants, and water features. I promise no sewage on the next family vacation.

Finally, I want to express my gratitude to Dick Luthy, Jörg Drewes, and the members of the National Science Foundation's Engineering Research Center on Reinventing the Nation's Urban Water Infrastructure (ReNUWIt). It's nice to know that there are so many talented people who are willing to devote their energy and creativity to writing the owner's manual for Water 4.0.

Water 4.0

1

Water Supply in Rome, the World's First Metropolis

I f water is the essential ingredient of life, then water supply is the essential ingredient of civilization. In ancient times, when people first began gathering in settlements for trade and mutual protection, they tended to locate within a short distance of their drinking water. But as settlements grew into villages and villages gave way to cities, people were forced to live farther away from their water source. Initially, the challenge of supplying areas of the city that were far from water was solved by digging a well or by paying for home delivery of water.[1] For the inhabitants of the first cities, obtaining water was just one more challenge that had to be overcome to reap the benefits of urban living.

As time passed, cities experimented with ways to import water. For example, around 700 BCE, inhabitants of the city of Erbil, in northern Iraq, dug gently sloping horizontal tunnels known as qanats to route groundwater into the city from a distance of approximately twenty kilometers (twelve miles) away.[2] Around the same time, the Greeks dug shallow canals to divert water into Troy and Athens from springs in the nearby hills.[3]

Densely packed groups of houses and the compressed soils that made up city streets also required drainage systems to prevent flooding. Early civilizations in the Indus Valley and Mesopotamia developed elaborate systems of gutters and covered channels for directing any water that accumulated in the streets into the nearest waterway. In many cases, the drainage systems included a way to collect drinking water: cisterns were built to capture clean water that ran off the roofs of buildings.[4]

These early prototypes made it clear that there were technological solutions to each of the major problems of urban water supply and drainage. But credit for the development of Water 1.0—a complete system of importing water, distributing it to homes and public spaces through a network of pipes, and returning used water to the environment—goes to the ancient Romans.

When it came time to take water to the next level, Roman water engineers didn't really have a choice: their city's water demand grew too big for the local sources. Before the Romans, the biggest cities in the ancient world rarely had more than 100,000 people. Provided that the climate was not too arid and the geology didn't preclude the use of shallow wells, cities of this size could usually manage by using local sources of water. But Rome was different. By around 300 BCE, the city's population had grown to somewhere around half a million people who not only needed to drink, but also loved baths and other forms of water recreation.[5] After Roman society began to thrive, the Tiber River (which runs through Rome), the shallow groundwater, and the local springs were no longer able to meet the needs of the thirsty city. In response, over the next five hundred years the city's engineers built a water system that ultimately imported enough water to supply Rome with a daily allotment comparable to that of our modern cities.[6]

When someone mentions ancient Rome's water supply, what first comes to mind are the graceful arches and elevated structures that crossed the arid valleys leading to the city. The iconic bridges, arcades, and viaducts of Rome are remarkable examples of the advances that Roman engineers made in structural engineering, hydraulics, and surveying. They also exemplify Rome's ability to create durable structures with concrete and masonry.[7] Yet the graceful, elevated sections of the aqueduct, while essential to the transport of water over long distances, are just a small part of the story: they made up only around 5 percent of the length of Rome's imported water system.[8] Furthermore, the Romans tried to avoid building them whenever possible, because they were costly and prone to failure. For example, the elevated section of the Aqua Claudia aqueduct took fifteen years to build and during its first two decades of use was only in service about half the time. Elevated structures were weak links in the Roman water supply chain. If the topography around the city had been more favorable, the Roman engineers would have avoided them entirely.[9]

Most of Rome's aqueducts actually consist of canals or underground pipes and tunnels that were made from masonry or cut into rock (the word aqueduct is derived from aqua—"water"—and ductus, "enclosed passage"). Although the entire Roman water system worked by gravity, maintenance of the reservoirs and aqueducts required vigilance so that damaged pipes and tunnels would be fixed quickly and debris that could block the flow of water would be removed. All of this maintenance and the construction of new aqueducts to meet the city's growing water demands required both funding from the emperor and donations by private citizens.[10]

Outside the city, much of the imported water system was hidden from view. The citizens of Rome could only see what their money had bought when the imported water entered the city on elevated structures, but these reminders of the infrastructure investment could get lost in the bustle of the city. To make the people aware of their accomplishments, Rome's leaders decorated the arches of the arcades where the aqueducts entered the city and built ornate fountains in public squares.[11] All of this extra effort can be seen as a political statement about the good works that the government had done rather than a tribute to the gods or an altruistic attempt to beautify the city. When Rome's aqueducts were rebuilt at the start of the Renaissance, the popes made sure that these decorative fountains were restored and updated for many of the same reasons.

In contrast to the Roman practice of building monuments to increase awareness of the city's hydraulic assets, most water arrives in modern cities with little fanfare. When fountains are built in public spaces, they are more likely to commemorate some nearly forgotten historical event or a deceased political figure than they are to celebrate the engineering prowess or institutional organization that was required to make the water flow. Perhaps if our water utilities took a cue from the Romans and advertised their accomplishments with beautiful fountains, they would have an easier time convincing the public about the need to invest in the upkeep of the system.

The aqueducts behind the fountains truly are engineering marvels when you consider that the Romans—without the aid of backhoes, concrete mixers, or satellite-enhanced surveying systems—built tunnels to exacting tolerances that followed the natural slopes of the hillsides. Placing the water supply underground avoided many of the challenges posed by viaducts. It also made the system more difficult for enemies to sabotage and minimized the likelihood that the water would be polluted as it flowed into the city.

Although the operation of a gravity-fed underground water delivery system may seem like a straightforward task, the Romans had to resolve a number of difficult problems in their quest to create a system that could reliably deliver water. Over a period of trial and error that spanned five centuries, the ancient Romans came up with concrete that could cure when exposed to water, arches capable of bearing the weight of massive volumes of water, and a number of other useful inventions.[12] For example, some sections of the aqueduct had to go down steep hills. Water flowing along these sections would move so fast that it would erode away the channel. The Romans solved this problem by installing stone structures in the aqueduct that made the bottom of the channel rough and so slowed the water's momentum.[13]

When the aqueduct crossed through a valley, it was necessary to move it up the next hill without the use of mechanical pumps. Roman engineers solved this problem by building massive inverted siphons that used the following downstream section of the aqueduct to help pull the water over the hill.[14] (If you have ever used a short length of garden hose to empty out an old aquarium or to take some gasoline out of your car's gas tank, you know how this works on a small scale: you fill the hose with water, or some other fluid, and as long as the place where the fluid leaves the hose is at a lower elevation, it will flow up and out. The Roman inverted siphons worked this way, except their "tubes" were made of bundles of lead pipes, each twenty-five centimeters [ten inches] in diameter.[15])

Roman engineers also had to grapple with changing conditions at the water source. Sometimes the water that they wanted to route through the aqueduct contained clay and sand that had been stirred up by a recent storm. If they let the sediment-laden water into the water distribution pipes, the pipes might clog. The Romans solved this problem by building wide troughs within the aqueduct system where the water velocity would slow enough to cause the particles to settle out (like sand in a lazy river) and where these particles could be removed easily by maintenance crews.[16]

Springs and streams located in the hills around the city fed the aqueducts and in most cases were easily connected to the water supply system. Sometimes, however, more complex engineering was employed. For example, the Anio Novus Aqueduct took its water from a reservoir that had originally been built to create a lake at Emperor Nero's villa. The forty-meter-high (130-foot) dam that held back the river remained the highest dam in the world for 1,500 years.[17]

A total of eleven aqueducts, with a cumulative length of over four hundred kilometers (250 miles), were built as Rome's water demand grew.[18] The Romans developed considerable expertise during the expansion of their water supply, because each successive project posed new and more difficult challenges. The knowledge that the Romans accrued while constructing their imported water systems allowed them to act as the world's first multinational construction company as they spread Water 1.0 to far-flung parts of the empire.

Ultimately, the aqueducts brought water into their capitol from distances as far away as approximately eighty kilometers (fifty miles). On a map of ancient Rome's aqueduct system, you can see the pattern that would later be repeated in the imported water systems of cities

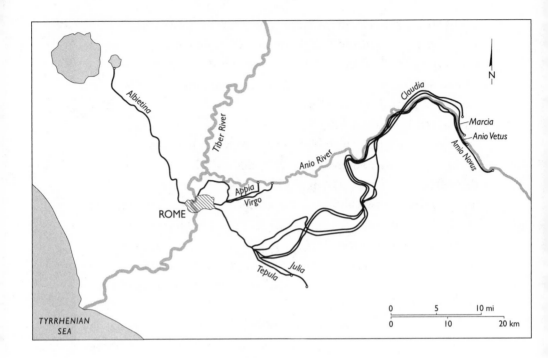

The aqueducts of ancient Rome.

like Paris, New York, and Los Angeles: as the population needing water grew, the water system's canals extended ever farther from the city center, much like the ever-expanding root system of a growing plant.

Delivery of imported water to the fountains was quite a feat, but it solved only part of the problem. Because there were advantages to living close to the heart of the city, Rome experienced the same housing pressures that we encounter in cities today. That is, as its population density increased, detached housing became a luxury reserved for the privileged class. For the average Roman, home was an apartment in a building three to six stories high, and because Roman tenements weren't equipped with indoor plumbing, water had to be lugged upstairs. It isn't much of a surprise, then, that most Roman water use happened at street level.[19]

In contrast to the masses, rich and influential Romans often had water piped directly into their homes, to a small fountain in a central courtyard. But the right to have piped water required official permission that could be difficult to secure. As a result, the rich often bribed local officials or surreptitiously connected their homes to the public water supply. In a survey of water use, Frontinus, the Roman water commissioner who served at the end of the first century CE, complained about the practice of "puncturing" the water system by making illegal connections. He wasn't certain how many illegal connections had been made in Rome, but he assumed that the practice was pervasive because of the large numbers of illegal pipes his workers had discovered as they repaired the streets.[20]

The fountains and water pipes that conveyed the water into Roman homes were made of lead, which seemed like a wonderful material for plumbing. Lead-containing ores are relatively easy to find, and lead is perfect for making into pipes because it melts at a low temperature and can be molded easily into all kinds of shapes. Unfortunately, lead is also a potent neurotoxin. The Roman engineer Vitruvius and his contemporaries were well aware of this problem and noted that lead pipes were unhealthy and should be avoided because they could cause water to "become corrupted." Even so, the Romans employed them everywhere because they were useful and convenient, and because there were few other choices for material from which to make pipes.[21] Indeed, the word "plumbing" is derived from the Latin word for lead, plumbum, which also provides us with its abbreviation on the periodic table—Pb.

In the late 1970s, when scientists were becoming increasingly aware of the health hazards associated with leaded gasoline and lead pipes used in modern plumbing, a number of books and papers were written in which the fall of Rome was blamed on exposure to lead.[22] Although this theory has not been embraced by classical scholars, who can identify many more viable explanations for the downfall of Rome, it is clear that the Romans were exposed to massive quantities of lead from sources unrelated to their water supply.[23] The Romans used lead salts to sweeten their wine, and they cooked and stored acidic foods in lead-lined containers under conditions that would leach large quantities of lead.[24]

The pipes that transported water around the city were another possible source of lead exposure for the ancient Romans. But when it came to water pipes, the Romans got lucky: the geology of the hills surrounding the city likely reduced the potential for lead to leach out of the water pipes. The region where the city's water supply was obtained had ample deposits of calcite—a relatively soluble mineral. The calcium present in the imported water appears to have precipitated inside the lead pipes, forming a protective mineral layer that prevented lead from leaching into the water.[25] In fact, contemporary engineers take advantage of this phenomenon when they manage water distribution systems that contain lead pipes and lead-soldered plumbing. By increasing the pH of the water to encourage the development of protective mineral layers, they prevent the lead from leaching out of those old pipes and soldered joints that are too expensive to find and replace.[26]

Once imported water was available, the Romans came up with all kinds of creative ways to use it. During the height of the empire, the Romans staged mock naval battles in which thousands of slaves reenacted historic fights, complete with real blood. One of the Roman aqueducts was even built mainly for filling up the artificial ponds used for the mock battles. It is notable that the Romans chose the water supply with the lowest-quality water for this purpose, saving the water sources with the lowest salt content and fewest suspended sediments for the fountains and private water supplies.[27] Although we no longer stage mock naval battles, we still use lots of water to entertain ourselves at golf courses, parks, and swimming pools. As we'll see, the Roman practice of building a separate water supply system for uses where quality is not as critical is becoming an increasingly popular approach in places where modern water supplies are limited.

The Romans also were enthusiastic about bathing: Rome was packed with public baths with hot water supplied through a sophisticated system of heaters and plumbing. The baths were social centers that served various recreational purposes, much like modern-day health clubs. In addition to getting clean, you could meet up with your friends, attend a lecture, or get some exercise at the baths. The typical Roman washed every day and took baths almost as often, especially before festivals and public holidays.

There is considerable uncertainty about Roman water consumption, with estimates of daily per capita water use ranging from approximately 200 to 1,200 liters (50 to 300 gallons), depending on one's assumptions about how the aqueducts were operated.[28] Whichever assumptions are correct, it is clear that Roman per capita water use was comparable to that of modern cities and far exceeded the amount needed for consumption and basic hygiene.

Because Rome's water supply relied on springs and streams whose flow varied according to the season, the city received less water during dry periods. As a way of prioritizing the various uses of water during times of drought, the tank where water from the aqueduct entered the city, known as the *castellum divisorium,* was designed with separate outlet pipes for the public fountains, private homes, and baths. This configuration ensured that after a minimum amount of water entered each of the three water distribution systems, the excess would flow to the public fountains where most people obtained their water, meaning that these public fountains would normally receive the largest water allocations. At Pompeii, the *castellum divisorium* had sluice gates that could be put in front of the pipes to cut off the flow during a drought.[29] Some modern cities also have set up priorities for water use during droughts, but we often rely on voluntary compliance or enlist utility employees and city workers to catch people who are illegally watering their lawns or washing their cars. If our modern water distribution systems prioritized among users as the Roman systems did, it would be a lot easier to ration water during droughts.

Opinions vary on whether the Roman water systems ran continuously or if there were valves to control the flow. The Roman water system almost certainly had a mechanism for stopping the flow to individual parts of the aqueduct by shoving an obstruction into the pipes or diverting the flow around a section to facilitate repairs. It is also possible that the aqueducts were shut off at night and sections were used for water storage.[30] It was, however, impractical to shut off the flow of water within the city, because the system was not built to withstand the high pressure that would develop if the flow was stopped at the distribution points.[31] Much of Rome's high per capita water use was really just water from fountains draining into the streets. But what did the Romans do with all of this water that was flowing out of the fountains and baths?

The used water had to be drained from the city to prevent flooding. Initially, much of the water flowed into the Cloaca Maxima, which was a drain that had been built earlier to help remove water from the low-lying areas adjacent to the river. In its early years, the Cloaca Maxima was a channel with reinforced masonry walls.[32] Over time, the channel was covered to make it easier to cross. Eventually, more drains were built to serve areas that were not already connected. Slowly, the cloacae, or sewers, of Rome were born. The gravity-fed sewer system was constantly supplied with lots of flowing water from the fountains, which kept it relatively free from noxious smells.

The Cloaca Maxima still drains the Roman Forum to the Tiber River, but it has been integrated into the city's modern sewer system. You can find an access point (which, unfortunately, is behind a locked gate) about thirty meters (one hundred feet) south of Julius Caesar's temple, and its final discharge point can be found just above the Ponte Palatino Bridge.

The Romans were pretty proud of their sewers: the Forum had been built on a swamp, but the Cloaca Maxima kept the center of the city dry and carried away the waste and debris that accumulated in the streets. Clean water was great, and the fountains celebrated it every day. But getting rid of the dirty water was also an important accomplishment and in typical Roman fashion, a goddess was needed: Cloacina, who bore a striking resemblance to the goddess Venus, and was

A Roman coin from around 50 BCE depicting the shrine of Cloacina.
Photo courtesy of Jon C. Schladweiler.

sometimes referred to as Venus Cloacina, even had her own shrine, coins, and prayers.[33]

Eventually, some enterprising Roman came up with the idea of cutting a series of holes in the ground above the cloacae. Thus the first public toilets were invented. Many of these facilities were conveniently located next to the bathhouses. Although they didn't have partitions between them like modern public toilets, they were preferable to the other option, which was to use a bucket or chamber pot that had to be carried to a central location, where it was emptied into cesspools or barrels that were ultimately dumped into the cloacae.

Rome also had a system of public urinals that was operated separately from the toilets. The operators of the urinals were happy to have visitors, because urine was a valuable commodity that could be sold to fabric shops and laundries. The high ammonia content of urine made it very useful for removing oil and dirt from wool, and presumably the urine smell didn't stay behind after the fabric was washed. The sale of urine from the public urinals was subjected to a special tax.

This practice gave rise to the saying attributed to the Emperor Vespasian, who ruled Rome from 69–79 CE. When asked about the lowly source of his revenues, he replied, "Pecunia non olet" (Money does not stink).[34]

The practice of collecting urine in a separate system and reusing it is coming back into vogue, but this time the proponents of urine collection are more interested in using it as a source of fertilizer.[35] Things are harder for the contemporary urine collectors, however: because modern technology and global trade routes have made it easier to acquire elsewhere the ammonia, phosphorus, and other essential nutrients found in urine, it is hard to make urine collection, treatment, and transport economically competitive.

Without regular upkeep, much of the city's water system failed as the Roman Empire crumbled. As Rome fell, its population decreased from a peak of around a half million to fewer than thirty thousand in medieval times, when only one of the city's aqueducts was maintained as a water supply.[36] The remaining aqueducts fell into disuse as scavengers hauled away many of the fountains and water pipes for scrap metal and used much of the aqueducts for building material. Eventually, the popes refurbished the aqueducts and built new fountains to beautify the city before turning the operation of the water system over to the municipal government. The water system in Rome has been upgraded over the years, but at its core much of it remains the system built by the ancients.

By the time the empire fell, the system that the Romans had built in their hometown had been replicated throughout the empire, thereby spreading the concept of Water 1.0 to Europe and Asia Minor. The blueprints for building and operating aqueducts and sewers were retained in church libraries, and the promise of a reliable and convenient water system lived on among people who resided in former parts of the empire where the abandoned aqueducts remained. Even so, much of the knowledge that Roman engineers had acquired on subjects such as matching water sources to their ultimate uses, surviving droughts by establishing priorities for water delivery among users, and separating wastes to facilitate more efficient recycling was forgotten in the rush to build bigger and better water systems. Perhaps the rediscovery of some of these Roman approaches will help us to design Water 4.0.

2

The Bucket Era

The Western world was very different after the fall of the Roman Empire. Without Rome's engineers, planners, and armies, cities faded into the background. Between 500 and 1400 CE, few places in Europe had populations that were greater than a fifth of the size of Rome at its peak. To our modern eyes, most medieval cities would seem like rural towns surrounded by a protective wall.[1] Houses were clustered in tight rows to protect city dwellers from the winter cold. The attached houses created the familiar narrow streets and town squares of old Europe, but hidden behind their facades were spacious backyards, where city dwellers grew food and tended livestock. Orchards, pastures, and a scattering of open fields were common sights within medieval cities. And the rural countryside started just outside of the walls, with plenty of open space for farming, which was the main occupation of most of the city's residents.

In the early years, local sources provided enough water for the people of medieval cities. More often than not, a bucket was all that was needed. Because waterways were important as a means of transportation, many cities were located on rivers, which meant that residents could simply walk to the water's edge to fill their buckets. If the nearest river was too far away, they would take their buckets to communal wells in the public square.

Well water may have been free, but bringing it up to the surface was often exhausting and dangerous. During this period, public wells were frequently little more than holes dug down to the water table. Laws requiring stone walls, roofs, and windlasses that made filling a water bucket safer and more convenient did not come about until the latter part of the Middle Ages.[2] Prior to the construction of these amenities, drawing water from a well was hard work and a simple slip at the edge of the hole could have fatal consequences, as indicated by the relatively large number of such deaths listed in records kept by English coroners.[3]

In places without easy access to surface water or an ample supply of groundwater, like the Italian hill cities and the coastal trading communities scattered around the Mediterranean, rain was the primary source of drinking water. Elaborate systems were developed to route rainwater from roofs into stone-lined underground cisterns. But the cisterns were often inadequate during dry periods, making drought a constant worry. In a pinch, water could be brought into the city in barrels, but this stopgap measure put considerable strain on a city's resources. As a result of the expense and uncertainty associated with the practice, cities that relied mostly on cisterns were often among the first to invest in more permanent kinds of imported water systems.[4]

Worries about inadequate local water supplies were not restricted to cities that depended on cisterns, however. For example, Kingston-upon-Hull, an English city located about thirty kilometers (eighteen miles) inland from the North Sea, obtained its water from rivers and creeks whose flows slowed to a trickle during the summer months. As the city grew during the late fourteenth and early fifteenth centuries, seasonal water shortages became so severe that people had to leave town during summer.[5] Even when local sources provided ample quantities of water, its quality left something to be desired. In the heart of medieval cities, wastes from slaughterhouses, tanneries, and stables drained directly into the water supply or were dumped into unlined pits.[6] To avoid the dirty water, people took their buckets farther upstream or walked until they found a clean well.

Better yet, people could avoid drinking water altogether. Because water often had an unpleasant taste and drinking it frequently caused an upset stomach or worse, it was considered by many to be the beverage of beggars. In Central Europe, beer was a popular alternative: average daily per capita beer consumption in Bavaria was around a liter in the 1500s. Farther south, wine was consumed in lieu of water. But not everyone could afford to drink beer and wine with every meal. And alcoholic drinks could not be used for cooking and washing. Like it or not, people had to have water.[7]

The drinking water in medieval cities may not have been the tasteless, odorless beverage that we are familiar with today, but in terms of disease things could have been a lot worse. In the early part of the medieval era, human waste was largely kept out of the waterways because it was valued as fertilizer. As long as homes had backyards with chickens and horses, human wastes were thrown onto the household dung pile, from which they were recycled back onto the land. Before the advent of synthetic fertilizer, manure was a valuable commodity, and distinctions were not often made among its many sources.

As cities grew, local water supplies and backyard waste disposal proved to be inadequate. With more people crammed within the city's protective walls, real estate became more valuable, leading to the disappearance of backyard gardens and their dung piles. As a result, local water supplies became more polluted as people began dumping chamber pots into streets and alleys.[8] The quality of local surface waters further deteriorated when streets were paved in an effort to control the mess created by all of the traffic passing through the mixture of mud, trash, and human wastes.

To address the need for larger quantities of clean drinking water, cities turned to water importation—and when it came time to build drinking water systems, Europe looked to the clergy for guidance. (Much of the Romans' knowledge about engineering and architecture had migrated to the church after the fall of the Roman Empire.) During the early medieval period, the monks who were responsible for building the church's ever-growing network of monasteries and convents developed their own approach to gravity-powered imported water supplies. Undoubtedly, the works of their Roman predecessors had informed their efforts. Monks learned about plumbing and water system construction by visiting those Roman aqueducts and pipe systems that had remained in service after the fall of the empire. They could also acquire practical knowledge about water engineering by reading Vitruvius's treatise on the construction and operation of water systems—a book that was a common feature of many a well-stocked monastic library.[9]

Monastic water systems were considerably smaller than the elaborate aqueducts and fountains that had been built during the Roman era. More often than not, they consisted of an underground pipe a few inches in diameter that brought water to the monastery compound from a source in the adjacent hills. Springs were the monks' preferred water source, because they flowed year-round and did not contain high concentrations of suspended particles, which could clog the pipes. After entering an intake structure at the source, spring water flowed downhill through lead or terra cotta pipes until it reached a fountain in the lavatorium—a room specially designed for personal hygiene—as well as the kitchen and a few other places within the monastic compound.

By the end of the twelfth century, dozens of these small systems for importing water had been built in monasteries throughout Europe, and the ruling class, taking a cue from the monks, had installed similar systems in a smattering of castles. Commoners were aware of these small-scale imported water supplies, because they were sometimes allowed to enter the monastery to collect some of the extra water that spilled from the fountains. City dwellers also learned about imported water through the reports of merchants, crusaders, and travelers who visited Rome, Antioch, Constantinople, and other cities where public fountains served as municipal water supplies.[10] But the existence of imported water technology was not enough to ensure the construction of municipal water supplies: for the citizens of medieval cities, a concerted effort was necessary to marshal the resources needed to scale up the small monastic water systems to projects that could serve tens of thousands of people at a time.

During the thirteenth century, increasingly crowded cities such as Paris, London, and Dublin built imported water systems to supplement their inadequate local supplies. The stories of how each of these cities financed, designed, and built their first-generation imported water systems demonstrate the ways in which technology and science remained alive in the medieval world.[11] Among the early adopters of imported water technology, the Italian hill city of Siena exemplifies the challenges and rewards faced by European cities as they entered the imported water era.

At the end of the twelfth century, Siena's cisterns and wells were unable to provide enough water to meet the needs of the expanding population. In response, sometime around the year 1190 the city used its tax revenue to build a network of underground channels to import spring water from the hills outside of town. To route water into the city, construction crews took advantage of a unique feature of the local geology: a layer of water-bearing, porous limestone, known as tufa, was present just below the surface, and beneath it was a layer of impermeable clay. By tunneling into the bottom of the tufa layer, it was possible to create tunnels—known as bottini—that would collect water as it percolated through the ground. By carefully constructing the bottini with a very gradual slope, the collected water could be routed down to the city. Yet while the local geology was conducive to construction of bottini, Siena's hilltop location proved to be a challenge for this gravity-powered water system. As a result, the first fountains had to be built at the base of the city's hills, several of which were located outside of Siena's protective walls.[12]

Recognizing the vulnerability of their water supply to attack, the city's leaders extended Siena's walls and posted permanent garrisons of soldiers to guard the fountains from outsiders.[13] Meanwhile, to protect the fountains from the masses within the city's walls, they hired wardens to enforce the numerous rules and regulations that had

A three-tiered spill fountain. Wikipedia.

developed around the use and cleaning of the fountains. Many of the rules were about how water could be taken from fountains. Most fountains were built with a series of spillover basins, each set at a different height and each of which had a specific purpose. The top basin, which contained the cleanest water, was reserved for drinking.[14]

According to the rules, those who wanted to draw water from the drinking water basin had to wash their jars in a separate cleaning basin before plunging them in. The second level was reserved for watering horses, but only those horses free of disease were allowed to drink from the basin. And the bottom level was reserved for industrial water uses or the washing of clothes (except at certain fountains where clothes washing was relegated to a special structure called a lavatoio, in which the overflow was directed through a shallow trough to a flat stone depression dedicated to laundry).[15]

The fountains made urban life much more pleasant, but after 150 years of walking up and down the hills, the tired citizens of Siena demanded a solution to their water-hauling problems. By this time, the keepers of the fountains had developed enough skill and confidence to tap into a mountain spring located a few kilometers north of the city, at a spot where the elevation was higher than that of the central plaza. Although the work of creating the new water system was undoubtedly harder, the payoff was high when water finally started flowing from the fountain in the central square. In celebration, the city held a party that lasted for fifteen days.[16]

In addition to serving as an excuse for a good party, Siena's fountains served a variety of civic functions. Fountains provided a place for young women to meet up with friends away from the ever watchful eyes of their parents. They also acted as an early form of fire hydrant. When a citizen sounded the verbal fire alarm, impromptu fire brigades would fill their earthenware jugs from the deep, lower basins that ringed the edges of the fountains and fling those jugs into the burning building. After the fire, the city would pay to replace the broken containers.[17]

Bringing more water into increasingly crowded medieval cities did not solve the problem of waste disposal. In addition to the fecal matter produced by people, there was plenty of waste produced by pigs, dogs, and chickens, which roamed the streets of medieval cities.[18] Because the wastes were still rich in valuable nutrients, an obvious solution was to find some way to transport them to the surrounding countryside.

Eventually, informal systems developed for collecting and distributing wastes to farms. While it was not necessarily a prestigious job, dung collector was a legitimate occupation for the people who made nocturnal visits to the alleys where people dumped their chamber pots. The human waste material dumped in the alleys came to be known as night soil. The word "night" referred to the time when it was picked up, and "soil" is thought to have referred to the fact that a layer of soil was sometimes added to the top of the chamber pot. Once the dung collector had a full load, he took the human waste by cart or boat to the countryside, where it was sold as fertilizer.[19] The trade in fertilizer from human sources was not very profitable, because the collection and transportation of wastes was labor intensive and because medieval farmers had ample supplies of manure from their own farm's manure pile. As a result of these unfavorable economics, the streets and waterways of medieval cities became increasingly polluted as the population boomed.

Efforts to remove wastes from city streets and alleys took on a new sense of urgency in the fourteenth century, when bubonic plague struck. From 1347 to 1352, the population of Europe decreased by around 30 percent as people succumbed to this mysterious and unforgiving disease. Lacking knowledge about the true cause of the plague, the populace searched for an explanation. The superstitious blamed witches or inauspicious astrological conditions. Using their rudimentary understanding of the connection between polluted water and disease, those inclined toward racist conspiracy theories concluded that the plague was the work of Jews who were poisoning the wells at night.[20] The more scientifically oriented, however, revived an ancient theory—popularized by Hippocrates—that the vapors emanating from rotting sewage and garbage were responsible for disease. According to this idea, wastes did not make people sick until they had time to rot and release their odors. In response to this explanation, which became known as the miasma theory, medieval cities stepped up their efforts to remove human wastes before they had time to make people sick.[21]

Despite its lack of scientific support, the miasma theory persisted for over five hundred years. Its longstanding influence is evident in the name given to the deadly mosquito-borne disease malaria—which literally means "bad air." It wasn't until the 1850s, when physicians and scientists grappling with cholera outbreaks demonstrated the role of polluted water in the transmission of disease, that the miasma theory was finally debunked.[22]

After the plague subsided, the removal of wastes from city streets was viewed as an important aspect of public health protection. To Leonardo da Vinci, the need to move wastes out of the city was a central design feature of the ideal city that he proposed to France's King François I in 1517.[23] Inspired by Rome's Cloaca Maxima, da Vinci included in his plan a rapidly flowing manmade channel as a means for ridding the city of its wastes before the miasmic vapors could infect the populace.[24] Although Leonardo's vision was never realized, he anticipated the return of the Roman cloacae in the nineteenth century, when the accumulation of wastes outpaced the ability of dung scavengers to remove them from the city streets.

On a more practical note, a few well-organized medieval cities succeeded in making the removal of accumulated wastes more efficient. For example, Flemish cities developed elaborate systems for transferring wastes from cities to farmers who were struggling to raise crops in nearby low-lying fields, where there never seemed to be enough manure to maintain good crop yields.[25] In Switzerland, similar schemes for getting wastes to the countryside were adopted. With characteristic zeal, the Swiss made the collection and distribution of wastes efficient and clean. The authorities made it easier for the night soil men to collect the wastes by designating on one side of each property special alleys—referred to as Ehgraben—where wastes were dumped.[26] And as multistory buildings became more popular, inventive builders created disposal chutes that extended out from the side of the building over the Ehgraben. These chutes made work a lot easier for the collectors, who removed the accumulated wastes during the night and sent them to farmers via boats or carts.

An etching showing an overhanging structure that medieval citizens of Zurich used to dispose of wastes in the alleys between their homes. Wikimedia Commons.

While Flemish and Swiss ingenuity made the collection of wastes more efficient, attitudes toward waste recycling were more ambivalent in other parts of Europe. Available evidence suggests that English farmers had little use for human waste—they preferred animal manure, ashes, seaweed, and even sweepings from pigeon cages as fertilizers.[27] More often than not, in these places the work of emptying cesspools and removing muck from the streets was a question of maintaining civic order and protecting public health. If farmers were unwilling to buy the wastes, they were given away, buried underground, or dumped wherever convenient.

In contrast to Europe, where with a few exceptions the recycling of human wastes provided limited economic benefit and informal waste collection systems were struggling to keep up with waste production, Asian cities by this time had developed a complex and efficient approach to waste recycling. In part, the elaborate waste recycling systems used in China and Japan succeeded because Asian farmers kept fewer animals—a factor that increased the value of human waste. In addition, Asian cities had more mouths to feed and correspondingly larger volumes of waste to collect: by the start of the eighteenth century, the cities that would come to be known as Beijing and Tokyo each had populations larger than any city in Europe, and cities such as Ghangzhou and Osaka were not far behind. Crowds flocked to thriving urban centers throughout Asia, and as these cities grew, enterprising merchants slowly transformed the activities of dung collectors into a successful industry.

In Japan, human wastes were separated prior to recycling. Fecal matter was the more valuable commodity, because solids were easier to transport. In the first stage of the recycling process, landlords sold the feces in their tenants' cesspools to merchants who were members of a guild that had secured the right to collect the wastes from that part of the city. The wastes were so valuable that the rent of an apartment would increase if the number of people living in the house, and hence the amount of solid waste produced, decreased. When it came time to renegotiate the price for the wastes, the guilds sometimes fought with each other for the rights to buy the increasingly valuable fertilizer.[28]

Urine—the less prized waste—was still a marketable commodity. Because of its lower value, tenants, who owned the rights to their urine, sold it to a group of merchants who were not part of the fecal waste guild. In the early years, urine collection was not a very lucrative business. But as the need for fertilizers continued to grow, prices increased, and the urine collectors were able to form their own guilds to set prices and exclude competitors from their territories. In Osaka, a poor village raised its prospects by establishing a monopoly on the collection of urine from barrels that were left on street corners to satisfy the needs of passing pedestrians.

It was a similar story in China, where a vigorous trade in night soil had developed over a longer period. Chinese households owned specially designed terra cotta jars with tight-fitting lids for the collection of wastes. The wastes were traded and shipped to the countryside, often on barges traveling through canals used almost exclusively for the purpose.[29] It was a complex system, but one that was essential to maintain high crop yields on fields that had been farmed for many generations.

Although the collection of human wastes resulted in cleaner drinking water, it did not eliminate risks from pathogenic microbes. The Asian system of collection and distribution of night soil included a step in which wastes were aged. Yet although storing wastes for up to a year before putting them on fields may have reduced the smells and lowered the infectivity of the pathogens, it did not eliminate the risk of disease. Gastrointestinal illness was endemic among farmers and their families. Conditions were not as bad for the city dwellers who bought the produce, because before it was eaten it was cooked or pickled—practices that substantially reduced the risk of infection.

As the urban populations in Europe continued to grow during the nineteenth century, some European cities struggled to develop approaches like those being used in Asia for moving wastes to the countryside. Modern manufacturing processes led to the use of metal containers that fit onto the bottom of a toilet seat, rather than simple buckets, which simplified the collection of night soil and reduced the smell, and to the development of mechanical pumps that made it easier to remove wastes from cesspools. By the late nineteenth century, this system was also losing its economic appeal as other sources of fertilizer were discovered and popularized. Nevertheless, the protracted early struggle to remove wastes from city streets and to find water that had not yet been contaminated had set the course for the development of the maze of water and sewer pipes underneath our modern cities.

3

Europe's Sewage Crisis

As Western civilization made the transition from medieval times to the modern era, the systems that had been developed to provide water and remove wastes struggled to keep up with increasing population densities. A new approach was needed if cities were going to continue their rapid growth. In response to the problems caused by inadequate and polluted water supplies, each city relied on its own ideas about public health, aesthetics, and the role of the state in civil affairs in order to develop urban water systems that were best suited for their particular climates and geographic features. The differences in the water infrastructures developed in various European cities have diminished over time, but they can still be seen in the practices and attitudes of modern Europeans.

These differences are best understood by exploring the development of urban water infrastructure in the two largest cities of the period—London and Paris. Both cities are located on the banks of major rivers (the Thames and the Seine, respectively), and both experienced rapid population growth starting in the sixteenth century, with populations crossing the one million mark near the beginning of the nineteenth century. When demand for water exceeded its supply and wastes from the densely populated cities started to foul the streets and pollute the water supply, London and Paris both started building up their water infrastructures.

But here the similarities end. London continued to rely on local water sources and to use its rivers for waste disposal, while Paris favored imported water and protection of its rivers by reusing human waste as fertilizer. By the early twentieth century, unrelenting population growth and economics forced both cities to adopt similar approaches for water supply and waste disposal, but even today subtle differences in attitude persist among English and French engineers about the design and operation of water systems.

London's population surged before that of Paris. As a result, it required improvements to its water infrastructure sooner. When London was growing in the Middle Ages, water was drawn directly from the Thames River, except at high tide when sea salt rendered it undrinkable. People who lived farther from the river pulled groundwater from shallow wells or paid vendors to deliver Thames River water directly to their homes. In 1236, a system of twelve pipes, known as conduits, was added that drew water from springs located a few kilometers outside of the city.[1] These local water sources were ample for a city with a population under 100,000. But as the population of London continued to grow, the shallow groundwater and local springs no longer met the city's needs. Some of London's growing water demand was fulfilled by the construction of a canal, known as the New River, which was built between 1609 and 1613 to deliver water from springs located approximately thirty kilometers (twenty miles) north of the city. When the New River Company was incorporated, the canal was considered a potentially lucrative business opportunity. But the company quickly adjusted its expectation as it learned that building a canal into the crowded city would be challenging: public concerns over the possibility that the canal would turn farms along its banks into swamps slowed construction; the cost of the canal increased because it had to follow a circuitous path around plots of land whose owners would not sell to the company and because wooden flumes were

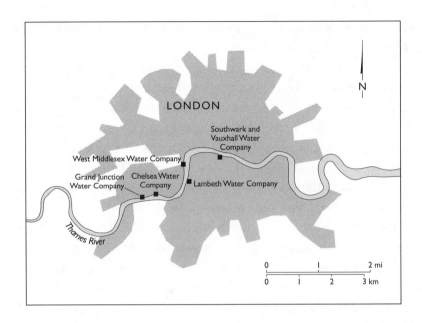

Locations on the Thames River of the drinking water intakes
used by water companies in 1840.

needed to carry it over existing roads. During its first few years, the
New River Company struggled to make a profit. By 1619, however,
business was better and the springs could no longer meet customer
demand. To increase the water system's capacity, the New River Company diverted a fraction of the flow of the River Lee into the canal.[2]

Despite the eventual success of the New River Company, the people of London were not particularly enthusiastic about the costs and
difficulties associated with building imported water systems when a
huge source of fresh water—the Thames River—was already running
through the heart of their city. To meet the public's demand for locally
sourced water, several private companies were established around
1720 to provide piped water from the Thames. Two of these companies, the Lambeth Water Company and the Southwark and Vauxhall
Water Company, had intakes located near the center of the city, which
meant that the water they delivered was polluted by runoff from the

city's gutters. In theory, runoff from the city's streets should not have been heavily contaminated because local laws prohibited dumping of human waste in streets and yards. But in reality the laws were rarely enforced and London's tenements had far too few outhouses. Consequently, human waste mingled with the mud, horse manure, and trash that both filled the city's yards and streets and eventually washed down the gutters.

As you might expect, the quality of the water delivered by the water companies left something to be desired. The title character in Tobias Smollett's classic novel *The Expedition of Humphry Clinker* comments about the choice of drinking water from the New River aqueduct or from the Thames during a trip to London in 1771:

> If I would drink water, I must quaff the mawkish contents of an open aqueduct, exposed to all manner of defilement, or swallow that which comes from the River Thames, impregnated with all the filth of London and Westminster. Human excrement is the least offensive part of the concrete, which is composed of all the drugs, minerals, and poisons used in mechanics and manufacture, enriched with the putrefying carcases of beasts and men, and mixed with the scourings of all the wash-tubs, kennels and common sewers within the bills of mortality.[3]

The private companies delivered this water of dubious quality through a network of approximately fifty kilometers (thirty miles) of wood and cast iron pipes that ran under the city.[4] And unlike the gravity-driven Roman and New River aqueducts, pumps were necessary to lift the water from the river's elevation to that of the city.

Initially, a set of pumps powered by water wheels was built on London Bridge for this purpose. By the start of the nineteenth century, the water wheels on the bridge were capable of delivering 16 million liters (4 million gallons) of water every day.[5] The water wheels, however, ultimately proved to be hazardous to the boats navigating the river, and the intakes were moved to the shore, where they were powered by a steam engine.

Although the wealthy preferred to drink spring water delivered by private companies, they were happy to have Thames water piped into their homes where it could be used for other purposes. Chief among these was the water closet. Access to piped water made the toilet possible, which in turn eliminated the need for chamber pots and trips to the outhouse in the dead of winter. Between 1850 and 1856, many wealthy homeowners in London connected their water closets to the sewer system, thereby doubling the flow of London's sewers and further contaminating the Thames with human waste.[6]

Throughout the first half of the nineteenth century, most of London's residents endured a dark existence: they worked in factories under bleak conditions, drank water from the polluted Thames, breathed air that was thick with sulfuric acid and ash from coal burning, and more or less suffered the dark side of the Industrial Revolution. With all of the stresses and strains of living in this Dickensian world it would have been hard to choose which of these many things to fix first if cholera had not struck the city.

Cholera, a waterborne disease, first reached London in 1831. During the first outbreak, the disease spread throughout the city, killing approximately three thousand people.[7] Following the medical ideas of the day, many people believed that the disease was transmitted by miasma, the infectious vapors emanating from rotting waste.[8] It seemed obvious to many that there was a connection between the trash and noxious odors in the streets and the infectious diseases that were concentrated in the city. In the years before microbes and the mechanisms of disease transmission were understood, efforts to prevent the spread of disease were thus focused on controlling what was believed to be the source of miasma: wastes from the city streets.

The increased efforts to clean the streets and to prevent the dumping of trash along the Thames, however, did little to stop the disease. As we now know, cholera is transmitted when water or food is contaminated with feces from people infected by the bacterium *Vibrio cholerae.* In nineteenth-century London, the disease spread because water from the Thames and the numerous shallow wells was often contaminated with feces. Street cleaning would have had little effect on cholera if the water supply were still contaminated.

Not until a second, much more severe cholera outbreak occurred in 1848 was the miasma theory finally debunked. A link between cholera and contaminated drinking water was established when John Snow, a London physician, produced a map showing that a cluster of cholera victims on London's Broad Street all had consumed water from the same shallow well. Snow reasoned that the disease was caused by the contaminated water and not miasma. By removing the handle from the well and forcing the local residents to draw their water from another place, he stopped the further spread of cholera in the area.[9]

As it turned out, the Broad Street well had been built about a meter away from a leaking cesspool.[10] The cholera outbreak was eventually traced to a single cholera victim who routinely used the outhouse there. Undoubtedly, the cesspool had been leaking for years before the cholera epidemic. That people thought nothing of drinking water from this well for so many years before the outbreak attests to the quality of water available to London's masses.

The story of John Snow and the Broad Street well provides a wonderful introduction to the science of epidemiology and so is repeated in many introductory biology and public health classes. But it is often told in a way that misses the influence of John Snow's discovery on urban water infrastructure. That is, removing the handles from the shallow wells located right next to cesspools was easy, but that wouldn't remove fecal contamination from the water supply. Fixing the Thames was a much bigger problem.

One obvious solution was to move the water intakes to a point upstream of the main sources of sewage contamination. That's exactly what the Lambeth Water Company did after the second cholera outbreak in 1849. When the next cholera outbreak occurred four years later, John Snow was once again proven correct when customers of the Lambeth Water Company fared much better than those of the Southwark and Vauxhall Water Companies, who were still using a downstream intake.[11] Under orders from the city's government, the Southwark and Vauxhall Water Company moved its intake upstream of the city in 1855.[12] But moving the intakes for the city's water supply upstream was only a partial solution, because London kept expanding and more sewage was finding its way into the upstream section of the Thames every year.

Another way of preventing the spread of waterborne disease was to install water treatment systems. Before the 1850s, water filtration had been practiced on a limited scale at London's Chelsea Waterworks and by a few other utilities in Scotland and Europe, mainly to improve the appearance and taste of the water.[13] But the people of London were desperate, and there was a chance that filtration would also help prevent cholera. In response to the second cholera outbreak, then, water filtration was mandated for all of London's water intakes. Fortunately for London, water filtration turned out to be more effective than they had hoped.

Six years before the second cholera outbreak, London had commissioned Sir Edwin Chadwick, a lawyer and journalist, to investigate long-term solutions to pollution in the Thames. When Chadwick began his assignment, the focus was on controlling the odors emanating from the Thames, which were thought to be the source of the miasma. Chadwick's report advocated the development of an integrated network of sewers that would share a common discharge point east of the city. Chadwick wanted to pipe the sewage from this central point to farms on the outskirts of the city, thereby eliminating the odors while simultaneously putting the nutrient-rich water to use.[14]

The idea of putting human waste—rich in nutrients such as nitrogen and phosphorus—to productive use was influenced by ideas of continental European scientists like Justus von Liebig, a German chemist who recognized that crops needed nitrogen and phosphorus to grow. Von Liebig and his coworkers advocated the more efficient use of nutrient-rich wastes, because they recognized that the amount of mineral fertilizers in the world was finite—which meant that farming would be very difficult after easily accessible mineral deposits were depleted.[15]

Chadwick also closely followed research being conducted on "sewage farms" in Scotland and Berlin. Researchers at these experimental farms showed it was possible to grow large quantities of vegetables and forage crops by applying sewage to the land. At that time, synthetic fertilizers were unknown, and the nutrients in the sewage gave the sewage farms large advantages over conventional agriculture. Using estimates from these initial projects, Chadwick reckoned that the sewage system and the pumps needed to move the wastes to farms on the outskirts of the city would grow enough food to pay for themselves.[16]

Despite support from the scientific community, Chadwick's ideas were criticized severely by engineers of the day as expensive and impractical, because a lot of extra piping and pumps would be required to send the sewage to the farms. The question of what to do with London's sewage continued to be debated until 1858, when an extended drought led to a low flow of water in the Thames and a two-year period known as "The Great Stink," when the smell of sewage overpowered all of the other odors of the city.[17] Parliament, which met on the banks of the Thames, deemed that it was high time to solve the problem. Expediency trumped complexity. By 1865, London's sewage disposal dilemma was solved by directing the flow through a few main pipelines that dumped it into the Thames well downstream of the city.

While London was struggling to find a cleaner water supply and manage its wastes, Paris was busy doing the same, with a slight twist. At the start of the nineteenth century, Parisian engineers were trying to integrate its water system into the orderly operation of the city. Unlike London, where the city's leaders seemed to be more interested in industrial progress than public health and urban planning, Paris was full of intellectuals and political philosophers who believed that cities should be comfortable and safe. These attitudes meant that Paris took the ideas of people like Chadwick and von Liebig more seriously and were willing to pay for systems that kept the city streets and waterways clean.

The need was great. By the late eighteenth century, the springs, shallow wells, and rainwater collection systems that had served as the local water supply for Paris were no longer adequate. The quality of water drawn from the Seine was rapidly approaching a point where it would no longer be drinkable. To address the city's water needs while simultaneously providing a route for barges to enter the city without navigating fast-flowing parts of the Seine, Napoleon Bonaparte commissioned the construction of the Canal de l'Ourcq in 1802.[18] The canal was fed by relatively clean Seine River water, and by local streams approximately a hundred kilometers (sixty miles) upstream of the city. The canal succeeded both as a means of shipping and as a water supply. As the water needs of the city increased, water from the River Marne was diverted into the canal to increase its flow.

With the construction of this canal and establishment of a public water system in 1823, Paris had built a water distribution network that brought water to eighty-four public fountains scattered throughout the city. Just as in Roman times, the decorative fountains served as public water distribution points. But unlike the Roman system, the French water pipes could withstand pressure, meaning that the fountains did not have to run continuously.[19]

The availability of large quantities of water in fountains distributed throughout the city made it possible to flush accumulated trash and dirt from the streets. Twice every day the fountains were drained into the streets for about an hour.[20] The street runoff also solved many of the odor problems associated with the sewer system that had been in place in Paris since the fourteenth century, by regularly flushing accumulated debris all the way through the system.[21]

With the advent of a piped water supply from the Canal de l'Ourcq, wealthy residents were able to bring water directly into their homes. But unlike the Romans, who enjoyed bathing communally, the Parisians preferred to bathe alone in the comfort of their homes.

The used bathwater had to go somewhere, but the use of the existing cesspools for bathwater disposal created a new problem.

Before construction of the water distribution system, urine and feces produced by Parisians were collected in cesspools and applied to farms. Wastes from cesspools in London and other cities had also been collected and reused in this manner.[22] But the system in Paris was different: for decades, the human wastes from the cesspools of Paris had been converted into a fertilizer known as poudrette by aging and drying it in pits near the city's dump. The fertilizer was popular among French farmers and was quite profitable for the company that ran the production facility.[23]

When the wealthy started bathing at home and using water closets, the liquid content of the city's waste increased. Between 1845 and 1858, per capita water use increased from around 13 liters to about 110 liters (3.5 to 30 gallons) each day.[24] Although not all of that water ended up in the cesspools, much of it did, making it harder to dry them out for the production of poudrette. In addition, the city had expanded beyond the foul-smelling suburb of Montfaucon, home to the city dump, the poudrette production site, and the city's main slaughterhouse. The city's leaders decided to relocate poudrette production to numerous sites in the outer suburbs, but this solution only succeeded in spreading the offensive odors beyond the city center. Moreover, the city itself kept expanding.[25]

During the 1850s, French chemists further refined the fertilizer production process by using distillation to extract pure ammonium sulfate fertilizer from human waste. This purified nitrogen-containing fertilizer was quite valuable, because few concentrated sources of nitrogen were available at that time. Somewhat ironically, much of it was exported to Britain.[26]

Like their counterparts in London, the sewers of Paris discharged a foul mixture of horse manure, trash, and mud to the Seine. But in contrast to London's sewers, the existence of the poudrette production system meant that the sewers of Paris contained much less human waste. This difference, coupled with the sewers' ample size—the main sewers

A boat tour of the Paris sewer system in 1896. Copyright © The Image Works.

of Paris were about 3 meters (9 feet) high and 5 meters (15 feet) wide—made the sewers of Paris less offensive. In fact, they were a source of fascination for writers like Victor Hugo, who set one of the climactic scenes of *Les Misérables* in the sewer. In the 1870s, public tours of the sewers of Paris, complete with a ride down the center of the channel in a boat, became popular.[27]

The local fascination with Paris's sewers did little to mitigate the impact of the city's discharge into the Seine. By 1874, the sewer system was creating a plume of black water that hugged the right bank of the river for a kilometer, continuously releasing gas bubbles and noxious smells as it traveled downstream. Even seventy-five kilometers (forty-five miles) downstream of the city, the effect of Paris on the Seine was still evident.[28] The city eventually built a tunnel to move the sewage six kilometers (four miles) farther downstream before releasing it to the river. Although this change moved the smelliest material away from the city, the problem remained unsolved.[29]

Influenced by the ideas of Edwin Chadwick and his contemporaries, the leaders of Paris started experimenting with sewage farming. The Parisian "sewage" that could be used for farming might better be described as street runoff mixed with household waste, because by this time homeowners were allowed to dump water from their sinks and bathtubs into the sewers. But although this sewage was not as well suited for farming as the organic-rich wastes produced by London, the political climate in Paris was more accepting of the idea of reusing wastes, because French intellectuals had been influenced by the ideas of writers such as Pierre Leroux, the political economist, who asserted that reuse of urban waste was essential for preventing the depletion of resources envisioned by Justus von Liebig and Thomas Malthus. Leroux's friend Victor Hugo applied these ideas to water by advocating a system of bringing clean water into the city from the countryside and returning nutrient-rich water to farmers who would use it to grow crops. Hugo explained:

> Those heaps of filth at the gate-posts, those tumbrils of mud which jolt through the street by night, those terrible casks of the street department, those fetid drippings of subterranean mire, which the pavements hide from you,—do you know what they are? They are the meadow in flower, the green grass, wild thyme, thyme and sage, they are game, they are cattle, they are the satisfied bellows of great oxen in the evening.[30]

The idea appealed to people throughout Europe and was even endorsed by Karl Marx in *Das Kapital*:

> Excretions of consumption are of the greatest importance for agriculture. So far as their utilization is concerned there is enormous waste for them in the capitalist economy. In London, for instance, they find no better use for the excretion of four and one-half million human beings than to contaminate the Thames with it at heavy expense.[31]

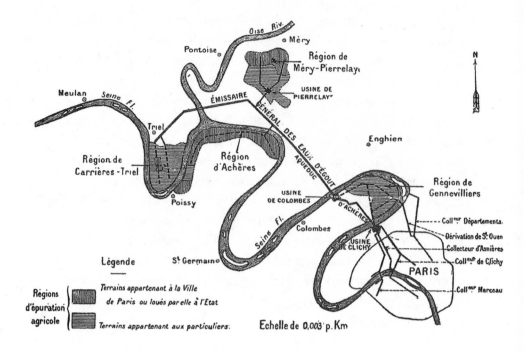

Locations of Paris's sewage farms on the Seine River. From Emile Gérards, *Paris souterrain*.

Like their counterparts in London, the engineers of Paris were not convinced that sewage farming was a practical solution to the waste disposal problem. They were aware, however, that percolation of the sewage through the soil would remove much of the pollution, and they reluctantly endorsed the venture. And so sewage farms were built starting in 1889 along the banks of the Seine in Gennevillers.[32] By 1893, close to a thousand hectares (2,500 acres) of cabbage, artichokes, and sugar beets were being grown on the sewage farms. Produce grown there was prized by the chefs of Paris and could be found on the tables of fine restaurants like the Grand Hotel.[33] In subsequent years, the farms spread beyond Gennevillers, and new sewage farms were set up further downstream. By the turn of the century, a fivefold increase in the area of the sewage farms ensured that almost all of the wastewater produced in the city would be reused.[34]

After passing through the soil, the water from the sewers percolated back into the Seine as shallow groundwater. Thus, the sewage farms served as a primitive type of sewage treatment system. This early form of wastewater treatment relied on the combined activity of microbes in the soil and the food crops: the microbes used the organic matter in the sewage as a source of food, converting much of the organic matter into carbon dioxide and water. In the process of breaking down the waste, nitrogen and phosphorus were released. The rapidly growing plants took up the nutrients, which were then removed from the land when the plants were harvested. The system was far from perfect because pathogenic microbes, especially tiny viruses, are only partially removed during their passage through the soil.

Was the food safe to eat? The sewage undoubtedly contained many types of waterborne pathogens, and it's not hard to imagine some of the irrigation water splashing onto the surface of the strawberries grown at the sewage farms of Gennevillers. But the other fields where Parisians' food was grown also were fertilized with animal wastes, and almost certainly also contained waterborne pathogens. Many of the vegetables grown in the fields were not consumed raw, and cooking should have made them safe to eat. Still, the strawberries and other prized fruits probably got contaminated from time to time. Maybe people were really careful about washing their fruit. Or perhaps the produce made people sick at about the same frequency as produce from other sources.

The success of the sewage farms helped bring an end to the use of cesspools and poudrette manufacturing in Paris. By 1894, the government had mandated the end to cesspools by requiring homeowners to connect their water closets to the sewer system.[35] But the existence of an alternative means of recycling the wastes was not the only reason the system was abandoned. The odors and nuisance associated with manufacture of dry fertilizers from human waste were objectionable to people living near the production facilities. In addition, the dry fertilizers were no longer as profitable after the widespread introduction of superphosphate (an inexpensive product in which the phosphate in minerals was converted into a form that was available to plants by treating it with sulfuric acid), and shortly thereafter nitrate-rich mineral fertilizers began to be imported from Chile.[36]

Although the attempt by Paris's leaders to reuse its citizens' wastes for agriculture was laudable, it was ultimately impractical, because continued growth meant that there was not enough land to spread all of the waste close to the city. Attempts to apply more sewage than the crops could handle would inevitably lead to decreased crop yields and foul odors emanating from the "sewage sick" farms. If sewage farms were to succeed, more land would be needed.[37]

In the 1920s, civic leaders proposed an ambitious plan to build a pipeline to take the wastes of Paris to sites in the Champagne region 140 kilometers (87 miles) west of the city.[38] The project would permanently solve the city's sewage problem by increasing the acreage of sewage farms tenfold. Ultimately, the project was never built, because the price of fertilizer had dropped too much to make the recycling of nutrients attractive.[39] In addition, by this time agronomists had realized that the mixture of nutrients in human waste contained less phosphorus than plants needed. When the lower cost of imported fertilizer and the need to supplement sewage with phosphorus were both factored into the analysis, sewage farms became less attractive.

By the end of the nineteenth century, Paris and London had both given up on the prospect of reusing human waste because other sources of fertilizer were readily available. To protect public health, sewage was being discharged directly into the Seine and Thames. The water intakes had either been moved upstream or water was being imported from less contaminated sources outside of the cities. The water supply was safe and secure. Problem solved—unless, of course, you lived downstream.

4

Growing Old Thanks to Water Treatment

During the nineteenth century, the United States matured from a sleepy, isolated country to a leading industrialized nation. New York grew from a city of fewer than 70,000 to a metropolis of over 3 million people. Chicago went from being a tiny military outpost to a city of 1.7 million people. And just as their European counterparts had decades earlier, cities throughout the United States suffered from cholera outbreaks, filthy streets, and inadequate water supplies during the first half of the nineteenth century.[1] In response, American cities made major investments in Water 1.0. During the last decades of the century, New York built the first sections of an aqueduct that would ultimately bring water into the city from a pristine watershed 190 kilometers (120 miles) to the northwest. The city also built a network of underground tunnels to convey its sewage to the ocean.

Chicago was thinking big, too. There was plenty of water in Lake Michigan, but as the city expanded, water from the sewage-contaminated Chicago River kept getting sucked into the city's drinking water intake pipes along the shore of the lake. After the city's engineers extended the water intake pipes as far from the shoreline as they possibly could, they embarked on a more radical solution: they raised the elevation of the entire downtown area and reversed the flow of the city's main river. The canals and locks of the Sanitary and Ship Canal were completed in 1892. Thereafter, the city's wastes flowed to the Mississippi River and not into Chicago's Lake Michigan drinking water intakes.[2]

Although much of America's growth took place in urban neighborhoods, like those that housed the sweatshops of New York's garment district and the stockyards of Chicago, manufacturing was also booming in small cities scattered throughout the northeastern states and the industrializing Midwest. Pittsburgh made steel. Minneapolis milled flour. And Cleveland, Cincinnati, and Detroit made machinery. It is in one of these small cities that we pick up the next phase of the urban water story.

The Merrimack River, which runs through southern New Hampshire and northern Massachusetts, was a hub of textile manufacturing in the region. The rapidly running river powered the water wheels that drove the looms of the factories. And once the goods were manufactured, the river provided a means of moving product-filled barges to the Middlesex Canal, which offered an easy route to markets in Boston.

Lowell and Lawrence were the two main mill towns on the Merrimack River. Both had been developed as water-powered manufacturing centers by investors from Boston. To make the cities suitable for textile mills, the investors had dammed the Merrimack just upstream of the cities and built canals to distribute water to the factories.[3] By 1850, Lowell had become the largest industrial complex in the United States and the second largest city in Massachusetts.[4] Building on the success of Lowell, Lawrence was developed about sixteen kilometers (ten miles) downriver in 1853. By 1890, the cities had populations of 78,000 and 45,000, respectively. And the abundance of immigrants freshly arrived in Boston made it easy to staff factories there.

Like most other American cities, the residents of Lowell and Lawrence got their drinking water upstream.[5] This approach was an obvious choice because the canals and river, in addition to providing waterpower, served as open sewers. The canals might have offended our modern sensitivities, but people who lived during the latter part

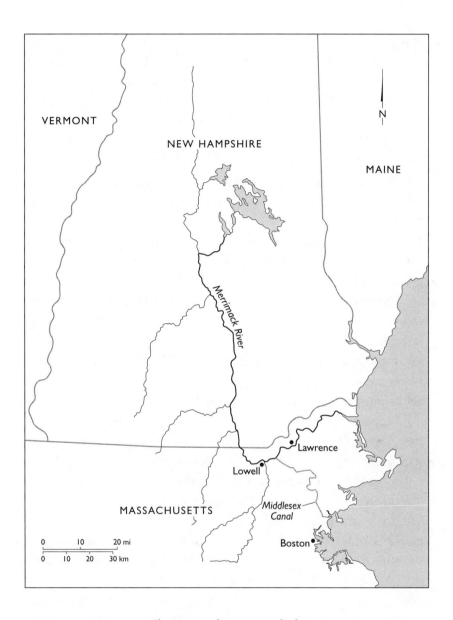

The Merrimack River watershed.

of the nineteenth century were accustomed to foul odors. Bad smells were not enough to discourage them from living in a town where there were good jobs. Moreover, the public health of these two cities was not much different from that in other American cities. Chronic disease was ever present, especially in the cities' crowded working-class neighborhoods, but these hazards were preferable to the poverty of the European cities and farms that the immigrants had left behind.

But in 1890 conditions got a lot worse in Lowell and Lawrence: an epidemic of typhoid fever swept through the two towns, infecting more than 1,500 people. In one year, the disease killed 150 people in Lowell and 83 people in Lawrence—rates of death that were roughly equivalent to those experienced during the height of London's 1832 cholera epidemic.[6]

Like cholera, typhoid fever is caused by contact with bacteria, in this case *Salmonella typhi,* in contaminated water or food. Typhoid fever was one of the most prevalent communicable diseases in America in the late 1800s.[7] It also occurred in the other cities along the Merrimack River in 1890. But people in Lowell and Lawrence were about four times as likely as their neighbors to contract the disease.

Recognizing the threat that typhoid fever posed to their cities, the town fathers of Lowell and Lawrence sought help from William Sedgwick, a biology professor from the Massachusetts Institute of Technology (MIT), whom many regard as the father of modern public health. Disillusioned with the mundane details of medical practice, Sedgwick had proceeded directly from medical school to Johns Hopkins University, where he had become fascinated with the new scientific discipline of bacteriology. Shortly after arriving at MIT in 1883, he had established the first course to train engineers in this new science because "a public [water] supply, if neglected, is a public danger."[8] With a fervor for challenging his students that matched his dedication to public health, Sedgwick became America's first sanitation detective.

After Sedgwick responded to the call to solve Lowell and Lawrence's typhoid fever problem, he and his team fanned out across the two cities, observing habits of the city's residents, interviewing doctors, and collecting water samples. Within a few months they had correctly diagnosed the problem: sewage contamination of the water supply.

Sedgwick's team traced the rapid spread of the disease to sewage originating in Stony Brook, a small tributary originating in a suburb five kilometers (three miles) upstream of Lowell. By the time the river reached Lawrence, it contained the *Salmonella typhi* from Stony Brook as well as bacteria from the sewers of Lowell. The problem was made worse because people working in the mills often quenched their thirst with water drawn directly out of the sewage-contaminated canals.[9]

Lowell's water utility solved the contamination problem by switching to a groundwater supply and discouraging people from consuming water directly from the canals.[10] If this approach had not worked, Lowell could have built an intake pipe upstream of the contaminated tributary or found a way to pipe the contaminated sewage to a location below the city's drinking water intake.

Lawrence faced a greater challenge. The city didn't have easy access to groundwater, and building an intake pipe extending upstream of Lowell and Stony Brook was too expensive for the downstream city. Lawrence was stuck with the Merrimack River as its water supply. And with Lowell's double-digit population growth, Lawrence could expect even more sewage in its drinking water in the future.

The typhoid fever outbreak in Lawrence challenged many scientists of the era who believed that flowing water undergoes a process referred to at the time as self-purification. Self-purification meant that there was no need to protect downstream cities from the discharges of their upstream neighbors, because the flowing river would remove contaminants from the water. In 1873, Charles F. Chandler, a chemistry professor at Columbia University who also served as the president of the New York Board of Health, summed up the conventional wisdom of the times: "Although rivers are the great natural sewers, and receive the drainage of towns and cities, the natural process of purification, in most cases, destroys the offensive bodies derived from sewage, and renders them harmless."[11]

Superficially, this line of thinking seems reasonable. Most of the noxious chemicals in sewage are in a chemically reduced form. In other words, they can contain energy that can be liberated by chemical reactions. While they are confined to a sewer pipe where the concentration of oxygen is low, the reduced chemicals tend to stay that way. Once the sewage is exposed to oxygen-containing river water, however, chemical reactions, aided by the actions of microbes that live in the river, convert the reduced chemicals into their oxidized forms. For example, hydrogen sulfide, the volatile compound that gives sewage the smell of rotten eggs, is rapidly oxidized to sulfate, an odorless compound, when it reacts with oxygen in a flowing river. Introduce sewage into a flowing river, and chemistry and biology will initiate the oxidation process.

The oxidation of reduced compounds in sewage leads to one of the most obvious problems associated with sewage discharges: oxygen depletion. If too many oxygen-consuming substances, such as hydrogen sulfide, ammonia, and organic matter, are added to a river, then chemical reactions can use up all of the dissolved oxygen. Once the oxygen disappears, the oxygen-breathing aquatic species—fish, crabs, and mussels—will suffocate. Add enough reduced substances to a river and noxious gases, such as hydrogen sulfide, will be released, as was the case in the section of the Seine River downstream of Paris before the sewage farms were built.

Luckily, the dissolved oxygen that is consumed by these processes is continuously replenished with new oxygen from the atmosphere. Actually, oxygen and other molecules are constantly colliding with the surface of water, sometimes getting trapped and dissolving into the water. At the same time, dissolved gases are constantly escaping from water back into the atmosphere. When oxygen, or any other gas, is depleted from water, the rate at which the dissolved molecules escape from the water decreases while the rate at which the molecules enter from the gas phase remains constant. Eventually, the concentrations of dissolved oxygen increase, and equilibrium is reestablished.

In a stagnant body of water, like a pond or a water tank, the process through which oxygen is replenished can be quite slow, often requiring days to return equilibrium to oxygen-depleted water. But the process is much faster in a rapidly flowing river, because air bubbles mix into the water as it flows over rocks and drops over ledges. This phenomenon is also why tropical fish aquaria always have those cute little divers and clams burping bubbles into the water. Flowing water may not always be cleaner than stagnant water, but it should contain more oxygen.

The idea that flowing rivers undergo self-purification was bolstered by the considerable dilution of sewage in most places as tributaries delivered clean water into a river. Dilution even occurred on rivers that didn't have tributaries as nearby groundwater flowed into the system through the sides and bottom of the river. Thus people saw and smelled the improvements in water quality as water flowed downstream, even if the contaminants in the sewage had not yet been removed by oxidation reactions. To remove those chemicals in sewage that would lead to algae blooms, foul odors, or the consumption of oxygen, self-purification by oxidation and dilution was often enough.[12]

In fact, self-purification was the law of the land in Massachusetts. Acting on the belief that self-purification alone was an adequate means of public health protection, an 1878 law allowed cities to dump their sewage into rivers as long as the intake of the nearest downstream water supply was at least thirty-two kilometers (twenty miles) away.[13] Lawrence's drinking water intakes were a little less than half the required distance from Lowell, but there was still no requirement to treat the sewage: the Merrimack River was specifically exempted from regulations due to the substantial dilution of waste that occurred in the river.[14]

But if oxidation and dilution were removing the visible effects of Lowell's sewage as it flowed downstream, why were people in Lawrence getting typhoid fever? The answer lies in simple math. A person can get typhoid fever if he or she ingests as few as a thousand *Salmonella typhi* bacteria.[15] Typhoid fever sufferers and even asymptomatic carriers of the disease released millions of the bacteria in their feces every day. (Perhaps the most famous asymptomatic carrier of the era, a cook in New York City named Mary Mallon, was given the nickname "Typhoid Mary" after public health workers discovered that she had infected about fifty people with typhoid fever around 1900.) During the outbreak, each liter of water flowing out of Lowell probably contained hundreds of thousands of *Salmonella typhi*. Some of the bacteria undoubtedly died from exposure to sunlight and cold river water; these both damage bacteria, which are adapted mainly for living inside of warm, dark places like the human body. But even after factoring in dilution and self-purification, Lowell's water still was not safe to drink.

To protect its citizens from *Salmonella typhi*, Lawrence turned to the same approach that London had adopted after its cholera outbreak three decades earlier: the city built a water filtration plant. To many public health experts the plant was an inadequate response born out of desperation. London had built a filtration plant during its last cholera outbreak, but this step also had been accompanied by relocation of the drinking water intakes upriver and installation of a centralized sewer system to move wastes out of the city. Although water filtration might improve the taste and appearance of drinking water, no one was sure if the process would actually stop the typhoid-fever-causing bacteria.

American civic leaders were influenced in their opinion of water filtration by the 1866 report of a prominent New York engineer, James P. Kirkwood. The city managers of St. Louis, Missouri, had sent Kirkwood to Europe on a fact-finding mission in preparation for the construction of a water filtration plant on the Mississippi River. Kirkwood visited over a dozen water filtration plants, taking copious notes on their design, operation, and water quality. Upon his return, Kirkwood was disappointed to find that his employers had already decided that building a filtration plant was expensive and unnecessary. Undeterred, he applied principles used in the European sand filters that had impressed him during his travels to design a water filtration plant for St. Louis. Although the plant was never built, his report and treatment plant designs raised expectations that water filtration might someday be used to improve water quality.[16]

Attempts to replicate European water filtration plants over the next two decades met with mixed results; sometimes the filters removed suspended particles, musty smells, and foul tastes from surface waters, and other times they had little effect on water quality. During the late nineteenth century, large filtration systems failed to live up to expectations in Columbus, Ohio (1871), Springfield, Massachusetts (1873), Toledo, Ohio (1875), and Brockton, Massachusetts (1880). Filters plugged up, or the plants delivered foul-tasting water.[17] Many of the projects were such debacles that the filters were simply abandoned. Water filtration plants were built successfully in 1873 and 1875 in Poughkeepsie and Hudson, respectively, but improvements in the taste and appearance of the water of these two communities on New York's sewage-polluted Hudson River were not enough to change people's minds. Most American engineers concluded that filtration could remove some of the suspended particles, but, as stated by the prominent engineer J. J. R. Crose in 1883, filters "do not make a polluted water fit to use."[18]

Luckily for Lawrence, the city had local experts who had not yet given up on water filtration. But maybe this advantageous situation wasn't only due to luck: the state had set up a water research facility in the city three years before the typhoid fever outbreak, in order to find remedies to problems caused by sewage in the rapidly growing state.[19] Lawrence had plenty of sewage-contaminated drinking water, and its location close to the state's leading engineering school (MIT) made it an ideal place to conduct research. Sedgwick and the engineers working at the newly formed Massachusetts State Department of Health's Lawrence Experimental Station turned to filtration as a possible solution to the typhoid fever outbreak, because it was the only viable means of water treatment at the time.

The field station's engineers' approach to water filtration was influenced by research on sewage treatment, which had been the mainstay of the lab during its first three years. The initial research at the station focused on the use of microbes to treat sewage—a logical extension of the principles of sewage farming pioneered in Europe. After all, water quality had been markedly improved after the sewage had percolated through soil on the farms.

By 1884, experiments conducted by London's municipal sewage authority also had demonstrated that microbes broke down the organic wastes after the sewage was discharged to the shallow estuary east of the city.[20] Furthermore, the experimental station's engineers knew that percolation of water through soil protected groundwater from contamination. Perhaps the self-purification process that occurred as water infiltrated through the soil could be made more efficient in an engineered system with a porous material like sand.

Early experiments in which sewage was applied directly to barrels filled with sand showed promise, but the process became less effective if the sand was not allowed to drain between sewage applications. The engineers correctly surmised that the rate of oxidation of organic compounds in the sewage slowed down after the microbes in the sand had used up all of the oxygen. These observations led to the design of the intermittent filter, a means of sewage treatment that was ultimately abandoned in lieu of methods that continuously introduced oxygen. Despite the failure of intermittent filtration, the idea of using microbes to treat sewage was firmly established.[21]

Experiments on the biological treatment of sewage proved that it was the microbes living on the filter and not the filter itself that were responsible for the improvement in water quality at sewage farms and in groundwater systems. Sedgwick's MIT colleague and fellow experimental station researcher Hiram Mills recognized that sand filters functioned the same way whether they were used for drinking water or for sewage treatment: the filter was actually a biological treatment system in which microbes growing on the sand oxidized contaminants. Sedgwick and Mills put on the project Alfred Hazen, a prodigy who had completed his degree at Dartmouth at age fifteen. Hazen and his fellow researchers demonstrated that the sand filter was much better suited for treating surface water than sewage because surface waters did not contain enough reduced organic compounds to deplete the dissolved oxygen.[22]

The organisms on the sand filter oxidized dissolved organic compounds, but could they remove *Salmonella typhi* and the tiny particles on which the pathogens often lived? The performance of the treatment plants in London suggested that waterborne pathogens were indeed being removed by filtration, but the way in which filters removed disease-causing microbes was unclear. Removal by straining seemed unlikely, because the pores between the grains of sand were simply too big to filter out bacteria in the way that a colander separates pasta from boiling water. If a sand filter was capable of removing pathogenic microbes, some other mechanism must be involved.[23]

The engineers working at the Lawrence Experimental Station set out to answer this question by applying state-of-the-art microscopy and chemical analyses to water filters. Their search focused on the jellylike substance that appeared on the first few centimeters of the sand filter after water had been flowing through the filters for a few weeks.

This slimy substance, which is now referred to as a biofilm, consists of thousands of microbes, most of which are harmless to people, covered with a mixture of polysaccharides and proteins (think of the bacteria as grains of rice living in a bowl of rice pudding). The biofilm protects microbes from microscopic predators by providing them with a place to hide. The MIT engineers discovered that the pathogenic microbes in the contaminated surface water and the suspended particles on which they frequently hitched a ride were being trapped on the sticky surface of the biofilm, where they became food for the microbes living there. Because the biofilm also slows the flow of water through the sand, this type of filter is referred to as a slow sand filter.[24]

Today's slow sand filters face the same problems as those used at the Lawrence Experimental Station: eventually, the accumulated gunk clogs the openings between the sand grains of the filter. When clogging occurs, the filter is taken out of service, and the pathogenic and benign microbes, particles, and biofilm are removed along with the top layer of sand. Some fresh sand is added to the filter, and water is passed through it until a new biofilm is established. The regenerated filter is put back into service, and the cycle is completed. The sand filters at a water treatment plant are built as independent modules, which means that individual units can be rotated in and out of service as they cycle among filtration, cleaning, and regeneration.

The research on sand filters was promising enough to extend it to a full-scale water filtration plant capable of treating Lawrence's entire water supply. That decision was instigated by the severity of the typhoid fever outbreak, and supported by the documented success of a similar water treatment plant in Hamburg, Germany, which had prevented a cholera outbreak a year earlier.[25] After Lawrence's water filtration plant started running in 1893, the rate of typhoid fever dropped by 80 percent, reducing the incidence of the disease to levels comparable to those of the surrounding communities that obtained their water from more pristine sources. Contaminated food and person-to-person transmission of the disease meant that typhoid fever would not disappear entirely, but the slow sand filter had made the water safe to drink.

Although sand filters were effective against waterborne pathogens, they had two distinct disadvantages. First, their low flow rate meant that a large surface area was needed for a treatment plant. A city like Lawrence needed a series of filters the size of a football field. For a larger city like Philadelphia, these early sand filters might take up the area of ten or twenty football fields. This wasn't an insurmountable problem when weighed against the suffering caused by typhoid fever and cholera, but it meant that water treatment plants were going to occupy large land areas, often in the heart of a city where real estate was most expensive.

The second problem with sand filters was that they were prone to failure if the water to be treated contained a lot of suspended particles.

This situation wasn't much of an issue in European cities, such as London and Paris, or in cities on America's East Coast, such as Poughkeepsie, but it meant trouble for America's inland cities, where spring runoff churned up clay-containing sediments that made the Mississippi and Ohio Rivers look like chocolate milk.[26]

Why was the removal of suspended clay particles so difficult for the early slow sand filters? Electronic charge and particle size. Clay is tough to remove from water because its surface contains hydrogen ions that are easily lost to the water through a process referred to as dissociation. For each H^+ atom that the clay particle loses, a single negative charge builds up. When a clay particle with numerous negative charges on its surface approaches a biofilm, which also tends to be negatively charged due to the presence of proteins and other common biomolecules that readily lose hydrogen ions when put in water, the two particles are repelled from each other because particles with the same charge repel each another. As a result of repulsion, sand filters are not very effective when it comes to removing clay particles.

In addition to the charge repulsion that makes them difficult to capture on filters, tiny clay particles are tough to treat because the tiny particles settle out of water very slowly. The types of settling basins that the Romans had built within their aqueducts, for instance, could not be used to remove clay particles because it takes days or weeks for clay to settle out of water. J. P. Kirkwood was well aware of this problem and had included a settling basin that would retain Mississippi River water for twenty-four hours before it entered the filters of the plant that he had designed for St. Louis.[27] This was not a very practical solution, however, because the huge settling basin would have been difficult to build and maintain.

To solve the problem of treating clay-containing water, engineers working for the Louisville, Kentucky, Water Company developed a new form of water treatment in which chemicals were added to the water to overcome the forces of charge repulsion and allow the tiny clay particles to grow into larger, more rapidly settling particles. This new process, which became the basis for most of the water filtration plants that were subsequently built in the United States, initially relied on the addition of an aluminum sulfate salt known as alum.

Although they had little appreciation or understanding of the complex and subtle surface chemistry of alum precipitation, Louisville's engineers were able to use trial and error to develop a reliable water treatment system. The approach works as follows: when alum is added to water it forms a positively charged particle. This particle, a precipitated aluminum-containing solid, attracts the negatively charged clay particles, which attach to form a larger precipitate. After it picks up some clay, the overall charge of the precipitate becomes negative. The negatively charged clay-aluminum hybrid particle then attracts another positively charged aluminum-containing particle, causing the mixed precipitate to grow.

After a few hours, the clay and alum precipitate grows into a large fluffy particle, referred to as a floc, that is heavy enough to settle out of the water by gravity. The flocs are even large enough to be filtered out by a coarse bed of sand without the aid of a sticky biofilm. Without a biofilm growing at the top of the filter, water flows much faster. Hence, the new treatment process came to be known as rapid sand filtration.

Subsequent experiments showed that metal salts other than alum, such as ferric chloride (a waste product from iron foundries) or lime (calcium hydroxide), also could be used to create flocs. The choice of which of these three inexpensive chemicals to use in a particular location was determined by trial and error or was dictated by their availability and price.

These new turn-of-the-century treatment processes were more complicated than their predecessors. When the water entered the treatment plant, alum, or one of the other metal salts, was added in a rapidly stirred mixing chamber. Next it passed through a series of wooden paddle wheels that gently agitated the water, causing the small flocs to collide, stick together, and grow into larger flocs. After spending about an hour growing, the water and flocs entered a swimming-pool-sized rectangular concrete basin that was a few meters deep.

The majority of the flocs settled to the bottom of the basin as the clean water flowed out through an exit near the surface. Those flocs remaining in the water were subsequently removed on a sand filter. To prevent the growth of a biofilm that would slow the flow of water, the filter was periodically backwashed, using pressurized water applied through a pipe beneath the sand to stir up the filter and scrape off the accumulated gunk. In this manner, the filters could be run at a higher flow rate, which meant that the new system took up about a quarter as much real estate as the slow sand filter.

Whatever type of filtration system is being used, visiting your neighborhood water treatment plant is like taking a trip back in time. With the exception of a few racks of modern sensors and maybe some mechanical alum-dosing pumps, the whole affair isn't much different from the plants that were built at the end of the nineteenth century: wooden paddle wheels, sand filters, and concrete basins still protect us from waterborne disease.

Over the past century, many water treatment plants have stuck to traditional designs because the system is effective and changing it might have unexpected consequences. Even small changes in the operation of water treatment plants can affect water quality, which in turn affects microbes living on pipes as well as the minerals that coat the interior surfaces of the pipes. These changes can lead to problems such as the release of lead or an excessive growth of biofilms within the pipe network.

Development of rapid sand filters coupled with the documented success of water filtration in combating waterborne diseases in Lawrence and Hamburg in the late 1800s quickly led to the construction of water filtration plants throughout the United States. Within twenty years, water filtration went from being viewed as an ineffective and unnecessary luxury to an essential part of the water supply of "downstream" cities such as Cincinnati, Philadelphia, and Pittsburgh.[28]

The effect of water filtration on public health was immediate and substantial. Cities that had suffered from typhoid fever throughout the second half of the nineteenth century repeated Lawrence's success in combating the disease. In cities where a water filtration plant was built, the incidence of typhoid fever immediately decreased to levels comparable to those of cities that obtained their water from pristine sources.

In addition to providing relief from typhoid fever, public health experts studying mortality statistics in Hamburg and Lawrence made an unexpected discovery: life expectancy in communities with water filtration systems increased much more than could be explained by the elimination of typhoid alone. Deaths from respiratory diseases, childhood illnesses, and even old age all decreased after water treatment plants were installed. Alan Hazen, the prodigy who was instrumental to understanding how water filters worked, proposed an idea that came to be known as Hazen's Theorem: "Where one death from typhoid fever has been avoided by the use of better water, a certain number of deaths, probably two or three, from other causes have been avoided."[29]

This remarkable finding, which was borne out by data from other cities, showed that many chronic diseases that plagued cities actually were due to poor water quality. Water filtration did a lot more than prevent outbreaks of typhoid fever and cholera; it improved the overall health of the community. From 1900 to 1947 the lifespan of the average American increased from forty-seven to sixty-three years. According to Harvard economists David Cutler and Grant Miller, approximately half of the increased lifespan among city dwellers was due to the treatment of drinking water.[30]

Every water treatment technology has its limitations. A well-designed drinking water filtration system might remove 99 percent of the pathogenic microbes from water, meaning that one out of every hundred organisms will pass through the filter. For a river like the Merrimack that contains modest amounts of pathogenic microbes, a treatment process that achieves 99 percent reduction in organisms will be enough to make the water safe to drink.

But filtration alone could not prevent disease in cities where the water was even more polluted. For example, the slow sand filters that had been built in Poughkeepsie, New York, improved the appearance and taste of Hudson River water, but they did not prevent typhoid fever.[31] In locations where water treatment wouldn't be fully effective in preventing disease, engineers and public health experts advised cities to find new, less-contaminated water sources. But what about places where highly contaminated rivers could not be avoided?

The new understanding of germ theory that arose from the research of scientists like Louis Pasteur, Robert Koch, and John Snow established the idea that living microbes were responsible for waterborne disease. Filtration saved lives by removing pathogens from the water. Perhaps water also could be made safe to drink by killing the pathogenic microbes.

This idea—making water safe to drink by treatment methods that don't physically remove microbes—is actually ancient. Sanskrit and Greek writings dating from 4000 BCE recommend boiling water as a way of making it safe to drink.[32] The addition of small quantities of silver and copper to water also was known to protect against pathogens. Cyrus the Great, king of Persia in the sixth century BCE, took advantage of two of these methods by boiling water and storing it in silver flagons when he went to war.[33] This technique is still used today— Brita® and other companies that sell home water filters impregnate the surface of their filters with silver to prevent the growth of microbes. While the levels of silver added to household filters are not high enough to kill off waterborne pathogens, they do prevent the growth of biofilms that would eventually reduce the flow of water through the filter and possibly make the water taste bad. In light of the new understanding of the role of microbes in waterborne diseases, it was reasonable to surmise that pathogens in drinking water could be killed by heat or exposure to small quantities of chemicals that did not pose risks to people.

Treatments that rely on killing microbes—processes that are sometimes referred to as disinfection or sterilization—could make water safe to drink, but none of the ancient methods were practical for the water supply of an entire city. After all, immense amounts of energy would be required to boil the water supply for a city, and adding silver or other metals to the millions of liters of water that a city consumed each day could get expensive. Was there an inexpensive way to kill microbes prior to sending it to the tap?

Chlorine was an ideal candidate for the job. Chlorine had been applied to London's sewage in the 1850s in an attempt to eliminate the odors that were thought to be the source of the miasma causing the cholera outbreaks.[34] But it was not until the 1890s that people began to recognize the potential for using chlorine to disinfect water.

The earliest applications of chlorine for drinking water disinfection were stopgap measures used during severe disease outbreaks. For example, chlorine was added to the water supplies of an Austro-Hungarian naval base on the Adriatic Sea and to the English town of Maidstone in the midst of cholera outbreaks in 1896 and 1897, respectively.[35] In these early days, chlorine treatment was restricted to emergencies because it had to be synthesized at a chemical factory, where it was converted to a powdered form, calcium hypochlorite, which was stable enough to ship to the water treatment plant. Furthermore, the public was resistant to the idea of adding chemicals to the water supply when there wasn't an immediate danger.

Not until 1902 was chlorine continuously added to a water supply. The engineers who designed the water treatment plant for Middlekerke, Belgium, took advantage of the disinfecting properties of chlorine by substituting calcium hypochlorite for lime in the flocculation process.[36] For the leaders of Middlekerke, the decision to use these more expensive chemicals may have been tied to the city's role as a tourist destination: any bad press associated with unsafe drinking water could easily undermine confidence in the city as a safe place to visit.

Over the next decade, chlorine became less expensive as new production and storage processes were invented. In particular, the development of an industrial-scale process for making chlorine in water by passing electricity through salt brine solutions made it possible to produce chlorine on demand at the water treatment plant, thereby avoiding the need to ship chemicals there or to set up a complicated calcium hypochlorite manufacturing facility on site. This electro-chemical process was eventually used to make chlorine at a large water filtration plant in Philadelphia.[37]

At about the same time, engineers figured out how to produce concentrated chlorine gas at chemical factories. After the chlorine gas was created, it was compressed until it turned into a liquid. The liquefied chlorine was put into steel cylinders that could be shipped by rail to the water treatment plants. The water treatment plant operators could then bubble the gas into water, where it would dissolve to form a solution of liquid chlorine.

The process for making concentrated chlorine gas was perfected just as Europe was gearing up for World War I. The military had followed the development of water treatment technologies because waterborne disease had always been a major problem during military campaigns. Military planners, however, also realized that the toxic properties of chlorine gas had potential uses as a weapon. Whereas most people are familiar with the way in which mustard gas was used in trench warfare, few recognize that the first gas attack of World War I involved chlorine gas, which under the supervision of Germany's leading chemist, Fritz Haber, was released from the same type of tanks that were used at water treatment plants.[38] The first German assault on the French with this new chemical weapon was very effective, but chlorine gas was quickly abandoned in favor of mustard gas because, among other reasons, the chlorine gas released from the cylinders could easily blow back into the lines of the attacking army.

The combination of low cost and proven disinfecting power made chlorine an attractive alternative to water filtration. But after unsuccessful attempts to use slow sand filters in muddy waters, water treatment engineers were cautious about adopting new technologies that might ultimately prove to be ineffective. It isn't particularly surprising, then, that the clientele of the first drinking water treatment plant in the United States that continuously added chlorine had cloven hooves: in 1908, the Bubbly Creek water treatment plant adopted the method to stop the spread of waterborne disease among the cattle held in

Chicago's stockyards.[39] While the customers of America's first chlorinated water supply shuffled on until they met the butcher without thanking the engineers responsible for the feat, the successful use of chlorine at the stockyards coupled with reports of the successful uses of chlorine in Europe increased confidence in the technology.

Although chlorine now seemed like a reasonable choice for water disinfection, early treatment plants employed chlorination as an extra safety measure to be used in concert with water filtration. It was not until a construction contractor struggling to make a profit on a contentious water supply project proposed installing a plant where chlorination would be used without filtration that the power of the new treatment technology came to be appreciated.

The Boonton Reservoir seemed to be a clean source of water, with no sewers dumping waste into the rivers that supplied it. So the East Jersey Water Company had not initially planned to treat the water that it was supposed to deliver from the reservoir to Jersey City, New Jersey. A few years of monitoring, however, made it clear that large rainstorms could deliver loads of waterborne pathogens to the reservoir from the nearby villages and farms—and once the data on waterborne pathogens were available, the contractor and the city could not agree about who was responsible for fixing the problem. The East Jersey Water Company argued that the city was responsible for controlling the pollution, while the city claimed that the contractor needed to build an expensive water filtration plant. After a lengthy lawsuit, in which almost every engineer and public health expert in the country testified, a settlement was reached: the East Jersey Water Company would build a treatment plant, but as a cost-saving measure, the plant could use chlorination without filtration.[40]

The resulting Boonton Water Treatment Plant produced water that was safe to drink, and moreover marked an important moment in the history of drinking water treatment. The water in the Boonton Reservoir was not nearly as contaminated as the Merrimack or the Hudson Rivers, but nonetheless chlorine had proven to be a valuable asset in the fight against pathogenic microbes.

Even if chlorine was not as effective as filtration, it was relatively inexpensive and offered an insurance policy against malfunctioning water filters. Some engineers believed that it could be used alone when waters were not severely contaminated. But George Johnson, the engineer responsible for building the Bubbly Creek Water Treatment Plant and many of the other early water chlorination systems, cautioned against reliance on chlorine as the sole means of water protection:

> The use of hypochlorites cannot be considered in light of a substitute for filtration. Where waters are uniformly satisfactory in appearance, but open to suspicion as regards their content in bacteria, the use of the hypochlorite process alone in many cases may prove sufficient. Where waters are unsatisfactory in physical appearance and are also polluted and require filtration, the combined use of filters and the hypochlorite process is called for.[41]

The one-two punch of filtration coupled with chlorine became standard practice for the treatment of sewage-contaminated surface waters. By 1941, fully 85 percent of the water treatment plants in the United States were using chlorine.[42] Today, drinking water filtration is always accompanied by chlorination or some other means of disinfection. Chlorine is only applied without filtration when drinking water is obtained from wells, where the aquifer itself serves as a filter.

How, exactly, does chlorine inactivate pathogenic microbes? Even today, after more than a century of using chlorine, we are still not entirely sure how chlorine disinfection works. We do know that chlorine gas and calcium hypochlorite both dissolve in water to form hypochlorous acid (HOCl). Hypochlorous acid has a proton that can dissociate to yield hypochlorite: OCl^- and a proton, H^+. Hypochlorite is the active ingredient in household bleach, sodium hypochlorite. We know that hypochlorous acid, and to a lesser degree, hypochlorite, can oxidize proteins. After proteins are oxidized by chlorine, they are no longer able to do all of the important things that proteins do, such as bringing reactants into close proximity with one another so they can undergo chemical reactions, regulating the flow of ions and nutrients across cell membranes, and keeping the metabolic processes of the cells intact.

We don't know, however, which proteins are most sensitive to chlorine. We also aren't certain how much damage must occur before a cell loses its ability to infect a host. And we don't know to what extent hypochlorous acid's ability to kill microbes is related to its ability to sneak across cell membranes and damage the cell. Finding answers to these questions might allow us to predict which types of untested microbes will be least susceptible to chlorine or how changes in water quality will alter the disinfection process. They also might give us more insight into the ways that other chemicals can be used to disinfect water.

The combination of water filtration and chlorination was the first major innovation in drinking water since the Roman aqueducts and sewers. The newly developed system of drinking water treatment—which we'll refer to as Water 2.0—made it possible for growing cities to obtain water from sources that would otherwise be unsafe to drink. Immense progress had been made between 1890—when Lawrence, Massachusetts, first had sought Professor Sedgwick's help in fighting typhoid—and the 1940s, when filtration and chlorination became the norm for treating surface waters destined for water utility customers. Through these efforts, waterborne diseases like typhoid fever and cholera were largely eliminated in the United States. Consistent with Hazen's Theorem, substantial decreases in death rates were evident wherever water treatment plants had been built. In fact, the U.S. National Academy of Engineering identified water treatment and distribution as the fourth most important engineering feat of the twentieth century, after electrification, automobiles, and airplanes but ahead of electronics and the Internet.[43] Filtration and disinfection revolutionized urban water.

5

Burning Rivers, Fading Paint, and the Clean Water Movement

n the 1860s, Edwin Chadwick, Victor Hugo, Karl Marx, and their fellow reformers campaigned vigorously for centralized systems to help farmers capture the nutrients in the sewage pouring out of rapidly growing cities. But by the end of the century the widespread availability of inexpensive synthetic fertilizers had taken away the economic incentives for sewage farming.[1] Without a market for the nutrients, it was hard to justify doing anything other than discharging sewage directly to surface waters. In locations where sewage posed obvious threats to drinking water, cities tapped new sources in distant watersheds, or they built drinking water treatment plants equipped with filters and chlorine disinfection systems.

Although these measures were effective in fighting waterborne disease, they did nothing to reduce the foul smells of sewage-polluted waters. In coastal cities located on rivers, such as London and Boston, where the odors of sewage made downtown living unpleasant, individual sewers were hooked together in regional systems with outlets draining to the ocean.[2] After these sewer networks were built, wastes discharged by upstream communities and local industries still caused smells along the waterfront, but the situation was vastly improved a few blocks from the water.[3]

During the nineteenth century few people paid attention to the odors caused by sewage discharges until they penetrated residential areas. While it may be hard to fathom for those of us accustomed to museums, restaurants, and condominiums situated on expensive waterfront real estate, the urban waterfronts of the early industrial period were bustling, low-rent zones where loading docks, factories, and power plants prevented the public from approaching the water. Even if people could get there, they might not be able to distinguish the smell of sewage from the boat exhaust, burning coal, livestock, rotting vegetables, and other items that moved along the docks and sometimes fell into the water.[4]

It was hoped that in addition to ridding the air of odors, sewer construction in London and other big cities would prevent the spread of disease by preventing the accumulation of unhealthy vapors in the city. Although the miasma theory had little scientific merit, it hastened the construction of integrated sewer systems to move wastes out of cities. The ascent of germ theory during the last decades of the nineteenth century added new energy to this movement. It was no longer acceptable just to connect sewers to the nearest creek or river and ignore the smells until they became unbearable. Modern theories about public health focused attention on actions that were proven to prevent disease, such as keeping pathogenic microbes out of drinking water and food. By the 1920s, for instance, scientists had proven a link between waterborne diseases like typhoid fever and sewage-contaminated seafood that allowed public health officers to keep contaminated food out of the marketplace. (This was progress even though it was still often deemed easier to abandon local shellfish beds and import seafood from less polluted areas than to solve the sewage problem.)[5]

Sewage washing up on expensive beachfront property sometimes provided a justification for taking action too. In Los Angeles, beach contamination convinced the city to tie the local sewers together in a network terminating in a 1.5-kilometer (one mile)-long pipeline into the Pacific Ocean near Santa Monica. The pipe eliminated some of the worst smells, but it did not dilute the waterborne pathogens enough to prevent swimmers from becoming sick.[6] As the volume of sewage dumped into rivers increased after the turn of the century, other cities, such as Philadelphia and Washington, D.C., followed the examples set by London, Boston, and Los Angeles. But joining local sewers together and discharging wastes downstream of the city only passed the smells and associated contamination problems on to someone else.

Perhaps the most extreme case of passing a sewage problem on to a neighbor was Chicago, where the city had put considerable resources into a plan to protect its Lake Michigan drinking water intake. Reversing the flow of the Chicago River involved the construction of a series of locks and canals to connect it to the Des Plaines and Illinois rivers. After Chicago's re-routed sewage flowed about four hundred kilometers (250 miles), it entered the Mississippi River just upstream of St. Louis. The 1900 opening of the Chicago Sanitary and Ship Canal was good news for Chicago, but it meant that the city's foul smells now plagued the small towns between Joliet and Peoria. St. Louis had attempted to use legal remedies to block Chicago's construction of the canal when it learned of the plan, but the upstream city had hurriedly completed the canal before the court could issue its decision. Chicago's leaders need not have worried: the U.S. Supreme Court ruled that Chicago's wastes posed less of a problem to St. Louis residents than did the wastes discharged by slaughterhouses and distilleries along the Illinois River.[7]

Although the idea of drinking Chicago's sewage offended the sensibilities of people living in downstream towns and cities, the odor of water carried by the new canal disappeared after about eighty kilometers (fifty miles) as the river underwent self-purification. According to Chicago's commissioner of health, who had hired scientists from the University of Illinois to investigate the issue, "running streams, adequately diluted, do purify themselves of sewage pollution. . . . All talk of Chicago sewage injuriously affecting the drinking water of St. Louis is thus completely and effectually disposed of by the work of these investigators."[8]

How did the sewage's trip downstream from Chicago ease—or even eliminate—its smell? To answer this question, an understanding

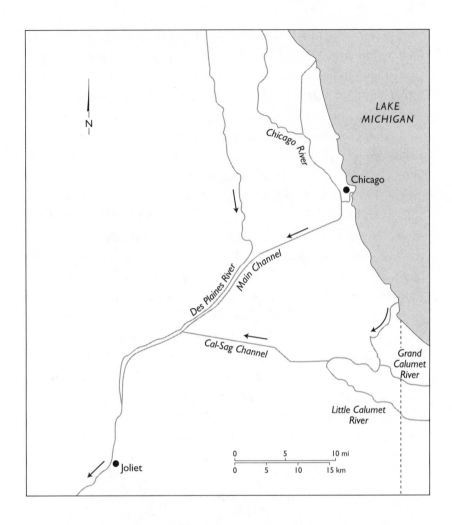

The Chicago Sanitary and Ship Canal.

of exactly how a sewage discharge causes unpleasant odors is helpful. The aroma of sewage is attributable to a mixture of about thirty different chemicals, including hydrogen sulfide (which smells like rotten eggs), skatole (which smells like feces), butanethiol (which smells like rotting cabbage), and butanone (which smells like green apple).[9] When this concoction temporarily binds to specialized receptors in our noses, we perceive the smell of sewage. Although the movements of each of the chemicals responsible for sewage odor in water and air are slightly different, we gain considerable insight into the smells of sewage-contaminated water by considering the most prominent chemical responsible for the smell of sewage: hydrogen sulfide.

This simple, reduced form of sulfur consumes oxygen as it is converted to sulfate by bacteria in rivers (Chapter 4). Because sulfate is odorless, many of the smells of sewage were eliminated when the oxygen-consuming microbes living in the river used hydrogen sulfide and related odorous compounds as a source of food. But if the oxygen was depleted by microbial activity as the water flowed downstream, not all of the hydrogen sulfide would get converted into sulfate. Instead, some of it would escape from water, moving through the air to human noses—superbly sensitive detectors that are capable of sensing the rotten-egg smell of hydrogen sulfide at concentrations as low as ten parts per billion. Our exquisite sensitivity to hydrogen sulfide is no accident: the compound is quite toxic. Hydrogen sulfide causes headaches and sore throats at concentrations about a hundred times higher than those where our noses can first detect its presence. At concentrations about ten thousand times higher than the odor threshold, hydrogen sulfide is lethal.[10]

Hydrogen sulfide is found in many places where chemical reactions happen in the absence of oxygen. For example, hydrogen sulfide leaking from the hot springs of Yellowstone National Park tells us that chemical reactions involving sulfur are occurring within the earth's crust. Most chemical reactions require the presence of an oxidant, which is also known as an electron acceptor. When oxygen is present, it normally serves as the oxidant, taking on electrons as it is converted into water. But when oxygen is absent, as is frequently the case underground, another electron acceptor is needed. Sulfate—one of the most common dissolved salts—often fulfills this need, accepting electrons as it is converted into hydrogen sulfide.

Bacteria living in the oxygen-free environment of the human digestive system also produce hydrogen sulfide when they too employ sulfate as a substitute for oxygen in their metabolic processes. In other words, the microbes "breathe in" sulfate, use it to accept the electrons acquired when they extracted energy from their food, and "breathe out" hydrogen sulfide. And yes, the strong tendency of dissolved hydrogen sulfide to move from the liquid to the gaseous phase is largely responsible for the smell of human intestinal gas. But the smell of flatulence is only a minor part of the story. More important for those of us interested in the odors experienced downstream of early twentieth-century sewers, wastes flushed down the toilet in cities like Chicago did not contain a lot of hydrogen sulfide. Most of the hydrogen sulfide in polluted rivers was actually produced within sewers and in poorly mixed sewage-receiving rivers where microbes had consumed all of the available oxygen. Adding large amounts of sewage to water thus depleted the oxygen and supported the activity of hydrogen-sulfide-producing bacteria that amplify the smells of sewage.

Despite the potential for sewage to produce hydrogen sulfide, not all sewage-receiving rivers stank, because the oxygen-breathing bacteria often degraded the hydrogen sulfide and organic compounds before all of the oxygen was consumed. For example, the section of the Merrimack River downstream from Lowell contained more than enough bacteria to spread typhoid fever to Lawrence, but the river did not emit strong odors because sewage discharged by Lowell was quickly diluted by oxygen-rich water flowing in from upstream. Except for the modest amount of hydrogen sulfide initially present in the sewage, which might have led to some odors near the sewer's discharge point, the river was able to eliminate the smells through self-purification. Of course, preventing oxygen depletion was also beneficial to fish, insects, and other oxygen-breathing creatures that couldn't survive in the absence of their favorite electron acceptor, but concerns about damage to aquatic habitat did not yet command much attention.

To predict how much sewage could be discharged to a river before its dissolved oxygen would be depleted, H. W. Streeter and his colleagues at the U.S. Public Health Service Laboratory in Cincinnati developed a system of mathematical equations to predict oxygen concentrations downstream of a sewage discharge.[11] The equations represented one of the first attempts to predict the ability of a natural system to purify water. By quantifying the capacity of rivers to remove reduced compounds in sewage, the government researchers took a crucial first step toward actively managing the water cycle to improve water quality.

To simplify the problem, they broke it into two parts. First, they estimated the potential for wastes to deplete oxygen by adding a few drops of bacteria-enriched water to a sample and sealing it in a bottle. After the bottle was incubated in the laboratory for five days, they measured the decrease in oxygen concentration. The amount of oxygen lost, which came to be referred to as the five-day biochemical oxygen demand, or BOD_5, provided a simple means of quantifying the amount of oxygen-consuming chemicals in the water sample. Next they estimated the rate at which the oxygen would be replenished by observing the relationship between characteristics of a river—such as its depth, temperature, and the extent of riffles and waterfalls—and the rate at which gases were transferred in and out of the water. They turned these two pieces of information into equations that could predict the rate at which oxygen was depleted from the water.

The mathematical balancing act between oxygen consumption and replenishment, known as the Streeter-Phelps dissolved oxygen sag curve, accurately predicted oxygen concentrations downstream of a city's sewage discharge. The model almost always predicted a gradual decrease in oxygen concentrations as water flowed away from a sewage discharge point due to the breakdown of reduced compounds by bacteria living on the surfaces of rocks and river sediments. At some distance downstream—often as little as eight kilometers (five miles)—the rate of oxygen consumption would slow as the organic compounds in the waste were exhausted. Eventually, the concentration of dissolved oxygen in the river water would reach a minimum value and begin to increase as the rate at which oxygen returning to the water from the atmosphere exceeded the rate at which it was being consumed by the microbes.[12]

If the oxygen ran out before the minimum oxygen concentration was reached, all of the fish and aquatic life in that section of the river would die off and the sulfate-breathing bacteria would take over. But the domain of the hydrogen sulfide-producing bacteria was usually restricted to a short reach of the river. Provided that no other wastes entered the river downstream from the sewer, oxygen concentrations would climb as the reduced compounds in the sewage were depleted. At some distance downstream the oxygen concentrations in the water would finally return to normal.

The Streeter-Phelps model provided engineers with a means of predicting the effects of increasing the amount of sewage released to a river. It also made it possible to predict when and where fish kills and hydrogen sulfide releases would occur. Armed with this new tool, engineers were able to tell city leaders how much waste could be discharged to a river before its oxygen would be fully depleted. But it didn't take a sophisticated model to predict the future: the rapid rate of population growth meant that many inland cities that were not already exceeding the ability of their rivers to self-purify would exhaust the environment's natural treatment capacity in the near future. For example, Chicago's sewage disposal canal had been planned when the city's population was projected to level off at around 3 million inhabitants. Unfortunately, the planners had underestimated: Chicago's population expanded from 1.7 million to 3.4 million between 1900 and 1930 and showed little sign of slowing.[13] For Chicago and other rapidly growing cities, it was only a matter of time before the downstream neighbors complained.

It was around this time that Progressive politicians began to turn water pollution into a political issue. Uncomfortable with the idea of cities not cleaning up after themselves, the Progressives picked up where Victor Hugo and Karl Marx had stopped. Believing that corporations and cities should do the right thing even if it took a toll on their profits, Progressives campaigned for worker protection, food safety, and stewardship of natural resources. They also espoused the idea that sewage treatment was the right thing to do. During a speech in 1909, the leading politician of the movement, Theodore Roosevelt, entered the fray when he said, "Civilized people should be able to dispose of sewage in a better way than by putting it into drinking water."[14] But Roosevelt and the Progressives had more popular and pressing injustices to fight. Sewage was a relatively low priority compared with trust busting, worker protection, and the establishment of national parks.

Other than giving a rousing speech about the injustice of sewage disposal, what could city leaders do after an upstream city's wastes had exhausted the ability of a shared river to self-purify? Reducing the volume of waste flowing from the sewers was not a popular idea, because no one was interested in giving up the flush toilet or returning to cesspools. In desperation, many cities turned to a rudimentary and inexpensive form of sewage treatment: settling basins. That is, some of the oxygen-consuming compounds were removed by putting wastes through rectangular basins like those used to settle flocs at drinking water treatment plants. Using gravity alone it was possible to remove about a third of the oxygen-consuming solids.[15]

To understand why settling basins could help prevent oxygen depletion in rivers, we need to return to the sewer and consider the composition of the easily settled solid material in sewage. In other words, we need to think like chemists about those bits and pieces suspended in early twentieth-century sewage. First the scatological part: some of the particles were exactly what you might expect—human feces, which is essentially all of the food that the body is unable to digest plus some of the bacteria that live in the oxygen-free world of the human digestive system. What is surprising is that bacteria account for up to half of the solids in feces. These tiny organisms are essential to human health and survival, because they convert large organic molecules into smaller pieces that our bodies can absorb. In addition to eliminating the food that humans are unable to digest, defecation provides a form of microbial population control. By removing some of the bacteria, the process prevents us from ballooning as intestinal bacteria grow and reproduce within our bodies. From a chemist's perspective, feces consists of difficult-to-degrade fibers from plants, undigested fats, inorganic salts, plus the carbohydrates, proteins, and nucleic acids that make up the bacteria inhabiting our digestive systems.

Sewage also contained more than just feces and random hunks of food washed down the sink: by the turn of the century, sewers were receiving a lot of industrial waste. If a business produced waste that could be carried down the drain with a healthy slug of water, it went into the sewer. As a result, sewers received waste from canneries, paper-making factories, breweries, and butcheries, all of which consisted mainly of cellulose, carbohydrates, proteins, and other easily oxidized organic compounds. During this period, organic wastes from industrial processes frequently contributed more reduced compounds to sewage than did wastes from homes.

The difficulties caused by oxygen-consuming industrial wastes eventually led to requirements for industries to remove organic-rich material from their wastewater before they put it into sewers. It is therefore ironic that General Electric's Garbage Grinder was developed in the 1940s as a means of using the sewer to dispose of organic materials in household waste. In 1950, after suffering from a cholera outbreak attributed to pigs being fed on the town's trash, local officials in Jasper, Indiana, passed a law requiring residents to install in their kitchen sinks the device that came to be known as the garbage disposal.[16] The devices put the pigs out of business and removed the cholera threat by putting an entire household's trash down the drain (this practice occurred in the era before plastic). The savings associated with the elimination of garbage pickups allowed the city to invest in a larger sewage treatment plant to handle the additional load of reduced organic compounds.

After the success of the Jasper experiment, other cities encouraged the installation of the labor-saving devices. Most, however, did not anticipate how much they would burden sewers and wastewater treatment plants with increased volumes of organic wastes. By 1960 Boston, New York, and Philadelphia had banned garbage disposals because their aging wastewater systems were unable to process the wastes. But quickly growing cities equipped with modern sewage systems such as Detroit and Denver actually required the devices in new homes built in the 1960s. Today many homes are equipped with these devices even though they put an extra burden on sewers and sewage treatment plants. And while they may save us an occasional trip to the garbage can, they certainly have not eliminated the need for trash pickup.

By preventing the suspended particles contained in sewage from entering rivers, settling basins kept a significant source of oxygen-depleting material out of rivers. Settling sewage in a basin was nonetheless a messy solution, because bacteria rapidly depleted the oxygen from these simple treatment systems—and if the oxygen disappeared completely, large quantities of hydrogen sulfide would escape. The construction of settling basins also brought about another problem: once again, cities had to dispose of large quantities of solid waste. But in contrast to the situation during the cesspool era, there was very little demand from farmers for the nutrient-rich but smelly fertilizer coming out of the settling basins.

By building settling basins at the end of the sewer pipes, cities essentially relocated some of the odors that would have been produced in the river to areas where people lived. Because of the smell of hydrogen sulfide and other odors wafting out of the basins, these early treatment plants were not popular with the neighbors. In Toronto, the owner of a candy and ice cream shop located opposite the city's new sewage treatment plant initiated legal proceedings against the city claiming that his business had been ruined by the smells emanating from the plant. The judge agreed, and in 1915 issued an order requiring the city to shut down the sewage treatment plant.[17]

Shortly after the turn of the century, an elegant solution to the problems of odors and solid waste accumulation was developed by the German engineer Karl Imhoff, who patented a simple device that retained

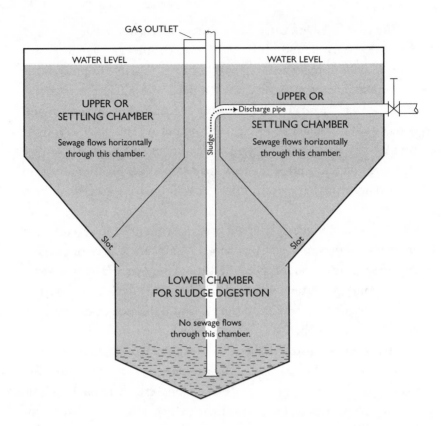

The Imhoff tank, which was designed to remove solids from sewage.

solids in a chamber isolated from the flowing water. By inserting a baffle to separate the organic-matter-rich solids from the water, the two-story-high Imhoff tank encouraged the growth of a different type of bacteria that could survive in the absence of oxygen.[18]

Unlike in the settling basins, the lack of flowing water in the lower part of the Imhoff tank meant that microbes would quickly use up the small amount of dissolved sulfate that managed to pass into the chamber along with the solids—and then bacteria that "breathed in" carbon dioxide would take over. The decomposition of organic-matter-rich solids by these organisms produced a different type of gas as the microbes "breathed out" methane. The carbon-dioxide-reducing bacteria were so effective at breaking down the organic-rich solids that the rate at which solids accumulated in the tank slowed to a trickle. And the carbon dioxide never ran out because the oxidation of organic matter released more carbon dioxide into the water. Particles not susceptible to the metabolic prowess of the bacteria only had to be removed from the Imhoff tank about once a year.

The engineers quickly realized another potential advantage: the Imhoff tank produced odorless methane—the main component of natural gas. Using methane for fuel, however, was not economically attractive in the early twentieth century because there was no inexpensive process for capturing and storing the gas. Methane produced by most Imhoff tanks was simply vented directly to the atmosphere or, better yet, burned as it exited to minimize the risk that a stray spark would turn the tank into a sewage bomb.[19]

The Imhoff tank and settling basins, which later came to be referred to as primary treatment, were built throughout Europe and North America during the first two decades of the twentieth century.[20] Although primary treatment did not solve the problems associated with sewage discharges, it decreased the amount of oxygen-demanding organic particles that was released into surface waters. In some cases, this simple approach was enough to eliminate the smells associated with oxygen depletion. In Chicago, an Imhoff tank capable of treating 1.5 billion liters (400 million gallons) of sewage per day was built in 1927 to reduce the odors from the city's sewage canal system.[21] But population growth soon overran the improvements from the primary treatment systems. More than just a gravity-settling process would be required to prevent oxygen depletion downstream of cities.

Although primary treatment was little more than a stopgap solution for many inland communities, the practice persisted throughout the twentieth century in coastal cities. Using discharge pipes up to eight kilometers (five miles) long fitted with outlets designed to maximize the mixing of sewage into deep ocean waters, primary treatment is only now being phased out in Honolulu, San Diego, and Sydney. (For this reason, the screenwriters for *Finding Nemo* may have set the film in Australia because Sydney is located on the same continent as the Great Barrier Reef and is one of the few places in the English-speaking world where a tropical fish flushed down the toilet could have made it out to the ocean alive—provided it didn't succumb to the hydrogen sulfide and other chemicals in the sewer.)

For much of the twentieth century it was hard to complain about the offshore discharge of sewage, because the system was inexpensive and solved the problems associated with noxious smells, pathogen-contaminated shellfish beds, and sewage washing up on beaches. While this out-of-sight, out-of-mind approach to sewage disposal was effective, newfound interest in recovering the water and nutrients from sewage is bringing about the end of the practice. The final chapter of the ocean disposal era has also been hastened by recognition of the damage to ocean ecosystems caused by the hundreds of millions of gallons of sewage pouring into deep ocean waters every day. In many coastal areas, pristine ecosystems have been damaged by the huge influx of organic matter, nutrients, and, maybe worst of all, salt-free water (which is very toxic to marine life).

Inland communities searched for approaches that were more effective at removing oxygen-consuming substances from sewage than primary treatment. The method used by Paris at the turn of the century—construction of a network of sewage farms—was not considered a viable solution in most cities, because farming required about a hectare (2.5 acres) to dispose of the wastes of a thousand people.[22] For a large city like Philadelphia, sewage farms would have required about a thousand hectares (four square miles) of arable land near the city center plus a massive infrastructure that was not considered practical by the city's leaders.

Although sewage farming had few proponents in the United States, the ability of soil to purify water planted a seed of inspiration that ultimately led to the invention of modern sewage treatment processes: perhaps the processes responsible for purifying water as it percolated through farm soils could be made more efficient in a carefully controlled system. Starting in the 1870s, engineers at the Lawrence Experimental Station had been trying to harness the self-purification properties of sewage farms.[23] Their early experiments demonstrated that microbes involved in the process became much less efficient when they ran out of oxygen. To overcome this problem, they applied the sewage to the land in batches, and were careful to stop adding the waste before the oxygen was depleted from the pore spaces between the soil particles. Between applications of sewage, oxygen would seep back into the soil pores. By doing away with crops on the land surface, it was possible to use fast-draining soils consisting of porous materials like sand and gravel. This new process, which the researchers referred to as intermittent filtration, required about half as much land as sewage farming for the treatment of the same volume of sewage.[24] While this was an improvement, there was little advantage to intermittent filtration if the local soils were not composed of porous sand and gravel. Several hundred intermittent filtration systems were built in the rocky soils of small New England cities at the turn of the century, but the approach never caught on in densely populated cities and towns that lacked the appropriate types of soil.[25]

To harness the power of microbes to purify water without having to set up vast networks of sewage farms or intermittent filters, an aboveground treatment process was needed. Numerous new approaches to sewage treatment were developed around the turn of the century, but only two caught on among design engineers. Both used primary treatment to remove particles, then exposed the sewage to large populations of oxygen-breathing microbes.

The first approach, which came to be known as the trickling filter, looked a lot like an intermittent filter in a concrete box. It had, however, one big advantage: by increasing the pore spaces in the filter through the use of gravel instead of sandy soil, oxygen depletion became less of a problem. The trickling filters used a rotating arm, like a windmill on its side, to apply sewage to the surface of a basin of coarse gravel 1.5 to three meters (five to ten feet) high. A drain at the bottom of the basin ensured that water did not pool in the open spaces between the gravel. By applying the settled sewage at a slow rate, the gravel would remain in constant contact with the waste while the spaces between the stones would always be filled with air. Under these conditions, a hearty biofilm capable of rapidly oxidizing reduced compounds grew on the surface of the gravel. As the sewage trickled over the gravel, the water was purified.[26]

The first large trickling filter sewage treatment plants were built in Manchester, England, and in Madison, Wisconsin, in 1893 and 1901, respectively. Over time, trickling filter treatment plants became more popular as engineers learned how to nurture the biofilms growing on the gravel. The trickling filters built in England and the United States during the first decades of the twentieth century were so effective and robust that many are still in service today. But few new trickling filter plants are currently being built because technologies developed later were less expensive. In fact, the early adoption of trickling filters in England committed cities to the technology and prevented them from abandoning inefficient plants when less expensive alternatives were developed.[27]

The second successful aboveground sewage treatment technology took a different approach. By bubbling air through sewage—much as air bubbles are introduced to streams as water plunges over rocks and ledges—it was possible to rapidly oxidize reduced compounds without the need for an attached biofilm. Freed from the oxygen limitations that normally retarded their growth in sewage-polluted rivers, the oxygen-using microbes multiplied rapidly. The resulting microbial community accomplished the self-purification process that Streeter and Phelps had modeled in rivers within the confines of a concrete tank. But instead of needing ten or twenty kilometers to oxidize the compounds, the activated sludge microbe got the job done in a few hundred meters.

The original idea for activated sludge treatment was inspired by a visit to the Lawrence Experimental Station by Gilbert Fowler. On his visit, Fowler witnessed a simple experiment in which reduced compounds were rapidly removed as air was bubbled into a beaker of sewage. Upon his return to the University of Manchester in 1913, Fowler

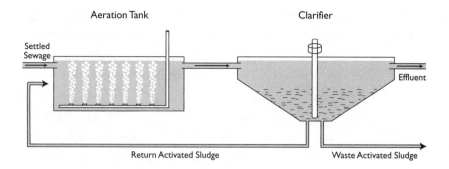

Aeration Tank   Clarifier

Settled Sewage

Effluent

Return Activated Sludge   Waste Activated Sludge

The activated sludge process.

and his students Edwin Ardern and W. T. Lockett turned this simple idea into a practical treatment system that they referred to as activated sludge. Although the name is not particularly appealing, the description is apt: the term "sludge" referred to the muddy brown appearance of the microbial colonies responsible for oxidizing the waste, while "activated" referred to the fact that the sludge was alive.[28]

In the new activated sludge system, tiny air bubbles introduced oxygen into a two-story-high tank that was continuously fed with settled sewage. Within the tank, colonies of suspended microbes fed on the reduced compounds. The bacteria and the treated sewage then flowed into a second tank known as a clarifier, which was much like the basins used to settle the floc particles formed in drinking water treatment plants. Because the bacteria grew in bulky colonies, they quickly sank to the bottom of the basin, which made it possible to separate them from the purified water. By returning some of the settled sludge to the first tank, it was possible to maintain a high population of hungry microbes in the aerated tank.

Just as humans need to eliminate excess bacteria growing in the digestive system, the activated sludge system needed to control the population of activated sludge microbes in the aerated tank. To avoid runaway growth, only about half of the settled activated sludge was returned to the first tank. The remainder of the activated sludge was typically dried and used as fertilizer.[29] Thus some of the nutrients in sewage were returned to the land. But unlike the solid material collected from cesspools and primary settling tanks, wastes from the activated sludge process did not smell like sewage. While the musty smell of activated sludge was not exactly pleasant, it was much easier to sell this nutrient-rich waste to farmers.

From the early developments in the 1880s until the period around World War II, settling basins, Imhoff tanks, trickling filters, and activated sludge became increasingly popular as means of treating sewage. By 1940, about half of the sewage in the United States was being treated in some manner prior to discharge.[30] Among the treatment plants, approximately half used only primary treatment. Activated sludge or trickling filters, the technologies that were eventually referred to as secondary treatment, were reserved for the toughest problems. A similar pattern emerged in Europe: during the first half of the twentieth century, as part of the continuing fight against oxygen depletion and the pollution of rivers, the United Kingdom rapidly adopted trickling filters and other countries gradually adopted activated sludge treatment as replacements for sewage farms.[31]

Before World War I, respected leaders in the engineering community, such as Alfred Hazen, the prodigy who documented the health benefits of water filtration, did not see wastewater treatment as a necessary part of a drinking water system:

> It is, therefore, both cheaper and more effective to purify the water, and to allow the sewage to be discharged, without treatment, so far as there are not other reasons for keeping it out of the rivers. It seems unlikely that a single case can be found where a given and reasonably sufficient expenditure of money wisely made could do as much to improve the quality of a given water supply when expended in purifying sewage above as could be secured from the same amount of money in treating the water. Usually I believe that there would be a wide ratio: that one dollar spent purifying water would do as much as ten dollars spent in sewage purification.[32]

While Hazen's logic was undeniable when the sole objective of treatment was to efficiently and economically prevent the spread of waterborne disease, an alternative viewpoint was developing. Arguments were made in favor of having sewage treatment as a second barrier against waterborne disease. Others noted that sewage treatment could eliminate the foul flavors often encountered in drinking water taken from sewage-polluted water, or benefit fisherman and recreational users of rivers. A new consciousness about the environment also was developing. As Aldo Leopold explained in his book *A Sand County Almanac,* rivers do more than "turn turbines, float barges, and carry off sewage."[33]

Despite the compelling need to build more sewage treatment plants, the nation put a low priority on sewage treatment relative to other pressing needs.[34] From 1925 to 1936, expenditures for sewage treatment plant construction averaged around a dollar a person per month, which was less than 10 percent of what was spent on highways and roads during the same period.[35] (To provide a basis for comparing expenditures in different periods without worrying about the effect of inflation, costs for infrastructure discussed in this and subsequent chapters have been adjusted for inflation. They are also expressed as if the costs were evenly distributed over the population served. These two assumptions are helpful for making comparisons but they are far from perfect in accounting for all variations.) Even after the U.S. government began funding massive infrastructure projects to counteract the effects of the Great Depression, sewage treatment plant construction struggled to keep up with population growth.

After World War II, the public was more sympathetic to the need for sewage treatment because the problem was becoming more difficult to ignore. In 1946, the U.S. Public Health Service estimated that the nation's inland waterways were receiving untreated sewage from 47 million people.

Perhaps nowhere was the need for sewage treatment more obvious than in the three booming cities located on San Francisco Bay: San Francisco, the region's commercial and cultural center; its less

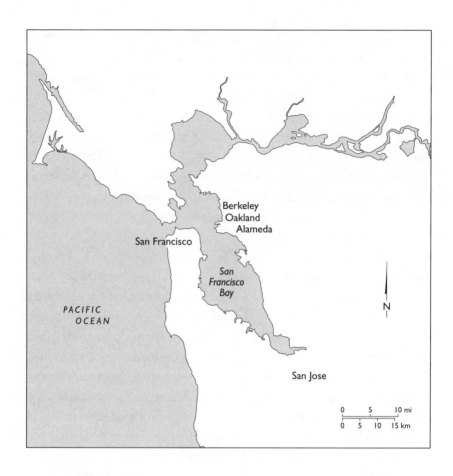

The San Francisco Bay region and the location of its major cities.

glamorous, hard-working industrialized sister, Oakland; and the sprawling agricultural community of San Jose. Because they were close to the country's main Pacific port, the three cities underwent rapid growth during the first half of the twentieth century.[36]

San Francisco Bay served as the repository for the region's sewage.[37] Engineers responsible for building and maintaining the sewer system for the Bay Area assumed that the timeworn approach of self-purification and dilution would be good enough for the region's rapidly growing cities. Initially they were right: in the early days, the bay's tidal flushing quickly sent sewage out to sea. But with an average depth of around six meters (twenty feet) and limited tidal circulation along the mud flats ringing the shoreline, the ability of the bay to self-purify was less than expected.[38]

San Francisco Bay's problems were particularly acute in the south, where the contents of San Jose's sewers discharged into a poorly circulating section of the bay where a narrow channel constricted water flow. The problem was exacerbated by the local canneries, which added tomato skins, juice-laden wash water, and rotten fruit to the sewer system's household waste. The bacteria living in the waters of the South Bay feasted on this rich mixture of reduced organic compounds, using up the dissolved oxygen and causing hydrogen sulfide and methane to bubble up from the sediments.

Hydrogen sulfide was so prevalent in the neighborhood near San Jose's sewer outlet that the color of freshly painted buildings faded after a few days of exposure to the polluted bay air.[39] (The fading was due to the widespread use of lead paint. Before we were aware of the hazards associated with childhood lead exposure, house paint contained between 10 and 50 percent lead in the form of lead carbonate, a white mineral. When hydrogen sulfide gas from sewage-fouled water came into contact with lead carbonate, it was converted into a gray lead sulfide mineral.) Although faded paint was inconvenient, the ever-present smell of hydrogen sulfide was literally a daily headache for residents of San Jose who lived near the bay.

Conditions were not much better in Oakland, where sewage was discharged to the edge of the bay. The sewage pooled on the shallow mudflats, creating a broad zone of hydrogen-sulfide-emitting sediments west of the city. The stink emanating from the mudflats made the ride on the new Bay Bridge connecting Oakland to San Francisco an uncomfortable experience. Luckily, the ride only lasted a few minutes. Residents of Alameda, an island south of the bridge that was home to Oakland's naval base, were not as lucky: they had to endure strong hydrogen sulfide odors whenever sea breezes shifted in their direction.[40] According to U.C. Berkeley professor Charles Gilman

Hyde, "because of this bad practice the shores and shore waters of the East Bay cities have become obnoxiously and notoriously foul and an affront to civic pride and common decency."[41]

Sewage odors were not confined to San Francisco Bay during the postwar period. The Hudson River below Troy, the Potomac River below Washington, D.C., the Mississippi River below Minneapolis, and the Delaware River below Philadelphia were all suffering from oxygen depletion due to excessive sewage discharges.[42] The problem had grown to a point where it could no longer be ignored.

In response to public outcry, the Water Pollution Control Act of 1948 was enacted. The new law established the idea that the federal government had a role to play in water pollution control. But political wrangling by representatives opposed to an expanded federal role in state affairs restricted the new statute to cases where interstate commerce was threatened. Ultimately the Water Pollution Control Act had little influence, because the promised grants and loans for sewage treatment plant construction never materialized.[43] Without federal grants as a carrot and regulatory enforcement as a stick, the law had little chance of changing the status quo. Between 1946 and 1949, only 646 new sewage treatment plants were built at a cost of approximately sixty cents a person per month.[44] Despite the growing problem and the existence of effective remedies (such as secondary sewage treatment plants), little progress was made in reversing the effects of sewage pollution.

The Water Pollution Control Act of 1948 had even less of an effect in California, where sewage discharges rarely affected interstate commerce. Because the state was so large, and the threats of Bay Area pollution to neighboring states were small, California was obliged to create its own system of water quality regulations, which gave California's regulators the ability to levy fines and prevent additional growth in cities when sewage discharges caused a public nuisance.[45]

The city of San Jose quickly realized that it would have to build a treatment plant if growth were to continue. After a construction bond failed to win the needed two-thirds majority in 1949, the state issued an order requiring the city to stop dumping its sewage into the bay.[46] The threat of daily fines and the prohibition of further land development galvanized the business community's support of the bonds. After the second bond measure passed in 1950, the city built a primary treatment plant. San Francisco, Oakland, and a handful of small communities circling the bay also built primary wastewater treatment plants during the early 1950s. Solving the sewage problem was not cheap: during this five-year period, expenditures on sewage treatment plants in the region rose to about twenty dollars a person per month.[47]

San Jose found a way of turning the hardship of financing a treatment plant to its advantage, however. The nearby communities, which also relied on the bay for sewage disposal, did not have the resources to build their own sewage treatment plants or the long sewer pipes needed to convey their wastes to the bay. San Jose offered these communities a solution that would allow them to keep growing. By accepting annexation, the neighboring communities were able to hook their sewers into the city's centralized system. In this way, San Jose shared the pain of funding sewage treatment plant construction among more taxpayers. In the process, the city doubled its population and increased its land area by 34,000 hectares (84,000 acres).[48] While Los Angeles had used access to drinking water to compel smaller cities to accept annexation, San Jose had gobbled up its neighbors with sewer hookups.

Elsewhere, cities were unable to keep up with their increasing volumes of waste without stricter laws and increased funding.[49] In 1956 Congress reauthorized the Water Pollution Control Act and in the process strengthened its enforcement provisions and provided financial support in the form of loans and matching grants for sewage treatment plant construction.[50] Between 1957 and 1969, approximately $5.4 billion was spent on sewage treatment plant construction, which works out to about $1.40 per person per month. Of these funds, about a quarter consisted of federal grants.[51]

Federal funding finally started to turn the situation around. By 1972, fully 98 percent of the country's urban population was served by sewage treatment plants. Not only were most city dwellers hooked up to treatment plants, but secondary treatment was becoming the norm as well: only about a third of the people living in cities were hooked up to treatment plants that did not employ some sort of biological treatment process.[52]

While increased funding during the 1960s alleviated some of the worst problems, many cities located on large bodies of water were still discharging their wastes into rivers, lakes, or estuaries after only primary treatment. For these cities, self-purification and dilution solved the problems that had once resulted in nasty smells along the shore—but they did not prevent problems farther away. For example, the sewage of Detroit and Cleveland as well as the wastes from automobile factories, steel mills, and chemical factories were discharged to Lake Erie with little or no treatment.[53] As a result, oxygen was depleted from the central part of the lake. In 1967 Senator Frank Moss wrote, "Today, about a fourth of Lake Erie is all but dead. This huge expanse encompasses 2,600 square miles in the central basin. It contains almost no oxygen, and no fish swim there; the surface is infested with scum."[54]

This dangerous cycle of building or upgrading sewage treatment plants only when conditions had deteriorated beyond a point of tolerance, and the public's skepticism about building treatment plants for anything other than eliminating odors or protecting drinking water supplies, quite likely would have continued had it not been for the birth of the environmental movement. Concerns about nuclear war, smog, and water pollution captured the public's imagination in the late 1960s. The much-publicized Cuyahoga River fire of 1969 and Rachel Carson's *Silent Spring* were rallying points for environmentalists campaigning against pollution.[55] Once the nation had turned its attention to the issue, it was possible for environmentalists to succeed where Progressives had failed sixty years earlier. On January 1, 1970, President Richard Nixon stated, "The 1970s absolutely must be the years when America pays its debt to the past by reclaiming the purity of its air, its water, and our living environment. It is literally now or never."[56]

In response to these growing concerns, a number of environmental protection laws were passed in the early 1970s.[57] Among these, the Clean Water Act of 1972 had the greatest impact on sewage treatment. By establishing a system of permits and regulations coupled with more generous grants and loans for sewage treatment plant construction, the law assured that almost every city built a sewage treatment plant equipped with both primary and secondary treatment systems. The new federal grants jumpstarted an era of sewage treatment plant construction. Between 1973 and 1981, federal grants covered up to 75 percent of sewage treatment plant construction costs. As a result, between $20 to $30 billion, or about four dollars a person per month, was spent on treatment plant construction during this brief period.[58]

Ironically, neither of the events that galvanized public opinion was directly related to sewage treatment. The 1969 Cuyahoga River fire was attributable to a layer of oil from the city's manufacturing facilities.[59] Although the river had caught fire on several previous occasions, the public's newfound interest in water pollution made the story newsworthy. Similarly, *Silent Spring* was an indictment of the chemical industry and not sewage pollution: with the exception of the sewage treatment plant near the chemical's main manufacturing site in Los Angeles, the main source of DDT in birds was aerial pesticide spraying and runoff from farms.

The support for sewage treatment plant construction during this period was in part due to the public's lack of understanding of the newly recognized challenges posed by synthetic chemicals. For a public anxious for responses to the threats posed by industrial pollution, investing in proven technologies, like activated sludge wastewater treatment plants, was more satisfying than banning DDT and hoping that the pesticide's replacement would be more benign.

After the investments spurred on by the Clean Water Act, the quality of the nation's waters improved markedly. For example, after

San Jose, Oakland, and San Francisco upgraded their sewage treatment plants, the amount of reduced chemicals entering the bay (as measured by the five-day biochemical oxygen demand) decreased by 88 percent, despite large increases in population. Fish kills became less common, and concentrations of bacteria in the bay decreased to the point that it became safe to swim in, provided swimmers steered clear of container ships and the occasional shark.

The sewage treatment plants built during the twentieth century can be thought of as the third revolution in urban water infrastructure—Water 3.0. Gradual progress began with a recognition that cities were becoming too big to rely on self-purification. Initially primary treatment plants were built as a means of eliminating the aesthetic problems caused by oxygen depletion. But as populations increased, more sophisticated treatment plants were needed to protect downstream drinking water supplies and aquatic ecosystems from the negative effects of sewage. Through the efforts of engineers at places like the Lawrence Experimental Station and the University of Manchester, reliable aboveground treatment processes were developed to harness the ability of microbes to purify water. But before the situation was perceived to be a major crisis, the public was reluctant to spend more than about a dollar a month per person to solve the problems posed by sewage. Ultimately, a public consensus to address sewage pollution at the national level coupled with a comprehensive set of laws and funding turned the situation around.

Our modern sewage treatment plants were built to eliminate oxygen depletion, and in achieving this goal they solved many of the more pressing problems of the day. But as cities have continued to grow, it has become clear that treatment plants also have to remove nutrients, toxic metals, and synthetic organic chemicals. Technologies are available to accomplish these tasks, but like the transition from primary treatment to secondary treatment, retrofitting sewage treatment plants will require additional funds. In addition, the initial rush to build treatment plants meant that adequate provisions were not made to support the maintenance and upgrades needed to keep the network of water and wastewater treatment systems working in the future. Now that our attention has moved on to other challenges, like greenhouse gases and climate change, additional regulations and government grants are unlikely to provide all of the means necessary to replace the worn parts and make the needed improvements. We must address these problems now if we wish to avoid reversing much of the hard-won progress of the mid- to late twentieth century.

6

The Chlorine Dilemma

fter the publication of *Silent Spring* and the much-publicized fire on the Cuyahoga River, all eyes turned to Washington, D.C., where concerned politicians pushed forward pollution-control legislation. Increased public attention and the lobbying efforts of environmental groups led to the allocation of federal funds to upgrade sewage treatment plants and to standards being set to control smog-producing gases emitted by factories and cars. But the energy and influence of the environmental movement did not stop there. The late 1960s was a time when idealistic people put their energy into making the world a better place—and among these idealists was a brash young lawyer and a group of scientists in New York who pioneered a new way of fighting pollution.

Alarmed by the effects of DDT described in *Silent Spring*, Victor Yannacone, a thirty-one-year-old lawyer, initiated a lawsuit against a Long Island mosquito control district claiming that in 1966 its use of the pesticide had caused a fish kill in a pond near his house.[1] Armed with his motto "Sue the bastards," Yannacone teamed up with an assistant professor of biology at nearby Stony Brook University and an ecologist from Brookhaven National Laboratory in an attempt to prove that the mosquito district's application of DDT was not in the public's best interest.[2] The group's approach of using the courts when a government agency failed to protect the public was a still untested legal concept. While it took twelve years for them to achieve their goal, the success of Yannacone and his associates gave environmentalists a new tool with which to fight pollution: the class-action lawsuit.

Shortly after the group's high-profile DDT case went to court, they formed the nonprofit Environmental Defense Fund. Over the next few years, this non-governmental organization engaged in an ambitious campaign of class-action lawsuits against the users of DDT and other pesticides suspected of harming wildlife. They also hired a team of full-time scientists to support their efforts to branch out into new areas such as land, water, and energy conservation.[3]

The actions of one of the Environmental Defense Fund's energetic young staffers would forever change the way in which drinking water treatment plants are operated, although he did not set out to remake urban water systems. Robert Harris, who had just received his Ph.D. in environmental science at Harvard, was among the first of the scientists hired by the Environmental Defense Fund. One of his initial efforts as an employee of the organization was to investigate the possible link between industrial pollution and cancer in New Orleans. Harris and Talbot Page, a scientist from the nonprofit group Resources for the Future, started by writing a three-part series for *Consumer Reports* entitled, "Is the Water Safe to Drink?" in the summer of 1974. By using the popular magazine to call attention to a little-noticed publication in which the newly formed Environmental Protection Agency had reported the presence of synthetic organic chemicals in the drinking water of New Orleans, Harris and Page awakened public concerns to wastes being discharged by the chemical industry.

After publication of the article, New Orleans officials asked Harris to determine if the chemicals were affecting people's health. Much in the manner that John Snow and William Sedgwick had identified the cause of cholera and typhoid fever, respectively, Harris and his team analyzed the relationship between the incidence of cancer and the source of drinking water in different parts of the city. Their results, published in November 1974, shocked the nation: men whose drinking water came from the Mississippi River had a 15 percent higher chance of dying from cancer than men who consumed well water.[4] Although he could not make a definitive link between the premature deaths and a specific pollution source, Harris suspected the cause to be wastes pouring from chemical factories upstream, runoff from Midwestern farms that were still using DDT, and the partially treated sewage of cities such as Chicago, Minneapolis, and St. Louis.

Harris's findings received widespread coverage on television and newspapers at about the same time that the Environmental Protection Agency released more data on the drinking water of New Orleans and a handful of other cities. Agency scientists had detected more than ninety commonly used synthetic organic chemicals, such as acetone, benzene, chloroform, and carbon tetrachloride, many of which were known or suspected to cause cancer.[5] Although no one knew for certain whether lifelong exposure to the low concentrations of the chemicals could cause cancer, most experts agreed with Harris that they should be kept out of drinking water. Moreover, the situation in New Orleans—which might have been exacerbated by the proximity of the water treatment plants to the region's many chemical factories—was hardly unique. The same types of chemicals were showing up in drinking water throughout the country.

Alarmed by the findings from the New Orleans study, Congress revived a piece of legislation that had languished in committee since 1969. Within two months of Harris's report and release of the Environmental Protection Agency's new data, President Gerald Ford signed the Safe Drinking Water Act into law.[6] The new legislation required utilities to monitor manmade organic chemicals in drinking water. Once a chemical was detected at an unsafe concentration, the utility was required to eliminate its source or to install additional treatment processes.[7] Although this approach seemed easy enough, deciding which chemicals to monitor and at what concentrations they posed an unacceptable risk would prove to be both challenging and contentious.

Initially, much of the effort of the scientific community was focused on chemicals that the Environmental Protection Agency had detected in its monitoring studies. In particular, researchers paid close attention to chloroform, a suspected carcinogen that was often present at concentrations about a hundred times higher than any of the other chemicals. As American scientists puzzled over why chloroform concentrations were so high, they became aware of the research of Dutch chemist Johannes Rook.

Several years earlier Rook had been asked by his employers to measure the concentration of organic chemicals in Rotterdam's drinking water. Luckily for the water utility they had hired a uniquely qualified chemist: Rook's experience at the Amstel brewery, where he was responsible for identifying the chemicals causing unpalatable tastes in beer, had prepared him well for the challenge of studying chemicals in drinking water. At the brewery, Rook always started his investigations by opening a bottle of beer. While many of his peers had been happy to concentrate on the beer, Rook had turned his attention to the air trapped under the bottle cap: it turned out that by sampling the air above the beer he could more easily detect the volatile compounds responsible for the undesirable flavors.

Rook employed the latest and most sensitive new instruments he could find to detect chemicals in Rotterdam's water. He used a gas chromatograph—an instrument that had been around for several decades—to separate the chemicals, before he passed them through a new device called an electron capture detector. This detector had an exquisite ability to detect chemicals that contained three of the elements in the halogen group of the periodic table—chlorine, bromine, and fluorine. In fact, the electron capture detector was often a thousand times more sensitive than any of the existing alternatives provided that the chemical being analyzed contained more than one halogen atom. Before this advance, chemists would have been happy to detect a few parts per million of a chemical in water, which might be useful if they were studying pollution coming out of a factory or an extremely polluted water source. With the electron capture detector, they stood a chance of detecting chemicals that were present at a few parts per billion—which is just what was needed to study drinking water.

The electron capture detector had been invented by James Lovelock—the enigmatic scientist who also came up with the Gaia hypothesis.[8] Lovelock used his invention to track air masses moving across the Atlantic Ocean. He reasoned that the trace amounts of manmade chemicals picked up by air as it passed through urban areas of North America's East Coast could be used to discriminate it from less polluted air originating in areas with lower population densities. Unexpectedly, the concentrations of two of the most prominent man-made chemicals measured by the detector—the chlorofluorocarbons CF_2Cl_2 and CF_3Cl—showed remarkably little variation in air masses originating over populated and remote areas.[9] Lovelock recognized that the nearly constant concentrations of chlorofluorocarbons in the atmosphere meant that the compounds were not breaking down upon exposure to sunlight and to the oxidizing conditions that normally removed organic compounds from air. In the absence of a breakdown mechanism, the compounds were being mixed throughout the atmosphere, where their concentrations would continue to increase as people released into the atmosphere chlorofluorocarbon-containing products like underarm deodorant and air conditioner refrigerants. Future Nobel Prize recipients Sherwood Rowland and Mario Molina took Lovelock's analysis one step further, reasoning that the unreactive chlorofluorocarbons would eventually diffuse into the upper atmosphere, where intense ultraviolet light would cause them to break apart, releasing halogen atoms that would catalyze the breakdown of the protective ozone layer.[10] The electron capture detector had led to discovery of the ozone hole.

Rook's analysis of Rotterdam's water with Lovelock's invention revealed that the high levels of chloroform in drinking water were actually an unintended consequence of disinfecting the water. In other words, in the process of protecting people from waterborne pathogens, the operators of drinking water treatment plants were inadvertently producing the chemicals thought to be responsible for increased rates of cancer.

What was particularly surprising to the scientific community was that chloroform production appeared to be related to reactions between chlorine and compounds released by decaying plants and algae and not some process involving the industrial pollutants that had been the initial source of concern.[11] Whereas the exact details of how chloroform is produced are still unresolved after thirty-five years of intensive research, we do know that chlorine's ability to inactivate microbes is related to its strong oxidizing power as well as its tendency to replace hydrogen atoms with halogens when it reacts with organic chemicals. During the water treatment process, chlorine was about a thousand times less likely to encounter a manmade organic chemical than it was to run into a member of a family of long-lived compounds produced when microbes and chemical reactions convert leaves, wood, and decaying algae back into carbon dioxide and water. These naturally occurring compounds are prevalent in surface waters because the microbes responsible for organic matter oxidation—the same process that resulted in oxygen consumption in rivers—create dead-end metabolites. Occasionally, the microbes cross-link long chains of carbon atoms, rendering them less susceptible to further oxidation. Over time, these dead-end metabolites—which often persist for thousands of years—become the major form of organic carbon-containing compounds in drinking water. This yellow-brown material, which we refer to as humic substances and German-speaking scientists used to call "Gelbstoff" (literally, yellow stuff), gives water rich in organic matter its characteristic color.

When chlorine reacts with humic substances, their color fades as light-absorbing compounds are oxidized. This type of reaction is the main reason that household bleach—which contains hypochlorite as an active ingredient—removes stains and colored dyes from clothing. Ultimately, a small fraction—typically around 1 percent—of the chlorine added to drinking water reacted with humic substances to produce chloroform. The remainder inactivated microbes and underwent reactions to produce chemicals that were not detectable by gas chromatography.

While scientists like Rook and Thomas Bellar of the Environmental Protection Agency were studying chloroform production in drinking water treatment plants, they also noticed the formation of a series of bromine-containing compounds when water was disinfected with chlorine.[12] Subsequent research revealed that the hypochlorous acid in the drinking water treatment plants had reacted with bromide ions naturally present in the water to produce hypobromous acid, a close relative of hypochlorous acid. Because hypobromous acid is considerably more reactive than its chlorine-containing cousin, the small amount of bromide naturally present in drinking water produced bromine-containing compounds during chlorination.

The entire family of chlorine- and bromine-containing compounds discovered by Rook, Bellar, and other researchers are referred to as trihalomethanes. In 1975, the Environmental Protection Agency released data showing the ubiquitous presence of trihalomethanes in the drinking water of eighty U.S. cities at concentrations up to around 300 µg/L. In contrast, most other organic chemicals detected in drinking water had been found at much lower concentrations or had only been detected in places with local sources of industrial chemicals.

Although passage of the Safe Drinking Water Act had been motivated by a desire to reduce the exposure of consumers to organic chemicals, it did not set standards for trihalomethanes or any of the other compounds detected in the tap waters of American cities. Rather, the difficult task of deciding which organic chemicals should be regulated was delegated to the National Academy of Sciences.[13] Typically, the National Academy takes one to two years to issue its opinions on weighty questions raised by government agencies. Setting standards for chemicals in drinking water was uncharted territory, and no one expected fast results. Impatient with the deliberative body's slow progress, the Environmental Defense Fund went to court to compel the Environmental Protection Agency to set enforceable standards in 1976.[14] The National Academy's first report, issued while the Environmental Defense Fund's lawsuit was still pending, did not provide the regulatory agency with much guidance on what constituted a safe level of trihalomethanes. There were too many uncertainties to provide a scientifically defensible answer. A year later, the federal court ruled in favor of the Environmental Defense Fund, instructing the Environmental Protection Agency to get on with the task of regulating trihalomethanes despite the absence of unambiguous science.

After another National Academy report and a series of hearings, the Safe Drinking Water Act was amended in 1977 with an interim trihalomethane standard of 100 µg/L. The chosen concentration represented a first step in what turned out to be a long process. As University of North Carolina environmental engineer Phillip Singer, one of the leading drinking water researchers of the period, explained: "Adoption of the 100 µg/L maximum contaminant level [standard] for total trihalomethanes was understood to be a compromise position. . . . It was presumed that a maximum contaminant level for total trihalomethanes as low as 10–25 µg/L would be adopted in the future."[15]

According to the Environmental Protection Agency's scientific analysis, which was used to justify the interim standard, a person who drank water containing the maximum allowable concentration of trihalomethanes for his or her entire life had an increased risk of developing cancer of 4 in 10,000.[16] But the drinking water implicated in high rates of cancer in New Orleans contained trihalomethanes at concentrations that were only slightly higher than the new standard. If the reasoning employed by the Environmental Protection Agency was correct, there would be only a small decrease in cancer rates in parts of the city where people drank chlorinated surface water after the interim standard was implemented.

Although much of the controversy about regulating the chlorine disinfection byproducts centered on the maximum concentration of trihalomethanes that should be allowed in drinking water, the Environmental Protection Agency's decision about *where* the trihalomethanes should be measured ultimately turned out to be just as important. The agency decided that water utilities should comply with the new rules for trihalomethane concentrations in water samples collected from homes and not at the water treatment plant. The decision to move the sampling location was related to the common practice of adding chlorine to the drinking water before putting it into the underground pipe network. While the extra chlorine made it easier to operate the drinking water distribution system, trihalomethane concentrations increased as water reacted with chlorine while traveling through the underground pipe network. In cities where only a few large water treatment plants had been built, drinking water could spend up to a week reacting with chlorine before it reached a water tap.

The biggest motivation for adding extra chlorine to treated drinking water was to prevent it from being recontaminated by microbial pathogens. In theory, underground networks of pressurized water pipes should have been watertight and thus immune from recontamination, but microbes routinely entered the system when broken pipes were repaired or when the pipes were opened as new homes were connected to the water system.[17] In addition, most drinking water distribution systems employed neighborhood storage tanks to maintain enough water in the system so that the pressure would remain constant even during periods of peak demand. The concrete, asphalt, or steel covers on the tanks usually had air vents or small cracks through which microbes could reach the stored water. The residual chlorine added at the end of the drinking water treatment process was usually enough to inactivate the modest amount of waterborne pathogens that penetrated the water distribution system through these weak spots.

Treatment plant operators added the residual dose of chlorine to the treated drinking water for another reason: to limit colonization of the insides of the underground pipes by microbes. This practice was deemed necessary because, from the moment water begins to flow in a newly installed water pipe, bacteria start growing on its interior surface. Left unchecked, the microbes in the biofilm coating the pipe's interior can accelerate the corrosion of the cast iron, serve as a source for chemicals that impart unpleasant flavors to water, and provide a hiding place for pathogenic microbes. While it is nearly impossible to eliminate all of the microbes living on the pipe surfaces, a small amount of chlorine added to the water was usually enough to keep biofilm growth in check.

The idea of controlling rather than eliminating the microbes in a biofilm by constantly exposing it to chlorine is similar to the modern practice of oral hygiene. Microbes living in biofilms on our teeth are responsible for the release of volatile compounds associated with bad breath as well as the production of the organic acids responsible for tooth decay.[18] Brushing two or three times a day and flossing when we feel guilty about an upcoming dental checkup reduce the thickness of the biofilm which, in turn, fights bad breath and tooth decay. Because we cannot employ a team of tiny divers to scrub the interior surfaces of the millions of miles of pipes running under our cities, we constantly expose the pipes to chlorine to control biofilm growth and to prevent the release of malodorous chemicals and corrosion-inducing acids.

As a result of the Environmental Protection Agency's compromise approach of setting the interim trihalomethane standard at 100 µg/L, only about a quarter of the nation's drinking water treatment plants were affected by the new regulations. For those utilities where trihalomethane concentrations were slightly higher than the standard, it was often possible to comply by lowering the amount of chlorine added during the disinfection process or by adjusting the coagulation and filtration processes to remove more of the humic substances from the water prior to disinfection.[19]

When a utility was unable to meet the trihalomethane standard by tweaking one of the treatment processes, the Environmental Protection Agency encouraged it to treat the drinking water with activated carbon before adding chlorine.[20] Many household drinking water treatment systems, like the two-chambered pitchers commonly found in refrigerators, employ a short column of activated carbon.

The carbon removes trihalomethanes and organic compounds responsible for unpleasant flavors. Residual chlorine also breaks down as it passes through the column, so that the unpleasant taste of chlorine is removed from the water.

Activated carbon is a form of charcoal produced when an organic-rich material, such as peat or lignite coal, is treated with acid prior to being heated in the absence of oxygen.[21] The process causes the carbon to activate by forming microscopic pores. The high surface area of the pores—up to a football field of surface area in every ten grams—gives activated carbon the ability to remove humic substances and many other chemicals from water. Although it was expensive to add an extra step to the treatment process, activated carbon provided utilities with a reliable means of reducing the concentration of dissolved organic matter enough to meet the trihalomethane standard.

While engineers were learning more about methods by which trihalomethane concentrations could be controlled, public health researchers were following up on the Environmental Defense Fund's study of cancer rates in New Orleans. In the early 1980s elevated rates of cancer of the bladder and rectum were also documented in parts of New York, Illinois, and Wisconsin where people drank humic-substance-rich water that had been disinfected with chlorine.[22] Unexpectedly, the high rates of cancer as well as the specific organs affected by the disease were inconsistent with studies in which laboratory animals had been exposed to chloroform. Furthermore, cancer data from factory workers exposed to high concentrations of the chemical did not show the types of cancers being reported in the new studies. While some researchers were content to explain away these discrepancies by invoking differences between the physiology of humans and rats or by noting the higher toxicity of bromine-containing trihalomethanes, a growing group of researchers started suspecting that there was more to the story.

Many of the scientists studying carcinogens in drinking water were also engaged in research on the question of whether pesticides, food, polluted air, and household products were causing elevated rates of cancer in developed countries. Faced with the daunting and expensive task of deciding which of the many chemicals humans encountered in everyday life could be responsible for high cancer rates being observed in advanced countries, University of California, Berkeley biologist Bruce Ames invented a rapid method for screening chemicals to determine their potential to cause cancer.[23] Cancer studies were notoriously slow and expensive because large numbers of test animals—typically rats—had to be exposed to test chemicals for many months before tumors developed. Reasoning that chemicals causing cells to mutate were also likely to cause cancer, Ames developed a test in which mutations within a population of fast-growing bacteria served as a proxy for a chemical's potential to cause cancer.

The key to the Ames test was a strain of bacteria lacking the ability to produce the amino acid tryptophan. Upon exposure to mutagenic chemicals, a few of the tryptophan-deficient bacteria would mutate back into a form capable of producing the missing amino acid. Detecting a handful of mutants from among the billions of bacteria present at the start of the test was easy, because Ames cultured the bacteria in a vitamin-rich growth medium that contained everything bacteria needed to grow except tryptophan. Only those bacteria that mutated back to the tryptophan-producing form could grow on Ames's tryptophan-deficient Petri dishes. In fact, the test was so easy that Ames's influential studies documenting the mutagenic properties of cigarette smoke and hair dye used data collected by an undergraduate laboratory class.[24]

Starting around 1980, researchers began applying the Ames test to drinking water. Samples of water collected at different stages of drinking water treatment revealed a substantial increase in mutagenicity after water was disinfected with chlorine.[25] Surprisingly, the mutagenicity could not be linked to trihalomethanes, because the technique used to concentrate the chemicals prior to conducting the Ames test did not recover the volatile trihalomethanes. The result of the

Ames test implied that the mutagenicity of the chlorinated drinking water was due to less volatile chemicals.

Initially, scientists did not know which less-volatile chemicals could be responsible for the mutagenicity. In part, the difficulty was due to the shortcut pioneered by Johannes Rook and his collaborators: the technique of sampling the gas above drinking water and analyzing it by gas chromatography allowed researchers to detect volatile compounds, but the nonvolatile compounds never made it into the gas chromatograph. Recognizing this limitation, researchers used an old trick to increase the volatility of the compounds in chlorinated drinking water: they added a highly reactive chemical known as a derivatizing agent to samples prior to analysis in order to convert the nonvolatile chemicals into volatile forms. Within a few years of developing this approach, the researchers had discovered a new family of nonvolatile compounds in chlorinated drinking water. Their biggest discovery was the detection of haloacetic acids, a group of compounds consisting of a molecule of acetic acid—the main acid in vinegar—on which one or more hydrogens had been replaced by chlorine or bromine. To the surprise of many scientists who were convinced that the trihalomethanes were the only game in town, concentrations of the haloacetic acids were often as high as or higher than those of the trihalomethanes. Furthermore, toxicity tests on lab animals indicated that the newly discovered compounds were substantially more toxic than the trihalomethanes.

Whereas the discovery of haloacetic acids proved that significant concentrations of nonvolatile compounds were present in chlorinated drinking water, researchers using the Ames test still could not explain the mutagenic signals detected in chlorinated drinking water. Redoubling their efforts, a team of researchers in Finland finally isolated a major source of mutagenicity in 1986, when they applied a technique known as liquid chromatography to isolate the compounds prior to conducting the Ames test.[26] By employing a patient lab technician or an overworked graduate student to collect the drops of liquid exiting the column, it was possible to separate the organic compounds into parts, or fractions. The fractions were then subjected to the Ames test, which in turn provided clues about the chemical properties of the mutagenic compounds. Fractionation also made it easier to identify the mutagens by the powerful forensic tool known as mass spectrometry because the individual samples contained fewer impurities that could confound the identification of chemicals in the untreated samples.

The tedious separation and analysis protocol led to the detection of a compound that researchers referred to as Mutagen X, or MX for short. The newly discovered chemical was incredibly potent, accounting for approximately 20 to 50 percent of the mutagenic signal detected in chlorinated drinking water, although its concentration was about ten thousand times lower than those of the trihalomethanes and haloacetic acids.[27] Unfortunately, measuring the concentration of MX in drinking water was a Herculean task that involved multiple steps to concentrate and isolate the compound prior to putting it through a gas chromatograph.

To avoid the nuisance of measuring exotic chemicals like MX, the Environmental Protection Agency relied on the idea that there would always be a correlation between the concentration of MX and those of more easily measured compounds, such as the trihalomethanes and haloacetic acids. Implicit in the correlation was the assumption that any steps lowering the concentrations of trihalomethanes and haloacetic acids would also take care of MX and other unknown carcinogens. Yet although there was little doubt that the concentrations of disinfection byproducts would decrease if less chlorine was added, no one knew definitively whether all the different approaches that might be used to reduce the concentrations of regulated disinfection byproducts would affect the formation of compounds like MX in the same way.

In anticipation of the adoption of stricter standards for the chlorination byproducts, utilities began experimenting with ways to avoid the expense of activated carbon treatment. Further reducing the amount of chlorine used during the drinking water treatment process seemed like a reasonable way of reducing byproduct formation, but it had a potentially serious drawback: less chlorine could lead to an increase in waterborne disease from pathogens that were not entirely removed by filtration. Lower concentrations of residual chlorine in the underground pipe network might also result in microbes surviving and growing in the water distribution system. To prevent this process, the Environmental Protection Agency modified its regulations in 1998: drinking water treatment plants would now not only have to meet the new standard of 80 µg/L for trihalomethanes and 60 µg/L for haloacetic acids, but also have to assure that the water had received more than a specified minimum dose of disinfectant.[28] The same year, the rest of the world started catching up to the United States in its effort to control chlorine disinfection byproducts. A directive passed by the European Union in 1998 set standards for chlorine disinfection byproducts that were almost as stringent as those that had been set by the Environmental Protection Agency. Elsewhere, countries began adopting standards that followed the approaches used in the United States or Europe.[29]

The easiest way for a drinking water treatment plant to comply with both aspects of the new standard was to make the chlorine less reactive. By adding a small amount of ammonia to the chlorine, the drinking water treatment plant operators were able to create a less reactive form of chlorine known as chloramines. Most of the chloramines consisted of a compound known as monochloramine, which was a molecule of ammonia on which one of the hydrogens had been replaced by chlorine. Chloramines still inactivated microbes, but they did not produce trihalomethanes, haloacetic acids, or MX when they encountered humic substances. The lack of reactivity of chloramines made them particularly well suited for use in the water distribution system, because they eliminated the need to add more chlorine as the water traveled to the distant edges of the underground pipe network.

To comply with the new standards, about 30 percent of the utilities in the United States switched to chloramines over the next five years.[30] The new disinfectant posed some minor logistical problems, such as the poisoning of kidney dialysis patients who failed to maintain the activated carbon cartridges designed to remove chloramines from their home dialysis machines.[31] Some consumers also complained that the new form of chlorine irritated their skin, but government experts were unable to identify a definite link between the complaints and the chloramines.[32] Although these and other concerns demanded the attention of water utility managers, neither problem could dissuade them from making the switch, especially because the new disinfectant allowed them to comply with the new drinking water regulations without adding expensive activated carbon treatment systems.

Coincident with the efforts to revise the rules on disinfection to improve drinking water safety, the Environmental Protection Agency was making a concerted effort to reduce human exposure to lead. The decision to focus on lead stemmed from research demonstrating that tetraethyl lead—a gasoline additive used to improve engine performance—was releasing fine particles of lead into the atmosphere. Children who breathed in the tiny, lead-contaminated particles or who ingested lead-containing dust or chips of lead-containing paint were showing subtle symptoms of lead poisoning, such as abnormal development of nervous systems and decreased scores on IQ tests.[33] Particularly troublesome were findings that the metal had adverse effects on children's health at concentrations much lower than previously imagined. As a result, a phase-out of leaded gasoline began in 1976 and the use of lead-containing paint was banned starting in 1977.

The new focus on lead exposure also turned the attention of the research community toward drinking water. Drinking water was a logical place to look for lead, because many of the older pipes connecting homes to the water mains running under the streets were made of pure lead. Although engineers of the nineteenth- and early twentieth-century water systems had been aware of the potential health consequences of using lead pipes, the metal that had been used by the Romans and medieval monks in their piped water systems was still their material of choice as well, because it offered substantial advantages over cast iron, wood, and concrete. Lead's malleability made it easy to connect a home up to the water main, and its resistance to corrosion meant that it would not be necessary to dig up the streets every ten to twenty years to replace leaking pipes. The designers of early water distribution systems were willing to take a risk on a potentially toxic pipe material because they knew that a protective mineral coating would form on the inner surface of the pipes after they were placed in service.[34]

The calcite mineral that deposited on the inside of pipes in water distribution systems was the same material that coated the interior surfaces of the pipes and conduits in ancient Rome's aqueducts.[35] As long as a city had mineral-rich ("hard") water, residents of modern cities would be protected from lead poisoning by this phenomenon. Unfortunately, not every city had water with a sufficiently high mineral content to form a layer of calcite. In cities with mineral-poor ("soft") water—exactly the places where the protective calcite layer would not form—engineers were more likely to use lead pipes, because they were worried about the corrosion of iron and concrete pipes. Unaware that the same chemistry that caused iron pipes to fail also resulted in elevated lead concentrations in drinking water, the engineers had set the stage for trouble.

According to University of Pittsburgh economist Werner Troesken, the use of lead in drinking water is one of the great underappreciated public health disasters of the modern era, causing elevated rates of childhood mortality, premature births, and early deaths through the first three decades of the twentieth century.[36] For example, his evaluation of public health data suggests that in 1923 approximately 10 percent of the population of Massachusetts suffered from chronic lead poisoning. Widespread lead poisoning went undetected because the common symptoms—headaches, stomach pain, and loss of appetite—were difficult to discriminate from problems caused by other common maladies of the era. Only those physicians who were alert enough to look for abnormalities in blood cells or the telltale blue line along the gums of affected patients became aware of lead poisoning.

Between 1890 and 1930, as doctors increasingly became aware of the prevalence of lead poisoning from drinking water, states began passing laws banning the use of lead pipes in water distribution systems. Public health officials also encouraged residents to replace the lead pipes that connected their homes to water mains. But few cities went through the effort and expense of digging up the streets or policing the removal of lead pipes. Instead, utility operators counted on a slow decrease in the concentration of lead as a protective layer of insoluble, oxidized material gradually built up on the inside surface of the lead pipe. Their hope that the problem would sort itself out was bolstered by data showing gradual decreases in concentrations in those cities that had phased out lead pipes.

Although the engineers of the early twentieth century did not realize it, the newly adopted practice of adding a residual dose of chlorine to water before it entered the distribution system probably played an important role in the declining lead concentrations. In places along the inside surface of lead pipes where a protective calcite layer did not form, a thin layer of a very insoluble form of lead was produced as the disinfectant oxidized the metal.[37] Or to be more precise, before chlorine had been added to drinking water, the surfaces of lead pipes were coated with a layer of relatively soluble corrosion products, such as lead carbonate, a mineral that includes lead in the +II oxidation state. After chlorine use commenced, the lead was oxidized to the +IV oxidation state, resulting in the formation of much less soluble forms of lead oxide. As long as residual chlorine was present in the drinking water, the lead pipes would not pose a problem.

Unfortunately, chloramines—the new substitute for chlorine— were unable to maintain the oxidized form of lead. When operators of drinking water treatment plants switched their residual disinfectant from hypochlorite to chloramines, lead gradually reverted from the less soluble +IV oxidation state to the more soluble +II form. A few researchers had warned that switching to chloramines could increase lead concentrations, but their worries went unheeded by utilities intent on lowering concentrations of chlorine disinfection byproducts.

By 2005, elevated concentrations of lead had been observed in the drinking water of a handful of cities, including Washington, D.C., and Greenville, North Carolina.[38] Studies conducted in these cities revealed a sharp increase in the number of children who had concentrations of lead in their blood that were high enough to cause learning disabilities and other health problems.[39] Facing adverse publicity, Washington's water supplier launched a $300 million program to remove the remainder of the city's lead pipes.[40] In Greenville, the source was lead-containing solder and brass fixtures that released lead when the disinfectant was changed to chloramines. Although these less-concentrated sources of lead were not as obvious, they were more numerous and virtually impossible to remove from the system.

To minimize the leaching of lead from lead pipes that managed to escape detection during replacement programs as well as from lead-containing plumbing fixtures, about half the drinking water utilities in the United States began adding phosphate to their treated drinking water.[41] In the presence of phosphate, the soluble coatings of lead in the +II oxidation state were converted into less soluble lead-phosphates. The public did not notice any strange tastes or changes in appearance of their water when small amounts of phosphate were added, but the change was enough to reduce the concentrations of lead in many situations. Incidentally, this process is similar to the way in which brushing our teeth with fluoride-containing toothpaste protects us from tooth decay: upon repeated exposure to fluoride the surfaces of our teeth are converted from a calcium hydroxide mineral known as hydroxylapatite to a form in which several of the hydroxy groups are replaced by fluoride. The resulting mineral is less soluble in the presence of acids produced by bacteria living in the biofilms coating our teeth.[42]

In locations with hard water and in newer cities where lead pipes had rarely been installed, lead was less of a concern. This difference, however, did not mean that chloramines were a trouble-free way of solving the chlorine disinfection byproduct problem. In 2000, scientists working at the Department of Health Services in California began to report the presence of N-nitrosodimethylamine, or NDMA, in drinking water that had been treated with chloramines.[43] The scientists had been testing for the chemical in groundwater near a couple of rocket engine testing facilities so they could track it as it moved toward nearby communities. When they applied the new testing method they had developed for detecting the chemical to water samples collected from other locations that they presumed would be free of contamination, they were surprised to find NDMA in many places far from the test facilities. Later inquiries revealed that some of the NDMA had been produced when chloramines reacted with chemicals in sewage effluent and with coagulants used during the water treatment process.[44]

Frustrated by the problems posed by chlorine and chloramines, many utilities contemplated a switch to a different disinfectant. Ozone offered the most practical approach for disinfecting water without creating chlorinated byproducts. Ozonation had become popular in France, Germany, and Switzerland after World War II because people had complained about the tastes imparted to drinking water by chlorine.

Despite the proven track record of ozone disinfection, attempts to introduce the technology to the United States were complicated by concerns about the expense associated with retrofitting existing drinking water treatment plants. Furthermore, retrofitted plants would still need to add chlorine to the treated water before putting the water into the distribution system, because any residual ozone disappeared within minutes through reactions with humic substances and other chemicals present in the water. Some northern European countries had been able to avoid the addition of chlorine because biofilms grow more slowly in cold water. In addition, the water often spent less time in the distribution systems of the more compact European cities. These two factors, coupled with the tendency of European countries to invest more resources in the maintenance of their water distribution systems, meant that residual chlorine was not always necessary. The utilities in the United States were hesitant to adopt this practice, however, because biofilm growth and recontamination of water were more likely to happen in America's warmer, sprawling cities.

As utilities have struggled to balance the need to disinfect water with the challenge of minimizing the formation of chlorine disinfection byproducts, ozone disinfection has become more common in the United States. Between 1990 and 2000 the number of drinking water treatment plants using ozone has increased from fewer than fifty to around three hundred.[45] But this change still represents a small minority of the drinking water treatment plants currently in operation. Engineers designing new drinking water treatment plants view ozone disinfection as a viable option that is suitable for those cities not particularly concerned with the slightly higher cost. In cities with existing treatment plants that employ chlorine, most engineers question the wisdom of investing in the retrofit if it will still be necessary to add chlorine to the treated water prior to distribution.

American engineers also are concerned about ozone because it has its own disinfection byproduct: bromate. This carcinogenic compound is formed when bromide present in natural waters is oxidized by ozone. The production of bromate during ozonation was first described in the early 1980s, but it only became a pressing concern after research showed that the compound is more carcinogenic than initially believed.[46] For water utilities whose source water is rich in bromide—which includes many cities in arid climates—the switch to ozone might mean exchanging one carcinogenic disinfection byproduct for another. As a result, many utilities have decided to stick with the devil they know.

We now face a dilemma. Chlorine protects us from waterborne pathogens present in rivers and lakes as well as those that penetrate our water systems after the treatment process. It also maintains a protective coating on lead pipes, which are expensive and difficult to remove. But the use of chlorine results in the production of disinfection byproducts that cause cancer and possibly other health problems, even if steps taken over the past thirty years have lowered the concentrations of these disinfection byproducts. The public's recognition that cutting back on disinfectants could increase the rate of infectious disease, as well as citizens' hesitancy to add new treatment processes, has meant that we may not be protected from the carcinogens that inspired Congress to pass the Safe Drinking Water Act.

The solution to the chlorine dilemma will require an upgrade of our drinking water treatment systems. We can think of it as Water 3.1. The least expensive upgrade probably would involve the removal of humic substances—the precursors of chlorine disinfection byproducts—followed by continued use of chlorine. Activated carbon, a treatment process that is already being used in some cities, offers a viable means of accomplishing this goal. New technologies like ultrafiltration also could be used to remove humic substances. Alternatively, we could switch to chloramines or ozone and operate our distribution systems without residual chlorine, though this change would require large investments in maintaining our distribution systems and removing lead from difficult-to-reach locations. Although an increase in the monthly water bill of a few dollars per month would likely be acceptable to people worried about the health of their families, there is not yet a cry for change from the public, because utilities and regulators continue to insist that our drinking water is safe and healthy.

7

"Drains to Bay"

On the curb across the street from my office there is a sign with a picture of a little blue fish ringed by the words, "No Dumping—Drains to Bay." Underneath the sign sits the storm sewer—an entry point for rainwater traveling through the underground pipe system designed to protect the city of Berkeley, California, from flooding. Any water flowing into the storm sewer makes a speedy trip under the city to a pipe that ends at the edge of San Francisco Bay. Along with the rainwater, anything else that has found its way into the street, like trash, leaves, or dirt, gets dumped into the bay and beyond.

The storm sewers in your neighborhood, which may or may not have a cute sign stenciled above them, might follow the same practice, draining rain and melted snow to a local stream, river, lake, or bay. Then again, they might be connected to the same underground pipe system that carries wastes from your home to the sewage treatment plant. Either way, these long-ignored systems are falling apart. And as they deteriorate, they will endanger our health as well as the habitats of fish, insects, and birds living in and around our inland and coastal waters.

Like the underground pipe networks developed to remove wastes from homes and streets during the nineteenth century, the urban drainage systems built over the past three centuries were an expedient means of moving unwanted water out of cities. But in the process of solving one problem, we created a new one: although the sewers quickly transported large volumes of water away from flood-prone streets, they often damaged the places where the water was discharged. In light of the difficulties faced by cities currently struggling to repair decaying pipes and to keep up with the increasing volume of water entering their existing drainage systems, it is evident that in the near future we are going to have to spend hundreds of billions of dollars on these concrete and cast-iron plumbing systems.[1]

The need for huge investments in urban drainage also represents an opportunity: by building new types of drainage systems that take advantage of the ability of natural systems to store and purify water, we might be able to end up in a better place. With a little ingenuity, we can reinvent storm sewers in a manner that saves money, improves the environment, and even replenishes our drinking water supply.

Why does a city need a drainage system, anyway? Consider what happens when rain lands in a park, a plot of forest, or a farmer's field. Much of the water percolates into the soil, where it provides moisture to plants and recharges groundwater. The water that does not soak into the soil flows gently downhill under the force of gravity. Along the way, it forms rivulets, which join together to form a network of streams and rivers.

Now consider the consequences of covering the land with buildings and other impervious surfaces that prevent water from soaking into the soil. If the hard surfaces were perfectly flat, the accumulated water would form gigantic puddles. But this rarely happens because most land is sloped, even after it is covered with asphalt or concrete. As a result, all the rainwater still flows downhill. If this large amount of water were to stay in a city, it would turn streets into rivers every time it rained and, much to the chagrin of homeowners and insurance agents, flood the basements of homes in low-lying areas. This process is exactly what happens in slums of developing countries that have been built without storm sewers.

The need to drain rainwater out of the streets was obvious to the builders of the world's first cities. Archaeologists have found evidence of extensive drainage networks among the ruins of Mesopotamian, Greek, and Chinese cities.[2] Most of the early drainage systems were simply ditches that collected water and routed it to the nearest stream or river. As cities became more crowded and the volume of water became too large to accommodate on the sides of the road, the ditches were expanded and covered over to create sewers.

By the time the Romans came along, urban drainage systems were quite sophisticated. For example, Roman engineers learned from their Italian predecessors, the Etruscans, how to build well-drained roads by using layers of crushed rock underneath the paved road surface. They employed curbs to keep water from moving into ground-floor dwellings, elevated sidewalks to provide pedestrians with a means of avoiding the water, and gutters to drain water away from the streets.[3] The Roman sewers, or cloacae (see Chapter 1), were originally designed to drain the waterlogged parts of the Forum: they also served as conduits for moving rainwater from the city's gutters to the Tiber River. After the aqueducts were built, the cloacae network was further expanded to remove the large amounts of water that flowed continuously into the streets from the public fountains.

The sewers of Paris, London, and other cities were built to protect homes from flooding and to minimize the accumulation of water in the streets. Prior to the advent of piped water systems and flush toilets, the water flowing through sewers mainly consisted of rainwater, horse manure, and the occasional piece of trash that escaped the watchful eyes of the city's scavengers. For builders of the early European cities, the challenge was to find a simple way to move runoff from the city to the nearest body of water. In fact, some students of sewer history (yes, there is an active group with its own website) claim that the word "sewer" is derived from the old English word "seaward," indicating that the purpose of a sewer is to move water to the sea as quickly as possible.[4] In Paris, the first sewers were little more than covered drainage ditches that had been dug to protect the low-lying neighborhood north of the Seine River from flooding. The small elevation difference between the sewers and the river meant that after it rained some water remained in the ditch, where it sat with whatever trash had been carried in with the previous storm. To remove the stagnant and smelly water, the city piped in fresh water from a nearby reservoir to continuously flush the low-lying sewers.[5]

After the sewers became repositories for human waste, the situation deteriorated. Suddenly the water flowing through the sewers posed a threat to the drinking water supply and caused a tremendous stink in the center of the city. As I described in Chapter 3, city leaders initially responded to this new form of pollution by building longer pipes to route sewage farther downstream. After they recognized that their sewage discharges were causing severe oxygen depletion in rivers, they decided it was time to start treating their household and industrial wastes. Thus, the third revolution in urban water involved the construction of sewage treatment plants.

As the engineers responsible for drainage in big cities got serious about Water 3.0, they realized that the dual function of sewers was going to pose a problem. When it was not raining, most of the water flowing through the sewers consisted of wastes from homes and businesses. This domestic and industrial sewage was rich in nutrients and organic matter—exactly the stuff that the microbes living in trickling filters and activated sludge tanks needed to survive. Except for some fluctuations in the flow and composition when people got ready for work in the morning and when the workers moved from the factories to the bars on Friday night, the composition of the sewage was quite consistent. But when it rained, the volume of water passing through the sewers increased, and its composition underwent a dramatic shift as the relatively clean rainwater mixed with a smaller amount of household and industrial wastes. In a typical storm, the flow of rainwater could be ten to twenty times higher than the volume of the household and industrial wastes, meaning that the sewage was no longer a rich mixture of organic matter and nutrients. In the days before treatment plants, the flushing action of the rainwater may have been a welcome respite from the constant flow of sewage, but the decrease in concentrations of nutrients and organic matter in the diluted sewage posed serious problems for wastewater treatment plant operators.

In addition to variability in the composition of the sewage, which made it difficult to keep the microbes growing in the biological treatment process, rainwater increased the rate at which water moved through the treatment plants. For plants designed to remove only easily settled particles (that is, primary treatment systems), the efficiency of the treatment process plummeted whenever it rained because the sewage and rainwater mixture streamed too quickly through the settling basins: the particles had fewer opportunities to settle out.

Treatment plants that employed biological processes to break down oxygen-demanding organic compounds faced even greater challenges when flows increased. The higher water velocity resulted in less efficient treatment because the sewage spent less time in the parts of the treatment plant where the microbes lived. If you can manage to think of the sewage treatment plant as a restaurant where the sewage pipes deliver a nourishing stew to perpetually hungry patrons (that is, the microbes in the activated sludge or trickling filter systems), you can understand why higher flows of diluted sewage were such a problem. Carrying this disagreeable analogy forward, every time it rained it was as if the waiters started bringing bigger servings of stew that the cook had diluted with copious quantities of water. Because the patrons were already eating as fast as they could, they couldn't possibly finish their bowls of stew before the waiters arrived with the next serving. This meant that more leftovers would end up in the dumpster behind the restaurant, which, in this case, was the river or coastal waters where the treatment plant discharged.

Engineers working in the early twentieth century considered two possible solutions to the problems posed by the increased volume of sewage. The first was to reduce the flows by holding back some of the waste within the sewers upstream from the treatment plant. With this approach, the excess water could be released slowly into the sewage treatment plant after the storm had passed. Alternatively, the treatment plant operators could admit defeat and send the untreated sewage directly into the river whenever it rained. Given the difficulty and expense associated with finding a place to hold millions of liters of sewage, coupled with the already degraded state of the surface waters where the new sewage treatment plants were being built, it is unsurprising that most cities were willing to throw in the towel (as well as everything else that flowed through the sewer) whenever it rained.

In reality it was a little more complicated than sending the sewage treatment plant workers home every time it rained. A bypass system was needed to protect the treatment plant from the high flows that could wash away the activated sludge or otherwise damage the facility. To provide a foolproof way to route the excess runoff and wastewater around the sewage treatment plant during large storms, early twentieth-century engineers modified an approach originally developed by the ancient Romans—the *castellum divisorium* (see Chapter 1), a plumbing invention that had been used to prioritize the way in which fresh water would flow to different users of the aqueducts.

In this modern incarnation of the device, the household and industrial wastewater flows along the bottom of the sewer, typically filling the lower 20 percent of the pipe under normal, dry-weather conditions. When a small rainstorm occurs, the level of the sewage flowing through the pipe rises as more water is carried to the treatment plant. If the rain continues, eventually the level of sewage approaches the top of the pipe. At that point some of the sewage escapes through an overflow outlet near the top of the sewer. The overflow pipe discharges the mixture of storm water and waste directly to the nearest waterway.

The overflow system also prevents sewage from backing up into homes. This pressure relief mechanism is needed because even if the treatment plant can handle the massive amount of water entering the sewer during large storms, at some point the amount of water will exceed the pipe's capacity, much in the way that water will accumulate in your bathroom sink if you dump in a large container of water while running the faucet at its highest flow rate. In fact, the overflow structure

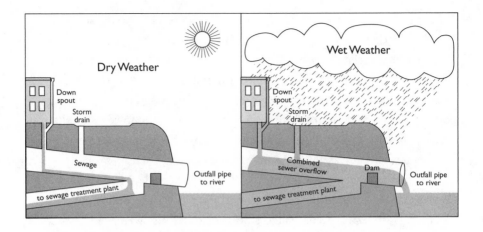

The operation of combined sewer systems under dry and wet conditions.

serves the same function as the little hole near the rim of your bathroom sink.

The release of the rainwater and sewage mixture to surface waters, which is referred to as a combined sewer overflow or CSO, only occurs when the capacity of the sewer system is exceeded. Originally, most systems were designed to accommodate all but the largest storms. As a result, combined sewer overflows should only happen a few times each year. But as the density of downtown areas has increased and outlying areas have been connected into the sewer systems, the ability of many combined sewers to treat storm water has diminished. After all, when it was time to allocate funding for sewer system expansion it was easier to cut a few corners than to raise taxes or dig up the streets to replace existing sewers with wider-diameter pipes. As a result, today many combined sewer systems are operating with pipes that are too small to accommodate wet-weather flows. In parts of London, New York, and a host of other cities, even the lightest showers cause the release of untreated sewage to surface waters.[6]

In the United States, combined sewer systems are clustered in the Northeast and around the Great Lakes—the regions where urbanization occurred prior to the 1920s.[7] In most of the rest of the country, engineers built separate drainage systems that have prevented human and industrial wastes from mixing with storm water. According to the U.S. Environmental Protection Agency, there are presently about eight hundred cities with combined sewer systems serving a population of around 40 million. In total, these systems discharge to the nation's inland and coastal waters approximately 3.2 trillion liters (850 billion gallons) per year of a mix of untreated sewage and stormwater runoff.[8]

Sewage treatment plants were built to solve the problems caused by household and industrial waste flowing into surface waters under dry-weather conditions. The engineers responsible for designing the first generation of sewage treatment systems did not consider it worthwhile to spend the extra millions of dollars needed to treat the few storms per year that would trigger overflows because these events did not contribute much to the problem they were trying to fix. The occasional sewer overflow, then, means that the combined sewer system is functioning exactly the way it was designed.

If combined sewer overflows were not a serious problem a century ago, is it worth worrying about them now? In terms of drinking water, the threat posed by combined sewer overflows is less than you might imagine. Although there are about sixty drinking water treatment plants in the United States located within 1.6 kilometers (1 mile) of a combined sewer overflow pipe, few episodes of waterborne disease outbreaks have been attributed to the contamination of drinking water by combined sewer overflows.[9] The relatively high concentrations of waterborne pathogens in waters subjected to overflows do not cause major problems because drinking water treatment plants were designed in the days before sewage treatment plants. As a result, they can provide safe drinking water even when they obtain their water from a pathogen-contaminated river or lake.

For swimmers, the mixture of stormwater runoff and sewage in the overflows contains more than enough viruses and bacteria to cause ear, nose, and throat infections.[10] But does it really pose a health risk? To understand the dangers posed by combined sewer overflows, public health scientists sometimes swap their lab coats for shorts and t-shirts and head out to the beach to ask people to fill out surveys on their health during the week following their visit. By comparing the reported incidence among beachgoers of illnesses such as ear infections and diarrhea with data from people who went to the shopping mall or stayed home, the scientists have learned that a child visiting beaches can expect to become sick from waterborne pathogens about once every forty visits.[11]

Although many of the beaches where the surveys have been administered were subjected to combined sewer overflows, it is difficult to blame these overflows for all of the infections. In fact, the few attempts to correlate waterborne illnesses among swimmers to specific sources point to cracked or leaking sewer pipes and upstream contamination from areas with high densities of farm animals as the most important culprits.[12] Nonetheless, many beaches located in areas with combined sewers ban swimming for several days after it rains as a precautionary measure because measurements of concentrations of waterborne pathogens and surveys of beachgoers have shown that combined sewer overflows can render beaches unsuitable for swimming.

In addition to polluting beaches, combined sewer overflows have become important sources of oxygen-demanding organic matter and nutrients, which pollute public water supplies. After a half-century of investing in sewage treatment plants to solve problems associated with household and industrial wastes flowing into waterways under dry-weather conditions, the biggest unsolved challenge may now be the pollutants emanating from these combined sewer overflows. For example, throughout most of the twentieth century, almost all of the oxygen-demanding organic matter and nutrients polluting Boston Harbor came from household and industrial wastes discharged by a primitive sewage treatment plant located close to the city. After the city spent close to $4 billion to upgrade the sewage treatment plant, extend the discharge pipe further offshore, and eliminate some of the worst combined sewers, the discharges from the city's treatment plants and the remaining combined sewer overflows now contribute approximately equal quantities of pollutants to the harbor.[13] If we want to further improve water quality in places like Boston, controlling this formerly unimportant pollution source seems like the logical next step.

While illnesses contracted at the beach and releases of pollutants from combined sewer overflows are certainly pressing concerns for many communities, perhaps the greatest objection to combined sewer overflows comes from public perception. Over the past forty years our expectations about rivers, lakes, and coastal waters have shifted. Before the Clean Water Act of 1972, society accepted the idea that untreated sewage might have to be dumped into surface waters. After all, most people making decisions during that era had come of age when dumping waste in surface waters was the norm. For this generation, releasing untreated sewage to a river or bay a few times a year was a vast improvement over sending it there all of the time. Four decades and many billions of dollars' worth of sewage treatment plants later, most people who are in positions of authority cannot conceive of building a system that would, by design, dump untreated sewage into inland waters a few times per year. As a result, combined sewer systems are no longer being built in most parts of the world.

Despite opposition to new combined sewer systems, there is much less support for retrofitting or replacing existing combined sewers, because most people remain blissfully ignorant of their existence and politicians are hesitant to raise taxes or monthly water bills to fix unrecognized problems. Until more people become aware of how combined sewers pollute our beaches and urban waterways, it seems likely that little will change. Consider this: during my childhood, my friends and I would use the little pieces of pink plastic we found on the beach as decorations in our sand castles without recognizing that they were tampon applicators that had washed up during combined sewer overflows. Needless to say, my attitude toward these and other pieces of trash that arrived on the beach by way of the toilet changed after I learned what they were and how they got there. I don't know about you, but I have a hard time swimming at a beach that has recently been subjected to a combined sewer overflow and am supportive of efforts to eliminate combined sewers, especially if it means that I won't run across those little pink pieces of plastic the next time I head out to the beach.

But fixing the problems caused by combined sewer overflows is going to require participation that goes well beyond engineers, city planners, and a handful of beachgoers who are fed up with finding sewer detritus on the beach. After all, previous efforts to fix combined sewer systems were thwarted by a lack of funding and an absence of innovative solutions. As early as the 1950s, engineers were sounding alarms about the pollution flowing from combined sewers. By the 1960s, these warnings had been translated into bans on the construction of new combined sewer systems in many cities.[14] The separate sanitary and storm sewer systems that were built in lieu of combined sewers had their own problems, but the new awareness of pollution emanating from combined sewers assured that they did not spread much beyond the Northeast and Great Lakes regions. Yet in most cities where combined sewer systems had already been built, engineers could do little more than tally the cost of separating the storm water from the household and industrial wastes: in 1964, the U.S. Public Health Service estimated that it would cost $30 billion to retrofit the nation's combined sewers. After more study, the estimate was increased in 1967 to $48 billion.[15] Throughout the 1960s, pledges were made to address the problem and a modest amount of research was conducted to identify cost-effective ways of controlling combined sewer overflows. But given the lack of support for funding the construction of sewage treatment plants for the treatment of dry-weather flows of concentrated household and industrial waste, only a few cities spent significant sums of money to fix their combined sewers.

The birth of the Environmental Protection Agency and passage of the Clean Water Act in 1972 initiated an era of gradual—make that glacial—progress on combined sewer systems. The Clean Water Act required every sewage treatment plant to obtain a permit to discharge its treated wastewater. According to the agency's interpretation of the law, combined sewers were also subject to discharge regulations.[16] But bond funding for upgrading or retrofitting combined sewers was a low priority compared to building and improving sewage treatment plants. Beyond projects that were supported by the federal government, which was underwriting up to 75 percent of the costs of building and upgrading sewage treatment plants, most big cities did little to fix their combined sewers.[17]

After a decade of overseeing the construction of sewage treatment plants, government regulators did turn their attention to combined sewers, but the ascendency of the anti-tax movements of the 1980s meant that there would be little financial assistance. Concerns about potential costs associated with future regulations on combined sewer systems struck fear into the hearts of mayors and city managers, who worried that they would be forced to raise billions of dollars in taxes and user fees to solve the problem. This fear led to the formation of groups like the Clean Water Partnership, an organization of cities and water utilities that lobbied Congress and met with the Environmental Protection Agency to make sure that major upgrades to combined sewer systems would not be required without substantial federal support. Because there was little appetite in Washington for subsidizing more sewage-related construction projects, politicians, regulators, and utility managers were unable to move forward in all but a few cities like Boston, where the overflows were causing problems that could not be ignored, and Chicago, where the city's influential politicians managed to secure federal funding to cover the bulk of the cost of their retrofit.[18]

Elsewhere the regulatory glacier kept moving. In 1989, and again with more details in 1993, the Environmental Protection Agency reiterated its policy of requiring state regulators and the operators of combined sewer systems to operate them as efficiently as possible. If the agency could not require cities to dismantle or upgrade combined sewer systems, at least it could make certain that they were being operated competently. The agency's policy set into motion a series of steps that utilities would need to take to avoid discharges from sewer overflow pipes when it was not raining. The Environmental Protection Agency also required cities to install screens on their discharge pipes to capture floating debris.[19]

If fully implemented, these new requirements would have prevented the little pink pieces of plastic and other floating debris from washing up on beaches, but they would have done little to prevent illnesses among swimmers or the foul odors, fish kills, and algae blooms attributable to nutrients and organic matter in the sewer overflows. To ease the public's concerns about the spread of waterborne disease, treatment plant operators attempted to decrease the amount of pathogenic microbes on beaches during wet weather through a controversial process known as blending.[20] As part of this approach, the flow coming down the sewer was split into two streams after it had passed through the primary settling basin. The larger portion of the flow was routed around the biological treatment system while the remainder was handled in the usual manner. Before discharge, the two streams of waste were recombined and disinfected with chlorine. Although disinfection of the blended sewage decreased the amount of pathogenic microbes entering surface waters, it was not a viable long-term solution because chlorine disinfection was less effective in the turbid, partially treated sewage. Furthermore, the process did nothing to decrease pollution from oxygen-demanding organic compounds and nutrients.

Blending and investing in solutions to some of the most egregious problems were about as creative as most cities got during the 1990s, because the Environmental Protection Agency's new guidance did not come with additional funding. Caught between the resistance of utilities to increased rates and pledges from politicians not to raise taxes under any circumstances, government regulators and utility managers muddled along trying to keep their combined sewer systems from deteriorating further. In 2000, the Environmental Protection Agency unveiled a regulatory framework requiring operators of combined sewer systems to develop short-term plans to assure that their systems were operated efficiently and long-term strategies to eliminate excessive pollution from overflows.[21] Under this formalized approach, combined sewer systems could continue to have overflows provided that they treated 85 percent or more of the water that entered the sewer system on an annual basis or if they limited the number of overflows to four or fewer per year. Systems that could not meet the new requirements also could avoid the need for costly upgrades by conducting studies to demonstrate that their discharges were not affecting surface waters. Essentially the regulatory agency blessed the continued use of combined sewers as long as they functioned as originally intended, and no one in the city complained too loudly.

While seemingly modest in scope, the policies developed over the past twenty years have forced some cities to initiate massive construction projects to rehabilitate their overburdened combined sewer systems. For example, the city of Indianapolis, which for decades had allowed housing developers to hook new homes into its existing combined sewer system without expanding the size of the downstream sewer pipes, experienced rivers of untreated sewage running through the heart of the city nearly every time it rained. Throughout the 1990s, regulators negotiated with the city to develop a plan that could achieve the goals set forth by the state's new regulatory policy, which had been dictated by the federal Environmental Protection Agency. Frustrated with the likely costs of coming into compliance, the Republican mayor, Stephen Goldsmith, broke off negotiations and sued the state in 1999, claiming that its regulatory agency lacked the jurisdiction to force the city to comply.

In the next mayoral election, Bart Peterson, the Democratic candidate running against Goldsmith's Republican protégée Sue Anne Gilroy, made combined sewers a campaign issue. He disputed claims from his Republican rival that the problem was too expensive to fix and highlighted that the people who were most likely to encounter sewage-laden streams and backed up toilets were members of minority groups who had moved into downtown areas during the previous two decades, as affluent residents had fled to the suburbs.[22]

After he was elected, Peterson reached an agreement with state regulators. Under his plan, the city would limit the combined sewer overflows to four to six times per year by building five underground tunnels, each eighty meters (260 feet) deep, to store the extra water entering the system during storms. The tunnels, which are 5.5 meters (eighteen feet) in diameter, are the most expensive and ambitious infrastructure projects ever attempted by the city and will be capable of retaining about 200 million liters (53 million gallons) of combined sewage.[23] When it is completed in 2025, the tunnels, which will be built in conjunction with a project to expand the capacity of the city's sewage treatment plants, will reduce the amount of overflowing sewage and make the combined sewers function as they were originally intended.

The total cost of rehabilitating Indianapolis's combined sewers will not be known until the project has been completed, but it is certainly not going to be cheap. The project has already resulted in an increase in average monthly sewer bills from just under $18 before the construction project began in 2008 to around $30 by 2012. In February 2013, the utility proposed to increase average monthly rates to $44.[24] While most of the city's residents already have come to terms with the increasing sewer rates, no one is certain when the rates will stop rising. An early version of the mayor's plan projected monthly sewer bills of over $100 per month when the project is completed.[25] Other cities also have built underground storage tunnels to rehabilitate their combined sewer systems, including Chicago ($3.0 billion), Kansas City ($2.4 billion), and Portland ($1.4 billion).[26] Perhaps Indianapolis will find a way to reduce the overall cost of its project. So far those cities like Indianapolis that are simply building gigantic concrete holding tunnels as a way of getting the combined sewers to behave as intended are proving that it is an expensive endeavor.

If you don't live in a city with a combined sewer system, you might feel a bit smug as you read about these problems. After all, the people who built your city had the foresight to avoid combined sewers or the city just had the dumb luck to grow after engineers had decided that they were a bad idea. Your city likely has two sewer systems: a sanitary sewer, which delivers only household and industrial wastes to the sewage treatment plant; and a storm sewer, which drains rainwater directly to the same streams and rivers that did the job before the land was covered with buildings, roads, and parking lots.

Unfortunately, you have little reason to gloat: separate sewers pose their own set of problems that might be even harder to fix. After all, the simple act of paving over land and installing storm sewers has numerous effects on wildlife habitat and water quality. Except for the absence of floating debris that has made its way to the stream banks by way of the toilet, it is often difficult to distinguish a stream that receives combined sewer overflows from one where the runoff arrives via a separate storm sewer.

Why would piping storm water to a stream have such a big influence on a body of water? Even when we decide not to replace natural drainage networks with underground sewer pipes, the quality of the stream habitat quickly deteriorates when a modest amount of land—typically as little as 10 percent—is covered over with impervious surfaces.[27] The character of urban streams changes as cities develop because paved surfaces quickly shed water. While the same amount of water falls on the city as what fell prior to development, it migrates off the land surface much more quickly because the movement of the water is no longer slowed by the long journey through the soil and shallow groundwater. Furthermore, the overall amount of water passing through the streams increases by a factor of two to five times relative to conditions prior to development because water is no longer either taken up by plants or allowed to recharge groundwater.[28]

In addition, to reduce the risk of flooding that could result when this larger volume of water moves through the stream network, engineers often dig new channels and straighten the flow paths of urban rivers to eliminate flood-prone meandering sections that can serve as bottlenecks. While the resulting channels protect property and, when sufficiently large and covered in concrete, make for great backdrops for car chases in Hollywood movies, the straightened rivers further increase the water velocity. The higher water velocities in the modified urban streams cause fine sediments and small stones on the streambed to get carried into the flow of the water more frequently. When the stream sediments are scoured in this way, bottom-dwelling worms and insects are unable to feed and reproduce. The absence of these tiny creatures in turn reduces the populations of fish and birds that rely on them as a food source.

The higher velocity and greater volumes of water gradually also erode the sediments from the walls of streams. When this erosion is coupled with the scouring of the sediments from the stream's bottom, the channel becomes deeper. Eventually, stream channels deepen until the banks become too steep for the soil to hang onto the sides. The eroding soil then falls into the water and gets flushed downstream.[29] As the stream banks become steeper, the vegetation that once shaded the channel disappears, increasing the amount of sun shining on the water. The increased light causes higher water temperatures, which is a big problem for species of fish that prefer colder temperatures. It also leads to more algae and to the growth of attached plants in the stream. Eventually, the urban stream becomes a deep, aesthetically unappealing channel with little value as a wildlife habitat.

In addition to degrading stream habitat through increased water flows, storm sewers introduce a host of contaminants into surface waters. The next time you are on a city street, take a look at all of the stuff scattered about: you may well see plastic bags, dog droppings, unwanted batteries, half-eaten sandwiches, candy wrappers, motor oil, and antifreeze dripping out of old cars. Because there is no treatment plant at the end of the storm sewer (in cities with separate sewers), all of that stuff is sent directly into streams, rivers, and coastal waters every time it rains. Although a properly functioning combined sewer will burp out a mixture of stormwater runoff and household waste a few times a year, a separate sewer conveys whatever is on the impervious surfaces of the city to urban waterways during every storm.

In addition to dumping trash into rivers, the water flowing through storm sewers has the potential to cause a host of other problems, including the spread of waterborne disease. The water flowing out of separate sewers typically contains concentrations of bacteria that are about a hundred times lower than that of combined sewers.[30] Nonetheless, discharges from separate storm water systems frequently result in beach closures, because the pathogen concentrations are still orders of magnitude greater than the standards for protection of swimmers. That water contaminated with microbes flows out of combined sewers a few times per year while separate sewers contaminate surface waters every time it rains makes it tough to decide which type of sewer is worse.

If storm sewers are not hooked up to homes, where do all of those bacteria come from? In many places, human waste that escapes from the sanitary sewer is the culprit. Sanitary sewers are meant to be watertight, but over time the thousands of kilometers of pipes under a city develop leaks. A major cause for the leaks is tree roots that work their way into the joints and small cracks in the pipes as the trees search for water and nutrients underground. Once a tree root finds its way into a sewer pipe, it expands, further cracking the pipe and eventually constricting the flow of sewage as it siphons precious water and nutrients.[31] Other causes for leaking sewer pipes include corrosion of the pipe material and damage from construction activities.

In dry weather, broken pipes allow some of the sewage to escape from the system, which can contaminate shallow groundwater with pathogens.[32] Damaged and partially blocked pipes are even more damaging in wet weather because they allow extra water to flow into the sewer pipe. To ensure the rapid movement of sewage and because city leaders wanted to save money on the initial pipe installation, the widths of the pipes used in sanitary sewers are just large enough to accommodate the normal flow coming out of homes and businesses. Therefore, any extra water can easily overwhelm the system. And because most sanitary sewers do not have the capacity to accommodate the higher flows, the extra water escapes in the only ways possible: by backing up into homes and by pushing up through manhole covers and onto the street. After flowing through the street for a short distance, the household and industrial wastes inevitably find their way into the storm sewer system before getting dumped into surface waters.[33]

This phenomenon, which is referred to as a sanitary sewer overflow, or SSO, occurs at a surprisingly high frequency. According to the Environmental Protection Agency, between 25,000 and 75,000 sewer overflows occur in the United States every year.[34] For a city of a million people, this translates into about a hundred sewer overflows each year. This means that during every rainstorm, one or more storm sewers are probably releasing waste from a sanitary sewer overflow in the city.

Storm water also acquires bacteria from household pets and wildlife that deposit their waste on the lawns and streets of the city. In fact, in terms of total numbers, the fecal matter of our furry friends is usually the main source of bacteria in runoff.[35] Fortunately, many of the pathogens that our household pets and neighborhood wildlife carry do not infect humans. Unfortunately, many of the simple tests that public health scientists use to identify waterborne pathogens cannot discriminate between bacteria from humans and other mammals. As a result, a considerable amount of effort is directed at a source of bacteria that poses little risk to swimmers.[36]

In addition to serving as a source of waterborne pathogens, urban storm water picks up a host of chemicals as it runs over impervious surfaces. Many of the chemicals come from cars: when you wander around the city after it rains, you might notice a sheen on top of the puddles in parking lots. The interesting refraction of light on the surfaces of these puddles is due to a thin film of petroleum products released from the road surface when it gets wet. Many of the compounds come from cars with slow leaks in their crankcases. In cities in the western United States that experience distinct wet and dry seasons, the first rain of the year can turn an innocuous hill into a veritable bobsled run as the oil accumulated during the dry period lubricates the road, making it difficult for tires to grip the surface. In addition to causing traffic accidents, motor oil contains a family of chemicals known as polyaromatic hydrocarbons, or PAHs, that are quite toxic to fish. Because of the presence of these and other chemicals that come from tires, diesel engine exhaust, roofing materials, and house paint, urban runoff can wreak havoc on the ecology of urban streams.[37]

Irrespective of whether an urban drainage system is attached to a combined or a separate sewer, addressing the problems associated with runoff requires that we reduce the amount of water entering the sewer during the peak period of a storm. Slowing the movement of water also provides an opportunity to remove contaminants. In cities where combined sewer overflows happen too frequently, the conventional solution has been to build underground tunnels to retain the mixture of rainwater and sewage and gradually release it to the wastewater treatment plant after the sewer flows decrease. While effective, these underground storage systems are expensive and continually need to be expanded as the population of the city increases. In cities with separate storm sewer systems, aboveground storage ponds are often used to prevent flooding. Such flood control measures often provide a secondary benefit by preventing the high flows that degrade habitat by eroding the banks of urban streams. The stormwater retention basins also can improve water quality as contaminants associated with suspended particles settle out during water storage.[38]

Given the massive investments needed to come into compliance with new government regulations on combined sewer overflows, many cities have begun to experiment with a less expensive alternative: by building a network of structures that retain runoff on individual properties, peak flows can often be reduced enough to allow combined sewers to function as intended, with overflows occurring only during the largest of storms. While there is currently less of a sense of urgency related to problems caused by separate storm sewers, many of the approaches being developed for combined sewers may be applicable to future efforts to fix problems associated with separate storm sewers.

This new approach for retaining the runoff from small and modest-sized rainstorms employs a design philosophy that has come to be known by various names, including low-impact development (United States), sustainable urban drainage systems (Europe), and water-sensitive urban design (Australia). Regardless of its name, the practice developed in response to a desire to use plants, trees, and soil to provide a cost-effective solution to urban drainage problems. In the United States, the low-impact development movement can be traced back to the early 1990s, when a real estate developer proposed an alternative approach for handling stormwater at a new development where he was going to be required to install a series of large water storage ponds.[39] Larry Coffman, associate director for planning at the Department of Environmental Resources in Prince George's County, Maryland, worked with the developer to come up with a viable alternative that could apply to other projects. By using a combination of native plants and unobtrusive manmade structures, they developed a means of returning the drainage patterns of urban and suburban properties to the state that existed prior to habitation.[40] Rather than relying on the traditional approach of quickly moving runoff from roofs, parking lots, and streets to storage ponds and underground holding tanks, low-impact development took advantage of the water-storage capacity of the soil. By routing runoff to retention systems that contained enough plants and soil to hold the water generated on nearby impervious surfaces, the designers of low-impact development systems were able to prevent the frequent combined sewer overflows that plagued the county's oversubscribed sewer systems.

Low-impact development caught on quickly in cities that were attempting to comply with the U.S. Environmental Protection Agency's new regulations on combined sewer overflows because it offered an alternative to spending billions of dollars on infrastructure hidden deep underground. In addition to being less expensive, the attractive vegetation used in the low-impact development systems was popular with members of the public. The new approach also appealed to government leaders and utility managers because the responsibility for retaining runoff could be transferred to real estate developers and property owners through zoning ordinances that required low-impact development in new construction.[41] Over the past twenty years, the momentum behind the low-impact development movement has increased and awareness of the benefits of this green infrastructure approach has spread beyond a small group of planners and engineers.

One of the most popular ways of realizing the promise of low-impact development is the installation of a green roof. To convert a conventional roof into a water-retention system, a thin layer of soil—typically fifteen centimeters (six inches) or less—is placed on the roof surface.[42] Drought-tolerant vegetation is then used to hold the soil in place and hopefully make the soil-covered roof attractive—at least during the growing season. During a small or moderate storm, the green roof's thin layer of soil and roots retain nearly all of the water. In larger storms, the plant and soil layer becomes saturated with water and any additional rain landing on the roof drains exits through downspouts and drainage pipes. After the rain stops, the plants slowly use the water retained in the soil.

In addition to reducing the amount of water flowing into sewers, green roofs can lower the costs associated with heating and cooling buildings because the soil and plant layer serves as an extra layer of insulation. The living blanket can also increase the interval between roof replacements by shielding the roofing materials both from sunlight and from the rapid swings in temperature that lead to deterioration of the rubber and asphalt roof covering. The extra savings associated with lower energy consumption and less frequent roof replacement are often used to justify the higher costs of constructing and maintaining green roofs.[43]

In addition to their functionality, green roofs are popular with architects because they help them accrue points in the system for rating the efficiency and sustainability of buildings known as Leadership in Energy and Environmental Design (LEED). If a design accrues enough points, the final construction can be classified as a LEED-certified green building, which is a highly coveted distinction valued by prospective tenants. Some commercial buildings even integrate into their green roofs public rooftop gardens complete with flowering plants, small shrubs, and places to enjoy the view. But rooftop gardens are less popular with the builders and engineers who are trying to solve problems associated with urban runoff because the thicker layer of soil needed to support large plants can greatly increase the cost and maintenance of the roof.

The other popular low-impact development approach converts the low spots on the property into underground water storage systems. Rain gardens, vegetated swales, and bioinfiltration systems are names used to describe low-impact development features that are variations on a common theme: by routing runoff from a property's impervious surfaces to a vegetated area, it is possible to store enough water underground to substantially reduce the amount of water leaving the property and the rate at which water leaving the property enters the sewer. To prevent the runoff-receiving area from turning into a gigantic mud puddle, it is often necessary to give the native soil in the low spot a makeover prior to planting. First the soil is dug out and a layer of gravel is placed at the bottom of the hole. If necessary, clay and poorly draining soils are replaced or mixed with sand before being placed back on top of the gravel layer. Finally, a layer of mulch is mixed into the surface soil prior to planting.

Once built, engineered infiltration systems function much like green roofs. In the initial phase of a storm, the soil and root layer retains the rainwater near the surface. After the surface soil becomes saturated, water fills the spaces between the gravel. Eventually, the pores in the gravel become saturated and water leaves the system through an overflow pipe connected to a sewer or an urban stream. After the rain ends, the plants gradually use the water in the soil layer. Provided that the ground underneath the gravel layer is permeable, some of the retained water will percolate into the groundwater.

In places where the underlying layer consists of low permeability clay or rock, it is possible to install a second drainpipe at the base of the gravel layer to remove the accumulated water after the rain stops.

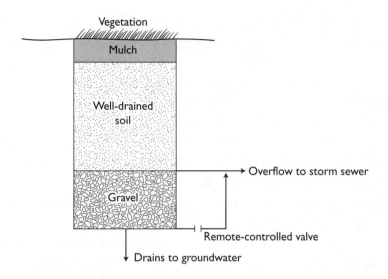

Vegetation

Mulch

Well-drained soil

Gravel

Overflow to storm sewer

Remote-controlled valve

Drains to groundwater

A typical bioinfiltration system used for treatment of urban runoff.

To avoid the need for a worker to run around town opening and closing valves every time it rains, the lower drain can be controlled by an electronic valve fitted with a wireless communication and control system.[44] Using the latest weather forecast to predict when the next rainstorm will occur, the valve can be operated in a manner that assures that the gravel layer will capture as much water as possible and that the time the stored water remains in the system will be maximized to facilitate the breakdown of contaminants by microbes growing on the gravel's surface. This approach has also been adapted for use with underground cisterns and rainwater storage tanks that store water for landscape irrigation and other applications where water is used for non-potable purposes. By using weather data to predict the amount of water that will enter the tank, the system can be managed in a manner that allows the greatest possible runoff capture and water storage.

In densely populated cities, there is often not enough land available to build the vegetated infiltration systems needed to control runoff. In these situations, the objectives of low-impact development can be achieved by replacing impervious concrete and asphalt surfaces with porous materials. One of the simplest ways of making parking lots, roads, and sidewalks permeable is to replace concrete and asphalt coverings with interlocking concrete blocks that have small gaps between them that allow water to percolate into the soil. Alternatively, concrete blocks with holes in the center can be used to create a permeable surface. By installing the blocks over a layer of permeable gravel, sand, or soil, runoff can be reduced. To prevent the ponding of water during large storms, an underdrain system is often installed with a connection to a sewer or an outlet leading to an urban stream.

Although this approach is often appropriate for sidewalks or small parking areas, where some grass poking out of paving blocks is not much of a concern, it is impractical for streets or parking lots where smooth surfaces are needed. Under these conditions, it is possible to reduce the amount of runoff with permeable pavement— porous materials that look exactly like familiar asphalt and concrete surfaces.[45] The key to making these special materials is to change the mixture of ingredients to maintain the tiny holes and cracks that develop as the surfaces harden. Porous asphalt and concrete are a little more expensive to install than conventional surface coverings and require occasional maintenance to prevent dirt from clogging the pores that make them permeable to water. If properly installed and maintained, however, they can provide an unobtrusive means of removing water from large areas that have the potential to generate considerable amounts of runoff.

Whatever the specific approach used to implement the principles of low-impact development, a coordinated effort involving wastewater utilities, city planners, builders, politicians, and members of the community is needed to implement a runoff control program. In the initial stage of the effort, demonstration projects are often needed to familiarize participants with the principles of low-impact development. To hasten construction of these more environmentally friendly systems, financial incentives and changes in zoning ordinances are necessary. And after the projects are finally built, a system must be put into place to ensure that they will be maintained. In addition to the logistical challenges associated with coordinating the efforts of all of the government agencies responsible for different aspects of the program, the benefits of low-impact development are often slow in coming: only after hundreds of projects are built over a period of years will their cumulative effect on combined sewer overflows become evident.

The public is usually oblivious to urban drainage problems. Consequently, if low-impact development is going to succeed at the scale of an entire city, committed advocates are needed from outside of the water sector. One of the best examples of the level of commitment needed to successfully launch a citywide low-impact development project is Philadelphia's "Green City, Clean Waters" program. Faced with the prospect of an expensive retrofit to address its combined sewer overflow problem, Philadelphia's mayor, Michael Nutter, decided shortly after his inauguration in 2008 to pursue low-impact development as an alternative to the conventional engineering approach.[46] But simply choosing low-impact development over underground tunnels was not enough. In addition to pushing for cooperation from the city's water department, which had led previous efforts to combat the city's combined sewer overflows, the mayor enlisted support from the government departments responsible for Philadelphia's parks, schools, transportation, and tax collection. After he got the buy-in from city agencies, he turned to selling his program to the public. To do this, he established a comprehensive program called "Greenworks Philadelphia" that explained his vision for the ways in which green infrastructure would transform every aspect of city life. In essence, he made a commitment to supporting green development as mayor.

The consent decree that the mayor signed in 2012 with the Environmental Protection Agency commits the city to a twenty-five-year program that will cover about a third of the city's impervious surfaces with green roofs, rain gardens, permeable pavement, and other low-impact development features capable of capturing and retaining the first 2.5 centimeters (one inch) of precipitation.[47] If everything goes according to plan, Philadelphia will invest approximately $2.5 billion in projects on city-owned land and private properties in its quest to reduce runoff. While the city's estimates suggest that the low-impact development approach will be more cost-effective than digging underground tunnels and expanding the capacity of sewage treatment plants, Philadelphia could still end up spending more than cities that followed the conventional path. But if Nutter's plan succeeds, the city will have gained more than a network of underground sewage tunnels. Low-impact development promises to offer energy savings, create attractive green spaces, and reintroduce residents of the city to the water cycle. Only time will tell if the investment was worth the extra effort.

8

Traces of Trouble: Hormones, Pharmaceuticals, and Toxic Chemicals

n 1995, I was invited to give a talk at a scientific conference fea-
turing the up-and-coming water pollution researchers. Of course
I agreed to go. After all, I was flattered by the attention, and as a
freshly minted assistant professor I knew that being identified as
someone who stood out from his peers would be useful when it came
time for tenure review. That the conference was to be held in Honolulu in mid-December had only a minor bearing on my decision to
accept the invitation.

Like most of the other speakers, I planned to slink off to the beach
for a week of rejuvenation after giving my talk. To be polite, I had to
attend a day of sessions with my colleagues, but that seemed like a
small price to pay. I wasn't expecting to learn much, because I already
knew most of the other presenters and had read their papers or seen
them give talks at other conferences. I certainly didn't anticipate that
one of the talks would change the focus of my subsequent research
and cause me to develop a deep skepticism about the ways in which
cities obtain, treat, and dispose of water.

The source of my trouble was a new graduate from Brunel University in England named Susan Jobling. I had never heard of any cutting-
edge research coming out this tiny school just outside London and
was surprised when she reported findings unlike anything I had ever
read. Jobling talked about research she had recently completed as part

of her Ph.D. under the supervision of John Sumpter, a biologist who had switched his research focus from the fundamentals of fish reproduction to water pollution upon learning of the alarmingly high prevalence in British rivers of male fish with eggs growing in their testes. Sumpter found out about this unusual phenomenon from British government researchers who had observed hermaphroditic fish in the River Lea, a tributary of the Thames River, starting in the early 1980s. Scientists working for the government-run utility, Thames Water, had quietly been trying to determine the extent of the phenomenon and its causes for several years when Sumpter and his students got involved. By the early 1990s, the combined team had documented the occurrence of male fish with eggs growing inside their testes in urban rivers throughout Britain. They also had learned that sewage treatment plants were the source of the problem: when they placed male trout in cages immediately downstream of treatment plants, the fish started producing eggs after as little as two weeks of exposure. Something in sewage was turning male fish into hermaphrodites.[1]

When I saw Jobling's talk in Hawaii, the feminization of fish by wastewater effluent was largely unknown outside of a small circle of British researchers. Jobling's talk and Sumpter's first paper on the subject, which had appeared a year earlier in a specialized scientific journal with a very limited circulation, were among the group's first attempts to communicate their findings to the scientific community.[2] To me, Jobling's descriptions of male fish with deformed testes seemed more like something from the pages of a British tabloid than a talk given by a serious researcher at a major international conference. But after word of the feminized fish diffused out to the scientific community, researchers around the world went into their labs and replicated the British findings.[3] Over time, a consensus was reached among scientists that wastewater could feminize fish, though the underlying cause of the phenomenon was still unknown.

At the time of the conference, Jobling suspected that fish were being feminized by manmade organic chemicals with structures similar to estradiol—the hormone that regulates the reproductive systems

Compounds that bind to the estrogen receptor: estradiol (a natural estrogen), ethinyl estradiol (a synthetic estrogen), DDT (a pesticide), and bisphenol A (a plasticizer).

of most vertebrates. The presence of excess estradiol or a chemical that looks like estradiol in the bloodstream of a mature male fish is problematic, because it can activate the organism's estrogen receptors—structures that trigger the development and growth of reproductive organs. This unnatural signaling, which is sometimes referred to as endocrine disruption, can have rapid and extreme effects on the appearances of fish, birds, and even humans.[4] For example, physicians have reported the feminization of pre-pubescent boys who used hair care products containing lavender oil or tea tree oil—two natural products that contain estrogen-like compounds. Apparently enough of the estrogen-like compounds had either passed through the boys' skin or had inadvertently been ingested in quantities sufficient to activate their estrogen receptors. Once this happened, the boys developed enlarged breasts, which stayed that way until they stopped using the estrogenic products.[5]

Although obvious alterations in reproductive organs are a clear sign of endocrine disruption, many estrogen mimics cause effects that are much more difficult to diagnose. The subtle ways in which endocrine-disrupting chemicals affect growth and reproduction have been a cause for concern since the 1990s in cases where health problems or decreased reproductive success have been observed among wildlife and humans. Theo Colborn's 1997 book *Our Stolen Future*, which has been compared to Rachel Carson's *Silent Spring*, popularized the idea that endocrine disruption is a widespread phenomenon that could explain a host of reproductive problems.[6] Her impassioned pleas for curtailing the use of estrogenic chemicals helped jumpstart efforts to ban chemicals such as bisphenol A from products like children's toys and drinking water bottles.

The two books have become even more closely linked by the emergence of a theory that ties the die-off of peregrine falcons, bald eagles, and other fish-eating birds described in *Silent Spring* to the endocrine-disrupting properties of DDT and related compounds. In the 1970s, scientists had explained the bird die-off through their observations that the shells of the bird eggs had thinned to a point where they cracked when their mothers sat on them.[7] Although these observations were a plausible explanation for the population declines, the mechanism through which the chemicals caused eggshell thinning was never entirely clear. According to the new theory, eggshell thinning occurs when high concentrations of DDT and its metabolites are passed from the mother to the developing chicks through the egg yolk. As the young birds develop, the estrogen-like chemicals overstimulate the estrogen receptor in the embryonic bird, altering the production of an enzyme that later plays a crucial role in the formation of the eggshell.[8]

When Jobling presented her talk in Hawaii, she and her fellow researchers were still unsure which of the many estrogen mimics that they had discovered—pesticides, plastic additives, and industrial chemicals—were responsible for the hermaphroditic fish.[9] Most of her experiments indicated that feminization of fish did not occur until the concentration of the manmade estrogen reached a concentration of a few parts per million. In modern sewage treatment plants, researchers had never detected manmade chemicals at such high concentrations. In fact, the manmade chemicals were usually found in sewage effluent at concentrations that were at least a hundred to a thousand times lower than those that feminized fish in the laboratory. Jobling and Sumpter speculated that this apparent discrepancy could be explained by chemicals that accumulated in the fat of the fish, much as DDT and its metabolites had built up in fish-eating birds before they laid their eggs. Given the huge differences in concentrations, it seemed unlikely that the chemicals could reach the concentrations necessary to cause egg production in the caged male fish after just two weeks of exposure. Upon reading these publications, it seemed to me that if estrogenic chemicals were feminizing the fish they would have to be a lot more potent than the agricultural and industrial chemicals that Jobling and Sumpter were studying.

The only chemicals that I knew of with that kind of potency were the estrogenic hormones themselves. Could hormones produced within the human body be responsible for the hermaphroditic fish?

It only took me a few minutes to find information on the concentration of estradiol in human urine. From the medical literature, I learned that urine from pregnant women contains about 75 times as much estradiol as that of women who are not pregnant and 150 times as much as men. The amount of estradiol produced in a day by a pregnant woman would raise the concentration of an Olympic-sized swimming pool to around 0.1 parts per trillion—which is high enough to feminize certain sensitive species of fish. Making a simple dilution calculation of how much estrogen could be present in sewage entering a treatment plant yielded a concentration of around ten parts per trillion.[10] According to studies conducted by the British researchers and fishery biologists, who had explored the possibility of using hormones to control the sex of fish in their breeding tanks, these minuscule amounts of estradiol would likely be enough to feminize certain sensitive species of fish.[11] Although a simplistic calculation suggested that estradiol could be the culprit, it would take several years of painstakingly refining the existing measurement techniques before it was possible to detect the presence of estradiol and related hormones in the effluent from sewage treatment plants.[12]

Could exposure to these low levels of estradiol feminize humans? All evidence suggests that exposure to nanogram-per-liter levels of estradiol in drinking water cannot harm humans because we metabolize the hormone before it can reach our estrogen receptors. Even for ethinyl estradiol, the synthetic hormone that is taken as an oral contraceptive, a much higher dose than would conceivably be present in water sources would be needed to cause endocrine disruption in humans and other mammals.

The concentrations of estrogenic hormones coming out of a typical sewage treatment plant are about ten times higher than the concentration at which sensitive species of fish, such as rainbow trout, are feminized.[13] In most rivers, however, the effluent from sewage treatment plants accounts for less than 1 percent of the overall flow. As a result, mixing estrogen-contaminated effluent with river water will dilute the concentrations of the hormones to a point where they can no longer feminize fish. Unfortunately for fish in the rivers studied by Sumpter, Jobling, and their colleagues, the British rivers were already contaminated with estrogens from upstream communities by the time wastes from the local treatment plants entered the rivers. The near absence of uncontaminated dilution water meant that the fish were trying to live and reproduce in rivers where most of the water had recently passed through a sewage treatment plant. Under these conditions, there were more than enough steroid hormones in the rivers to feminize the fish.

If steroid hormones have always been present in human waste and sewage has been discharged to rivers since the early days of piped water and flush toilets, why did it take so long for us to discover the hermaphroditic fish? After all, the flow of many of London's rivers had been dominated by effluent for decades before Thames Water scientists discovered the deformed fish. The answer lies in when sewage treatment plants were built: prior to the installation of modern sewage treatment plants, there would have been few, if any, fish living in London's effluent-dominated waters, because the untreated or partially treated sewage would have contained more than enough organic matter to deplete the dissolved oxygen. Even those fish that were hardy enough to survive at low oxygen concentrations would have had a hard time living in the presence of the high concentrations of toxic ammonia that are in sewage. But after the environmental movement of the 1970s spurred large investments in water pollution control technology, wastewater treatment plants improved to a point where fish could survive in pure wastewater effluent. Their ability to success-fully reproduce, however, may be jeopardized by the presence of estro-gens. In 2007, a group of Canadian researchers published a paper describing a study in which they added the synthetic hormone that is the main active ingredient in the birth control pill, ethinyl estradiol, to a small lake for a couple of years. After the hormone treatment the lake still contained fish, but one of the key species—the fathead minnow—disappeared because it is sensitive to the endocrine-disrupting hor-mones and failed to reproduce under the conditions in the lake.[14]

Perhaps the rivers around London are the exception to the rule. After all, London and its surrounding suburbs are among the most densely populated places in the developed world. Most other big cities are found on the coast where wastewater is quickly diluted into the ocean. While there is probably little reason to worry about estrogens under these circumstances, there are still plenty of effluent-influenced rivers downstream of major cities. For example, the Rhine River trav-els around 1,100 kilometers (700 miles) from its headwaters in Swit-zerland through the industrial heart of Germany and Holland before flowing to its outlet at the North Sea. In the process, the river receives the wastewater effluent of around 50 million people. The effluent con-tent of the river varies according to the amount of rain or snowmelt entering the river, but during periods without much rain or melting snow, wastewater accounts for 10 to 30 percent of the overall flow along many sections of the river.

Other prime examples of rivers where wastewater effluent now accounts for much of the overall flow can be found in Japan, where the Yodo River carries the wastes of Kyoto and surrounding cities through Osaka and the Tama River—a body of water that serves as a conduit for effluent from areas outside of Tokyo on an eighty-kilometer (fifty-mile) journey to the sea.[15] There are also numerous smaller river systems in Europe, Japan, and Australia where wastewater accounts for a significant fraction of the overall flow downstream of a sewage treatment plant.[16] In addition, there are many small, effluent-dominated creeks that flow for a short distance before effluent is diluted into a

The Rhine River flows from Switzerland to the North Sea. On the way,
it serves the needs of millions of people as both a drinking water source
and a place to discharge wastewater effluent.

river. No one has bothered to look for hormones or feminized fish in
most of these places, but it is quite likely that both would be found.

If effluent-dominated rivers now occur in Europe and Japan, what
about in the United States? In terms of length and the presence of
major cities, our closest analogues to the Rhine and Yodo are probably

the Mississippi and Ohio rivers, where wastewater from Minneapolis and Chicago or Pittsburgh, Cincinnati, and Louisville enter the water before the rivers combine and flow from St. Louis to New Orleans. Fish living in the areas immediately downstream of the sewage treatment plants in the Mississippi River basin do sometimes show symptoms of feminization.[17] But the large distances between the cities and the presence of multiple tributaries that contribute water from less populated areas assure that effluent rarely accounts for more than a few percent of the overall flow. Despite the presence of 70 million people who discharge their wastes into the Mississippi River, wastewater effluent is a relatively minor contributor to pollution of this great water system compared to agriculture and industry.

The absence of densely populated cities lined up along a single waterway in the middle of the country does not mean that there are no effluent-dominated river systems in the United States. In many river basins a lack of precipitation means that there is simply not enough water flowing down the river under normal circumstances to dilute away the wastewater effluent. To gain an appreciation of the inability of rivers in arid regions to dilute chemicals, you need to forget the static thick blue lines that are used on maps to represent rivers in all kinds of climactic regions. For rivers in arid regions, two different types of lines would be more realistic: in spring and early summer, a thick blue or brown line could represent the often fast-flowing torrents that churn up the sediments on the bottom of their streambeds, but after the melt ends, the maps should probably use a thin blue line to represent the diminished flows that occur in rivers where it might be possible to wade across them after rolling up your pants. During these low-flow conditions, the wastewater effluent from an upstream community might become the primary source of water. And if the upstream community has constructed dams and reservoirs to trap the spring flows, wastewater might just be the main source of downstream flow all year long.

We often fail to appreciate the natural state of surface waters in arid regions, because it is difficult to find rivers flowing through cities that have not already been modified by dams, canals, and sewage treatment plants. As a result of these unnatural conditions, rivers in arid regions often have relatively stable flows like those encountered in places that receive a lot more precipitation. Superficially the rivers might seem like their free-flowing cousins, when in reality they have more in common with pipes used to convey sewage effluent from the treatment plant to the river.

A Texan eventually cured me of my ignorance about how the flows of arid-region rivers are now controlled by cities, but he had to be persistent. Within five years of hearing Susan Jobling's talk in Hawaii, I was giving talks about research that I had been conducting with my graduate students on the fate of hormones in surface waters. After one of those talks, a soft-spoken, distinguished man approached me and, with a charming Texas accent said, "Y'all really oughta be studying the Trinity River."

By this time, steroid hormones had become a hot issue for biologists, water utilities, and environmental groups, and I was being overwhelmed by requests to study wastewater treatment plants or rivers in far-flung places. Texas was unfamiliar territory for me, and I had enough trouble keeping track of my projects in California. I politely accepted the gentleman's business card, stuffed it into my top desk drawer, and promptly forgot about it. The soft-spoken Texan showed up two more times at my talks before I decided that I should hear him out, if nothing else to save him the trouble of tracking me down me at future conferences.

It turned out that my pursuer was Alan Plummer, president and founder of Alan Plummer Associates, an engineering consulting company based in Fort Worth with about a hundred employees. For decades, Plummer had been intimately involved in water resource planning in the Dallas–Fort Worth area, which the locals refer to as the Metroplex. As a result, he was well acquainted with the Trinity River. He explained to me that downstream of the Metroplex, the Trinity normally consists of nearly undiluted wastewater effluent. The wastewater from the Metroplex travels approximately 320 kilometers

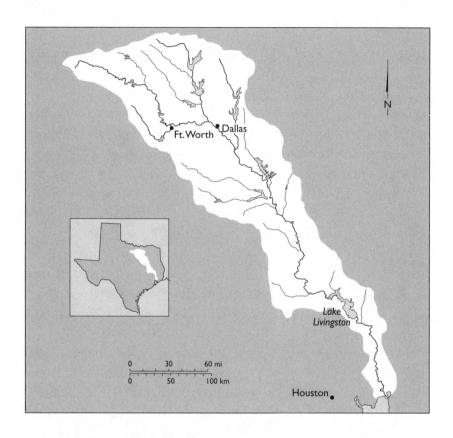

The Trinity River system in Texas. South of Dallas and Fort Worth, much
of the flow of the Trinity River consists of wastewater effluent. Lake Livingston
is one of Houston's main drinking water reservoirs.

(200 miles) south to Lake Livingston—one of the main drinking
water reservoirs for Houston—with only a few small tributaries adding to the flow. After a summer thunderstorm, the flow in the river
might not be dominated by wastewater, but most of the time, the waters of the Trinity consist of around 75 percent wastewater effluent.[18]

Before the Texan engineers arrived, the Trinity was a typical arid-
climate river that occasionally dried up during the summer. From the
time of the founding of the republic to the end of the nineteenth century, the river served as a water supply for Dallas, but as the volume of

untreated sewage being dumped into the river increased, the city's residents stopped drinking from the Trinity. In the mid-1950s, sewage treatment plants were finally built to alleviate the stench wafting out of the river just as the state was hit by the worst drought in its recorded history. By 1959, the cleaner water flowing down the Trinity was being used to solve Houston's drinking water supply problems through the construction of the Lake Livingston Reservoir.[19] Recognizing that Dallas might someday decide to retain the waters of the Trinity for other uses, Houston's engineers made contingency plans to work with their counterparts upstream in the Metroplex to share the valuable water that wastewater treatment plants were dumping into the river. They need not have worried: explosive population growth in the upstream cities ensured that there would be plenty of effluent flowing down the Trinity. Over the next four decades, the base flow of the river tripled, turning the river and reservoir into an effluent-dominated system.

Like many aspects of Texas, the Trinity River is distinguished by its exceptional size, but it is hardly unique. Effluent-dominated rivers can be found downstream of major cities throughout the arid western United States, including the Platte River below Denver, the Salt River below Phoenix, and the Santa Ana River, which flows from the growing cities of Southern California's Inland Empire to a discharge point near one of the surfing beaches immortalized by the Beach Boys.[20] Effluent-dominated systems are even starting to occur in rapidly growing parts of the humid Southeast, such as the Chattahoochee River near Atlanta and Little Econlockhatchee River outside of Orlando.[21]

While feminization of fish was the first problem to be documented in effluent-dominated waters, researchers have long hypothesized that chemicals in wastewater that are a lot less potent than the estrogen hormones might also be taking a toll on fish and wildlife.[22] For example, in 2009, Baylor University professor Bryan Brooks reported the presence of antidepressants and perfume fragrances in the livers of fish living in the Trinity River and several other effluent-dominated systems.[23] These and other studies documenting the presence of hundreds of pharmaceuticals and household chemicals in the rivers of the United States and Europe have raised concerns that continuous exposure of wildlife to these chemicals could result in subtle, unexpected effects on wildlife reproduction, behavior, and survival.[24] A few studies have even shown shifts in behavior at concentrations approaching those detected in effluent-dominated rivers, though unambiguous signs that chemicals in wastewater are harming fish have yet to be documented.[25]

It is quite possible that the concentrations of these less potent, manmade chemicals are too low to harm fish and other wildlife. Perhaps the take-home lesson from these reports of pharmaceuticals in rivers that have been published over the past decade is that with a sensitive instrument a talented chemist will be able to detect the presence of a few molecules of manmade chemicals in all but the cleanest systems. After all, we are talking about concentrations of about a part per trillion, which corresponds to something like a few grains of salt dissolved in an Olympic-sized swimming pool. Even the most potent fish endocrine disrupters—the estrogen hormones—can be measured at concentrations at which they have been diluted beyond the point where they affect fish. Therefore it should not surprise us if the same measurement technologies allow us to detect the presence of these less potent chemicals at concentrations that have no effect on fish and wildlife.

In fact, when toxicity data are available, scientists often conclude that the levels of pharmaceuticals and consumer products in fish livers and river waters are well below the levels where toxicity occurs.[26] This makes intuitive sense, because many of the compounds were designed and tested by companies that had a strong incentive—the threat of a lawsuit—to be certain that their products will not harm humans who ingest them in large quantities. Because fish and other wildlife share many of our biological systems, it is usually the case that a dose that is many times lower than what a person is likely to receive would not damage a fish. In other words, if a person can ingest around a gram of ibuprofen each day to relieve pain and reduce swelling with few ill side effects, wildlife that share many of the same biological systems can likely tolerate an amount that is a hundred billion times lower.

Nonetheless, we have to recognize that our knowledge of wildlife is incomplete. The systems that we do not share with wildlife, such as the enzyme that controlled the development of eggshells of birds or the olfactory receptors that allow salmon and other fish species to find their home spawning streams from great distances, may respond in a much different manner than those of humans. Furthermore, it is difficult to detect the subtle effects of a chemical on the ability of a fish to avoid a predator, outcompete a rival for a mate, or recover from an infection. But sometimes scientists can conduct sophisticated experiments that reveal the subtle effects of chemicals on wildlife. For example, in 2007, scientists working at the University of Minnesota conducted a clever experiment in which they showed that male fish that had been exposed to estrogens were unable to reproduce when placed in a tank with unexposed males because the estrogens made them less aggressive than their fellow suitors.[27] The jury may still be out on the potential effects on wildlife of every one of the thousands of chemicals in wastewater, but the feminization of fish by estrogens and the presence of a cocktail of other chemicals in fish livers are probably reasons enough to be concerned.

Although the feminization of fish by chemicals in wastewater inspired much of the recent scrutiny of effluent-dominated rivers, the effects of wastewater effluent on drinking water might end up being an even greater concern. After all, as in the case of the Trinity River, effluent-dominated rivers frequently serve as drinking water supplies for cities. Since piped water first enabled us to easily dispose of our wastes in rivers, drinking water supplies have frequently contained sewage. But until recently, the contribution of sewage to the drinking water supply was relatively modest. Recall the contamination of Lowell's water supply by the wastewater from Lawrence described in Chapter 4, in which the outbreak of typhoid fever in Lowell was attributed to Lawrence's relatively small contribution (just a few percent of the river's total water) of waste upstream. The engineers at the Lawrence Experimental Station were able to remove the typhoid-fever-causing bacteria from the waters of the Merrimack River with sand filters, but the drinking water treatment technology that they pioneered was not good enough for effluent-dominated rivers. The one-two punch of filtration and disinfection that was perfected over the next three decades was capable of removing most waterborne pathogens from effluent-dominated rivers. But chemicals would not have been much of an issue to the early drinking water engineers because there would have been few manmade organic chemicals worth worrying about in the sewage prior to the second half of the twentieth century. By the time that modern activated sludge treatment plants had transformed effluent-dominated rivers into seemingly fishable and drinkable water supplies, sewage contained a vast array of manmade chemicals in addition to the oxygen-consuming organic matter, nutrients, and pathogens that then spurred the development of water pollution control technologies.

Do the birth control pills, antibiotics, perfumes, detergents, plasticizers, and other household chemicals that we pour down the drain survive the trip from our sinks and toilets to the taps of our downstream neighbors? The answer to this question depends on the chemical in question and the gauntlet of treatment systems that it must navigate on its journey through the hydrologic cycle.

Sewage treatment plants were not purposefully designed to remove manmade chemicals, but many of the compounds are still removed as the sewage-loving microbes go about their business of breaking down oxygen-demanding organic matter. The ability of microbes in sewage treatment plants to remove trace amounts of pharmaceuticals and manmade chemicals is related to the fact that the bacteria are equipped with an arsenal of enzymes that they employ to attack a variety of chemicals. When the microbes encounter a molecule of an unfamiliar, manmade chemical, they will attempt to use it as a source of food. As long as part of the molecule looks like a naturally occurring compound that the microbes know how to use as a food source, they will be able to initiate its breakdown. Quite often, a successful attack on part of the molecule makes the remainder much more likely to react with other enzymes. Even if only part of the molecule can be broken down, its toxicity will likely diminish significantly through partial degradation.

Just how effective are modern sewage treatment plants at removing trace amounts of chemicals? Many chemicals are removed about as well as the rest of the oxygen-demanding organic matter in sewage. Thus if a modern wastewater treatment plant was designed to remove 90 percent of the oxygen-demanding organic matter, the concentration of a manmade chemical that is just as easily degraded as the natural organic material will also decrease by around 90 percent. This is the case for chemicals such as estrogens and painkillers like ibuprofen and naproxen (also known as Advil and Aleve, respectively).[28] When you purchase dish soap or laundry detergent that is labeled biodegradable, it is likely that the chemicals in the bottle have bonds that microbes can break about as easily as they handle natural organic matter.

While many manmade chemicals are removed just as well as natural organic matter, others pass through sewage treatment plants untouched. Over the past decade, scientists have discovered a number of compounds in wastewater effluent at concentrations above one part per billion. (Recall that the presence of manmade chemicals in this concentration range was originally thought to be the cause of cancer among people who drank surface water in New Orleans.) In many cases, the chemicals detected at the highest concentration are those that were designed to resist enzymatic attack. For example, artificial sweeteners in low-calorie foods contain bonds that the enzymes in our digestive systems have trouble breaking. As a result, the sweeteners sucralose, acesulfame, and saccharin—which are also known by their respective trade names Splenda, Sweet One, and Sweet'N Low—are present in wastewater at relatively high concentrations.

The concentrations of artificial sweeteners in effluent-dominated waters appear to be too low to affect wildlife, most likely because the same properties that protect the molecules from enzymatic breakdown also prevent them from binding to receptors or otherwise wreaking havoc inside of cells. What about that sweet taste? Despite their ubiquitous presence in effluent-impacted drinking waters, the highest observed concentrations of artificial sweeteners are still less than 0.01 percent of the levels at which they can be detected by our taste buds.[29] People would have to consume a lot more diet soft drinks and sugar-free candy before sewage effluent acquires a sweet taste.

The stable bonds in artificial sweeteners also prove to be useful outside the food and beverage industry. Chemicals with stable bonds are routinely used in products such as flame retardants, pharmaceuticals, and coatings that make fabrics stain resistant. Through routine use, many of these compounds find their way into and through sewage treatment plants. For example, about a decade ago a team of scientists at the Technical University of Berlin noticed that a group of iodine-containing organic compounds was present at relatively high concentrations in wastewater effluent. It turned out that the scientists were detecting a family of unreactive chemicals commonly used in medical imaging. These chemicals—which are referred to as contrast media—consist of a benzene ring on which all of the hydrogen atoms have been replaced by iodine or carbon chains. The stable carbon-iodine bonds make them nearly impossible for microbes to break down.[30]

When doctors want to create an image of a patient's digestive system, they pump large quantities of a concentrated solution of contrast media directly into the patient's stomach, intestine, or bladder before taking an X-ray. The presence of the iodine in the organic molecule causes the organ to preferentially absorb X-rays and stand out from the adjacent tissues. At the end of the imaging procedure, the concentrated solution is dumped down the drain. As a result of the many grams of phase contrast compounds that are used to create medical images, it only takes a handful of clinics around the city to explain concentrations of a few parts per billion of the compounds in effluent from a city's sewage treatment plant.[31]

It is a bit of a simplification, but we can envision wastewater effluent as containing two types of manmade chemicals. The first group consists of compounds broken down almost as easily as the oxygen-demanding organic matter that comes from our bodily wastes and bits and pieces of the microbes living in the treatment plant. The concentrations of these readily degradable compounds will typically decrease by 90 to 99 percent as they pass through a sewage treatment plant. For the second group, which includes the artificial sweeteners, contrast media, and a small group of pharmaceutical compounds, little or no change in concentrations will occur as sewage undergoes treatment. Even though some of these compounds are used only in small quantities, their resistance to treatment means that they will be among the compounds detected at highest concentrations in wastewater effluent. In fact, one of the most reliable ways to estimate the contribution of wastewater effluent to the overall flow of a river is to measure the concentration of artificial sweeteners or X-ray contrast media.[32]

After passing through sewage treatment plants, the manmade chemicals still have to survive the trip downstream and through drinking water treatment plants before they can show up in our drinking water. During this second part of the trip, a number of different processes can decrease the concentrations of manmade chemicals as they flow down a river. For example, the enzyme-catalyzed chemical breakdown processes that occur within sewage treatment plants continue within the river as microbes degrade manmade chemicals while feeding on the residual organic matter in the effluent. In addition, sunlight causes some of the compounds to break down through a process referred to as photolysis. (The fading of color in a fabric that has been exposed to sunlight for long periods is an example of photolysis. In the case of colored fabrics, sunlight-induced chemical reactions cause bonds in the dye molecules to break. The resulting products no longer absorb sunlight.) Both of these processes occur over days or even weeks under the conditions encountered in most rivers. Microbial and photochemical breakdown processes are often difficult to study in rivers, because the dilution of effluent with water from tributaries has a bigger effect on chemical concentrations than do these relatively slow chemical reactions. Therefore, the best laboratory for studying the removal of wastewater-derived chemicals is one where dilution is minimal over a lengthy stretch. The effluent-dominated river with the longest stretch of tributary-free water in the United States is probably the Trinity.

In 2005, I finally took Alan Plummer's advice and sent a couple of my students to Texas to figure out how well microbes and sunlight remove manmade chemicals from the Trinity River as it travels to Houston's reservoir. By finding places where roads intersected the river between the Metroplex and Lake Livingston, they were able to collect a water sample about every eighty kilometers (fifty miles) along this path during a single day. By repeating this procedure for a week, they were able to follow a slug of water down the entire length of the river. Averaging the concentrations of manmade chemicals in the daily river water samples allowed us to be certain that the trends we were seeing were not attributable to day-to-day fluctuations in the use of chemicals by the residents of the Metroplex or some quirk of the river's flow.

Our data from the Trinity taught us a lesson that in retrospect should not have been much of a surprise: the chemicals that were susceptible to breakdown in the sewage treatment plant continued to be removed by bacteria in the river, albeit at a slower rate because of the lower density of microbes in the river water. Several of the other compounds also degraded upon exposure to sunlight, but the limited penetration of sunlight in the river's muddy water meant that the process was only important for the chemicals that were most susceptible to breakdown by sunlight. By the time the water reached Lake Livingston, the concentrations of the degradable chemicals had decreased by 90 percent compared to their levels right after treatment. Those compounds that did not degrade in the sewage treatment plant, however, such as the contrast media, remained at nearly the same concentrations we measured at the exit of the sewage treatment plant after a week of exposure to microbes and sunlight.[33]

The Trinity River water spends about a year in Lake Livingston before it enters Houston's drinking water treatment plant. It would seem reasonable to assume that the concentrations of the readily degradable compounds, like ibuprofen and naproxen, continue to decrease in the reservoir through microbial breakdown and to a lesser degree, photochemical reactions near the water's surface. In contrast to the degradable chemicals, the concentrations of artificial sweeteners, contrast media, and other compounds probably undergo little decrease other than those related to dilution of the effluent with rainwater runoff. Rivers and reservoirs can help break down the manmade chemicals in wastewater effluent, but those compounds that were difficult to remove in the wastewater treatment plant are likely to survive the trip downstream.

The final barrier to wastewater-derived chemicals is the drinking water treatment plant. As we learned in Chapter 4, drinking water treatment plants employ two main processes: particle removal—typically with a slow or a rapid sand filter—and disinfection. Because the chemicals that made it through the wastewater treatment plant have little affinity for suspended particles, disinfection is the only process where we expect to see any significant removal of chemicals in a conventional drinking water treatment plant.[34]

In the United States, the most common form of disinfection is chlorination. Through the same types of chemical reactions that cause plant-derived organic matter to produce disinfection byproducts, some of the manmade chemicals in wastewater are transformed during chlorination.[35] For example, under the conditions typically employed in drinking water treatment plants, 17β-estradiol, ethinyl estradiol, and several of the other estrogenic hormones are converted into products in which one of the hydrogen atoms on the molecule's benzene ring has been replaced with a chlorine. As a result of the high specific-ity of the estrogen receptor, these transformed versions of the steroids have only a fraction of the estrogenic activity of the parent compound.[36] Chlorination of water means that drinking water obtained from rivers with effluent will not contain estradiol or ethinyl estradiol. The discovery that chlorination of water eliminates endocrine-disrupting compounds may also prove to be a simple solution to the problem of feminized fish: wastewater treatment plants that discharge to effluent-dominated rivers can protect the fish by adding a small dose of chlorine prior to discharge.

The practice of adding chlorine to wastewater effluent is already common in parts of the United States where wastewater is disinfected to protect downstream recreational waters. To disinfect water, chlorine is added at one end of a channel or long pipe. After it reacts with the effluent for about an hour, a slight excess of a benign chemical that reacts with chlorine, such as sodium bisulfite, is added to the water to protect fish in the receiving water from the toxic effects of chlorine. Because of concerns associated with the safe storage of chlorine gas, chlorine is gradually being displaced by ultraviolet light and other disinfectants. In many European countries, wastewater effluent is discharged without disinfection.

Although it's reassuring to know that chlorine can protect us from endocrine-disrupting steroid hormones and many manmade chemicals that go down the drain, we have to consider the prospect that the products of the reaction will be more toxic than their parents. One obvious place to look for toxic products of a reaction between chlorine and a manmade chemical is among the family of disinfection byproducts discovered in the years after Johannes Rook discovered the presence of chloroform in Rotterdam's tap water.

Certain pharmaceuticals or consumer products produce chlorine disinfection byproducts such as trihalomethanes and haloacetic acids when they react with chlorine.[37] There is, however, little reason for concern because most of the manmade chemicals that serve as the precursors of these mildly toxic compounds are present at concentrations that are too low to cause a problem. It is possible to reach such a broad conclusion because the concentrations of the manmade compounds rarely exceed one part per billion in effluent-dominated water supplies. If each organic molecule produces one or two molecules of trihalomethanes or haloacetic acids during its reactions with chlorine, the maximum possible concentration of the trihalomethanes and haloacetic acids formed by chlorination will be around 1 percent of the value that is considered safe in drinking water. For most drinking water supplies, the increase in concentration of the disinfection byproducts that are formed from manmade chemicals will be negligible compared to those produced from reactions with naturally occurring humic substances.

As a result of the substantial differences between the concentrations of manmade chemicals and the concentrations of the disinfection byproducts that are subject to government regulations, drinking water treatment plants that rely on effluent-dominated waters generally do not have problems complying with government drinking water standards. That does not mean that there is no risk: for example, MX, the super-toxic compound that some researchers believe to be responsible for increased rates of cancer and spontaneous abortions in communities with chlorinated drinking water, rarely occurs in drinking water at concentrations above around one hundred parts per trillion.[38] Conceivably this and other yet-to-be-discovered toxic compounds could be formed when wastewater-dominated rivers are disinfected with chlorine, but no evidence of this kind of toxicity has been found.

While there is no evidence that MX and related mutagens are produced when effluent-dominated water supplies are disinfected with chlorine, in 2011, a team of researchers from the U.S. Environmental Protection Agency and a German research institute reported the formation of elevated concentrations of highly toxic disinfection byproducts in drinking water treatment plants that receive effluent-impacted river water. The researchers attributed the source of the toxic compounds to a reaction among iodine-containing contrast media, naturally occurring humic substances, and chlorine.[39]

If conventional drinking water treatment plants cannot remove all of the unreactive manmade compounds and a few of them are transformed into toxic byproducts during the disinfection process, or if we are just plain worried about the presence of all the manmade chemicals in our tap water, it might be prudent to alter the way we operate drinking water treatment plants. The two easiest changes to make are identical to those that we came up with in response to the discovery of chlorine disinfection byproducts in water that is rich in humic substances—namely, using activated carbon to remove the byproduct precursors prior to disinfection, or switching to an alternative disinfectant like ozone.

These two treatment technologies have a long track record. Activated carbon was first widely applied to drinking water in the 1920s as a means of removing tastes and odors. Ozone also has been used to disinfect water for decades, especially in Germany, Switzerland, and other parts of Western Europe where consumers dislike the strong taste that chlorine imparts to the water. After the discovery of chlorine disinfection byproducts in the 1970s, the use of both technologies began to expand in the United States, but despite their growing popularity they are used by only a small number of large drinking water treatment plants: currently, about 10 to 15 percent of the large drinking water treatment plants in the United States use activated carbon or ozone.[40]

Both technologies are quite effective at removing the manmade chemicals. But the compounds that are difficult to remove in wastewater treatment plants and do not break down during downstream transport, such as phase contrast media and artificial sweeteners, also are the ones that are hardest to remove with activated carbon and ozone.[41] Under typical conditions, the concentrations of these compounds decrease by less than half after passing through the treatment process. There is, however, still ground for hope: the application of ozone prior to activated carbon treatment is proving to be an effective means of removing these stubborn manmade chemicals.[42] The synergy between ozone and activated carbon is attributable to the fact that the ozonation step partially degrades some of the humic substances in the water, and these partially degraded substances become a source of food for microbes living on the surface of the activated carbon particles. While the prospect of adding both technologies to drinking water treatment plants strikes fear into the hearts of penny-pinching utility managers, it is the most reliable and cost-effective of the currently available strategies.

Despite its efficacy, ozonation coupled with activated carbon may not be a panacea. A 2006 study conducted by researchers in Karlsruhe, Germany, showed that ozonation of water contaminated with trace amounts of a manmade chemical produces high concentrations of the super-toxic disinfection byproduct N-nitrosodimethylamine, or NDMA.[43] On the basis of its high potential to cause cancer, regulatory agencies have set drinking water standards for this compound at concentrations around ten parts per trillion.[44] In a forensic investigation with more twists and turns than a television crime drama, the German researchers painstakingly determined that microbes living in the soil near vineyards partially degraded a fungicide that had washed off of the grapes. When groundwater contaminated with the breakdown product of the fungicide migrated to the wells, it reacted with ozone to produce NDMA. Although this fungicide is unlikely to find its way into wastewater, a number of pharmaceuticals and household products have structures similar to that of the fungicide. Someday we may learn that ozone reacts with manmade chemicals in wastewater to create NDMA or some other super-toxic disinfection byproduct that cannot be removed by activated carbon.

My encounter with Susan Jobling in 1995 led me to question the practice of using rivers as a dumping ground for sewage effluent. Initially, it was the presence of steroid hormones in effluent-dominated surface waters and their ability to feminize fish that drew my attention. After my colleagues and I learned that the problem could be solved by relatively simple measures, like improving the ability of the sewage treatment plant to remove organic matter or by adding a relatively inexpensive additional step, like chlorination, at the end of the treatment process, we turned our attention to the less potent manmade chemicals. We still do not know which, if any, of these chemicals might be causing subtle effects on the growth and reproduction of fish and other aquatic organisms that make their homes in effluent-dominated rivers, though it is clear that some of the compounds survive their trip to our drinking water treatment plants. In most cases, the concentrations of the difficult-to-remove compounds are so low that it is exceedingly unlikely that they will affect our health. But in a few cases, the manmade chemicals react with chemical disinfectants during drinking water treatment to produce potent mutagens or carcinogens. Initial evidence suggests that we might be able to eliminate some of these chemicals by upgrading our sewage and water treatment plants, but the total cost of such improvements is high.

In addition to activated carbon and ozone, there are numerous up-and-coming water treatment technologies that might be more effective than the retrofits that are currently being contemplated. Before we start investing in Water 3.1—an upgrade of our aging wastewater and drinking water systems to address the problems caused by trace amounts of chemicals in wastewater—we should consider approaches for breaking free of the nineteenth- and twentieth-century practice of using our rivers and drinking water supplies for waste disposal.

9

Paying for the Fourth Revolution

My water bill is just one of many that land in my physical and virtual mailbox every month. In addition to telling me what I owe, it helpfully points out the amount of water my family used and the breakdown of fees for different tasks that my local water company does to keep the water flowing to and the sewage flowing away from my home. Fifty dollars a month puts it in the same price range as the monthly bills for cell phones, electricity, and Internet service. In fact, if I calculate the cost by volume used, my family spends a little less than half a cent per liter (two cents per gallon) for our water. That's not bad if you consider all of the hard work that went into solving the problems of thirsty cities, cholera outbreaks, and sewage-choked rivers.

Although most of us give little thought to the details of the humble water utility bill, it may well hold the key to our urban water future. If the ways in which our utilities collect money prevent them from investing in new infrastructure before water systems reach a state of emergency, the problems described in the previous chapters are going to get a lot worse before anything is done about them. And if patching up the existing system ultimately proves to be a lot less expensive than adopting radically new approaches to supplying clean water and treating wastewater, we may end up investing in repairs to the weak points in the system for decades before we upgrade to Water 4.0.

Historically, utilities in the United States have almost always struggled to raise the money needed to improve water treatment and delivery systems, but in recent years it has become tougher. Unbeknownst to most people, the ways in which water utilities fund their operations has shifted over the past twenty-five years: before the late 1980s, operating costs were paid mainly through utility bills, while much of the investment in new reservoirs, pipelines, and treatment plants was paid for by federal grants. A shift away from federal funding, coupled with increasing costs of operation, means that water bills are rising at rates faster than inflation just to maintain the status quo.

The last major investment that the United States made to its urban water systems—the sewage treatment plants built in the fifteen-year period after passage of the Clean Water Act of 1972—were paid for mostly with federal grants. Correcting for inflation, the federal contribution to local utilities amounted to around $80 billion during this brief period. Throughout the construction boom, the government provided about 70 percent of the funds needed to build and upgrade treatment plants.[1] The logic seemed reasonable at the time: by putting money on the table, the federal government took the sting out of complying with tough, new water pollution laws. Unfortunately, the grants also led people to become accustomed to the idea that clean water does not require a financial sacrifice from the local community.

After the initial round of building and upgrading sewage treatment plants was completed, the political will to continue the grant programs dissipated.[2] Starting in 1988, the federal government transitioned to a new system in which grants were replaced by subsidized loans from a "revolving fund," so named because as utilities paid off their loans, the returned funds were lent out to new projects elsewhere.[3] This less costly federal incentive, initiated after some of the most egregious problems had already been fixed, ended the sewage treatment plant construction boom. Overall, the general consensus among economists, political scientists, and lawmakers was that the new pay-for-service system was a success.[4] In fact, the popularity of the revolving fund led to the creation of a second revolving fund when drinking water laws were tightened in 1996.[5]

After the modern water and wastewater systems were built, keeping them running should have been easy; all the utilities had to do was cover the costs of their operations and maintenance. In theory, the monthly bills should have been set at constant levels that covered all of the anticipated costs of running and maintaining the system. The current situation is similar to what would happen if you and your siblings inherited a vacation cabin from your grandmother. Because granny had already paid off the mortgage, you and your siblings would only have to chip in money to cover things like painting the walls and fixing the occasional leaky faucet. You would also have to put aside a little money every year to replace the roof when it eventually wears out. As long as you had accurately estimated the costs of keeping the house going, your monthly contribution to the "cabin fund" would remain constant after correcting for inflation. If the operators of our urban water systems have correctly accounted for operations and maintenance costs, our water bills should also remain steady, after accounting for inflation, and there should always be enough extra money left over to pay for anticipated repairs and system upgrades.

Unfortunately, these assumptions have not gone according to plan for many water agencies. Water bills are rising at rates well in excess of inflation just to maintain the status quo. For me, this means a water bill that will increase by 30 percent over the next five years. Elsewhere, water and wastewater rates are following the same trend, with average annual increases of approximately 5 percent nationwide over the past decade, which is about twice the rate of inflation.[6] The increases are not restricted to the United States. Just about every country that has a modern water system is experiencing substantial water rate increases. At the extreme among countries in the developed world, Australia has experienced a near doubling of water rates over the past five years to start paying off investments in new water supplies made in response to a severe drought.

What happens when water utility rates increase faster than inflation? Although residents of a community cannot switch to another supplier who offers lower prices, water utility managers still do their best to slow the rate at which bills increase because they hope to avoid political fallout. The pushback comes from a variety of sources, including irate mayors, who worry about losing their edge in attracting new development; business leaders, who see increasing water rates as a threat to their bottom line; and anti-tax lobbying groups, which are convinced that part of their utility bills are going to overcompensated union workers, lazy managers, and services that should be paid for with existing tax revenues.

Starting in the 1990s, concerns about water rate increases have even resulted in laws that make it even harder for utilities to raise their rates. For example, an anti-tax group in California orchestrated the passage of a statewide initiative in 1996 that created a formal mechanism for fighting utility rate increases. As a result, certain increases in water rates now have to be approved by a majority of the utility's customers.[7]

The success of groups that resist water rate increases means that it is becoming difficult to cover the operations and maintenance costs of urban water systems. The U.S. Conference of Mayors estimates that cities take in only about 80 to 90 percent of the funds needed to repair their water and sewer pipes.[8] The same holds true for the utilities responsible for the operation of drinking water and sewage treatment plants. Starting in the 1990s, this investment shortfall has turned into a funding gap. According to the Environmental Protection Agency, water and wastewater utilities in the United States will have to come up with about an additional $300 billion to make up for the difference between what they collect and what they will actually need to spend between 2010 and 2030.[9]

The funding gap in water infrastructure has been the subject of considerable lobbying by groups that want to reestablish the federal grant programs. Utility-sponsored advocacy groups and the Congressional Budget Office have analyzed the implications of the funding gap on the financial health and viability of water and wastewater utilities. Despite some differences in the assumptions that the two organizations made about improvements in efficiency and the true costs associated with borrowing money, their findings are quite similar: the difference between what utilities currently collect and what they will need to spend to comply with pollution control laws while still keeping the water flowing means that they will have to come up with an additional $26 billion of annual revenue in the near future, assuming that utilities comply with current and future regulations and replace their worn-out equipment in a responsible manner. The Congressional Budget Office also considered a low-cost scenario that assumed a decrease in service, more water main breaks, and less aggressive pollution control. The low-cost scenario yielded additional annual expenditures of $4 billion per year. Put another way, to fill the gap without federal help, a typical water and wastewater bill will increase by a total of about $18 per month over the next two decades.[10] Although there is considerable uncertainty associated with these estimates, when we couple the infrastructure spending gap with other factors that are pushing up water costs, it is quite possible that the 5 percent annual increases in our water bills that many of us are experiencing are too small or that some other source of revenue will be needed to keep urban water systems going.[11]

To survive under conditions in which they are unable to raise rates as much as needed, utilities often cut corners on the maintenance of pipes and treatment plants.[12] Although the strategy of deferring maintenance may be effective in the short term, eventually the pipes and treatment plants fail, resulting in property damage, injuries, and a loss of consumer confidence. The most vivid reminders of the price of deferred maintenance are the spectacular geysers of water that occur when pressurized drinking water pipes break, such as the pipe break that happened in the suburbs of Washington, D.C., on Christmas Eve in 2008. When a major water distribution line ruptured under the streets during rush hour, nine people had to be rescued by helicopter from the torrents of water streaming from a broken pipe that had turned a road into a river.[13] Not counting the 220 million liters (55 million gallons) of treated water lost during the break, damage to vehicles, or the costs of deploying rescue crews, the pipe break cost the utility about $1.4 million.[14] According to the *Washington Post,* the blame could be partially attributed to cutbacks in the staff in the office responsible for pipe inspections and maintenance—cutbacks that were made in an effort to avoid rate increases when the community was considering the possibility of privatizing the utility.[15]

The more frequent, less spectacular water and sewer line breaks that keep the repair crews scurrying around my neighborhood at all hours of the day and night are inconvenient—especially for people who live next to the broken pipe—but they are not necessarily more expensive than replacing the entire pipe network. From the perspective of a utility's bottom line, it may be more efficient to allow a certain number of pipe breaks to occur each year than it is to replace all of the pipes before they wear out. Of course, this savings is partially due to the fact that the utility does not pay the full costs of flooded streets, illness associated with the introduction of waterborne pathogens into the drinking water supply, and damage to the environment. Pipe breaks can wreak havoc on rivers and streams because much of the drinking water and sewage that escapes from broken pipes eventually finds its way into a water body. When sewer pipes leak, untreated wastewater can introduce waterborne pathogens, nutrients, and organic matter into surface waters. Perhaps surprisingly, drinking water pipe breaks also can pose serious threats to the environment: at the concentrations present in drinking water, both chloramines (the residual disinfectant used in many drinking water systems) and copper (from corrosion of pipes) are toxic to many species of fish. Just like an aging car that needs a repair every few weeks, the pipe network will eventually reach a breakeven point when it makes more sense to replace the remaining pipes than it does to keep repairing the leaks.

If utilities are struggling to finance their current operations and maintenance despite hefty annual increases in rates, what does the future hold? In many ways, the current investment shortfall is just the tip of the iceberg. Additional financial pressure is going to be placed on utilities from the increasing costs of personnel and energy, climate-change-induced droughts or floods, and ever tougher treatment requirements. Given the tenuous state of our existing water systems and the magnitude of the coming challenges, simply pouring more money into the system in an attempt to maintain the status quo may be the wrong approach: in fact, I believe that the impending costs of maintaining the status quo will be the push needed to start the fourth urban water revolution. Although the operating manual for Water 4.0 is incomplete, the promise of a less expensive and more sustainable alternative should serve as an incentive for working out the details.

Before we start a revolution, we need to convince ourselves that it will not be possible to solve our problems through modest investments in our existing water systems. If incremental improvements—call it Water 3.1—turn out to be much less expensive than major changes, the revolution can wait. To figure out whether or not our financial situation will clear a path to investing in Water 4.0, we need to dig below the surface of the water bill to understand how our money is being spent and how much it is going to cost to address all of the urban water challenges that we will face in the near future.

Let's start by investigating the ways in which utilities currently spend the money that they collect. Most of a water utility's budget is allocated to one of three purposes: daily operations, system maintenance, or the construction of new infrastructure.

Running a water utility is a labor-intensive endeavor, especially when it involves maintaining a network of hundreds of kilometers of canals and underground pipes while simultaneously complying with a complex set of regulations concerning land use, public health, and the environment. To operate our existing water and wastewater system, you need teams of construction workers to fix pipes, along with scores of engineers, lawyers, and lab technicians to ensure that the system meets all of the government's requirements. Salaries and benefits for the large number of skilled workers needed to operate a modern water system typically consume about half of the operations and maintenance budgets of water utilities.[16]

Let's take my local water utility as an example. The East Bay Municipal Utility District (EBMUD) provides water for about 1.3 million people and wastewater treatment for about 650,000 people in and around Oakland, California. It has approximately two thousand full-time staff members, which makes it one of the largest employers in the area.[17] Put another way, about one of every five hundred people in my community works for the water utility. If we were to count the people who rebuild reservoirs and treatment plants—workers who are often employed as contractors—the number would be considerably higher. For comparison, the U.S. Census Bureau estimates that there is about one doctor for every five hundred people in the United States. This means that the chances are about equal that a child born in my city will grow up to work for EBMUD or will become a doctor.

As a result of increasing costs of health benefits and pension plans, the labor costs borne by water utilities have increased quickly in recent years. While salaries for working at a water utility are nowhere near as high as those in medicine, law, or finance, most utility workers receive decent compensation packages. In part, this is because many of them have specialized training in engineering or in one of the construction trades.

Although this situation may be appropriate for the people who protect our health and environment, it means that personnel cuts are a logical step for leaders to consider when trying to balance budgets in tough times. In fact, hiring freezes and cuts to employee benefits were often the first responses of water utilities to the economic downturn of 2008. Further reducing salaries and benefits in the future might help utilities deal with funding shortfalls, but strong unions and the good relationships between management and labor at many utilities mean that further reductions of this kind won't be easy.

In the long run, automating operations or outsourcing nontechnical jobs may help, but many of the more immediate savings are likely to come at a price, because water treatment plants are already pretty lean when it comes to staff. In my travels to treatment plants, it is not unusual to run across fewer than a dozen workers running a treatment plant that provides drinking water to a million people. Therefore reductions in staff size will likely come from the maintenance department, where a large number of managers, engineers, and construction workers are responsible for labor-intensive activities designed to prevent pipe leaks and to ensure the smooth operation of the system. Almost certainly, then, simply cutting back on maintenance staff without introducing radical new approaches for accomplishing the work with fewer people will lead to more pipe breaks and a decrease in water quality.

After labor, much of the remaining money for operations and maintenance is used to purchase and install replacement parts—underground pipes, pumps, and settling tanks—when they wear out. Water and sewer pipes can survive underground for a long time, but eventually they develop leaks or undergo catastrophic failures. The cumulative effect of leaks on the overall operation of a water system can be quite large. Typically somewhere between 10 and 20 percent of the treated drinking water leaks out of the distribution system before it can be used.[18] Think about it: after all of the work that goes into acquiring and treating drinking water, we allow it to escape through leaking pipes that are not adequately maintained. But leaking sewer pipes can have consequences beyond lost water. Modest-sized leaks in sewers allow waterborne pathogens to penetrate shallow groundwater, and sometimes these pathogens even seep out at the shoreline, where they contaminate shellfish, fish, and swimming areas.[19] In addition, the leaks go both ways—they also allow groundwater to flow into sewers where they greatly increase the volume of water passing through the system. The increased flow is particularly problematic in cities that have separate sewers for human wastes and storm runoff systems because the increased volume of sewage can overwhelm the sewage treatment plant during periods of wet weather.

It takes somewhere between 75 and 120 years for the walls of a metal or concrete pipe to wear down to the point where the overlying weight of the soil or a spike in pressure will cause it to break or to develop a leak. The exact lifetime of an individual pipe depends on a variety of factors including temperature, water pressure, the nature of the soil and rock surrounding it, and the composition of the water flowing through it. It also has a lot to do with the way that it was manufactured.

As a result of a quirk in the manufacturing process, the old-fashioned cast-iron pipes installed near the beginning of the twentieth century last a lot longer than the pipes installed during the postwar wave of suburbanization of the 1950s and 1960s. The longevity of the older pipes is due to the imprecise ways in which the pipes were made in the early days: prior to the 1920s, cast-iron pipes were manufactured by pouring molten metal into a mold that was made out of sand. As you might imagine, this primitive process was imprecise, which meant that walls of the pipes had to be made extra thick to compensate for irregularities that could develop if the molten iron did not flow through the mold evenly. Starting in the late 1920s, the thickness of pipes was reduced by a new manufacturing process: by rotating the mold as the molten iron was poured, it was possible to achieve a more uniform thickness in the pipe walls. The resulting product was lighter and less expensive to manufacture. Unfortunately, the thinner pipes wear out faster than their heavier predecessors. During the 1960s, further innovations in the manufacturing process resulted in the development of thin-walled pipes that corroded more slowly. As a result, water pipes that are currently being installed last about as long as those installed in the early years of the twentieth century.[20]

The pipes, pumps, and concrete basins used to build our water and wastewater treatment plants also have finite lifetimes. Because of the timing of water infrastructure investments, many treatment plants are around fifty years old. Just like underground pipes, the concrete and steel structures that are the backbones of our treatment plants are due to be replaced.[21] Many of the other components at treatment plants are also ready for upgrades: the mechanical and electrical systems used in treatment plants are typically designed to last fifteen to twenty-five years.[22] While many of these systems can limp along beyond their planned lifetimes, even after they are repaired the vintage technologies require more oversight and consume more energy than their modern counterparts.

Unfortunately for us, the thick cast-iron pipes installed in the early twentieth century, the thinner pipes and drinking water treatment plants that were built during the postwar wave of suburbanization, and the first generation of wastewater treatment plants built during the Clean Water Act construction boom are all reaching the end of their useful lives at the same time. The need to simultaneously replace the first generation of urban water infrastructure is going to mean a lot more floods, detours around dug-up streets, and work for construction crews as we enter what the American Water Works Association refers to as the "Replacement Era" for water systems.[23]

As you might imagine, it is going to be expensive to get urban water systems through the Replacement Era. For my local utility, annual expenditures for replacing pipes and aging treatment plants are expected to double over the next thirty years. This translates to an additional monthly cost of around eight dollars per household over this thirty-year period, which would account for about one-sixth of the increase that I am currently experiencing in my monthly water bill if it were spread out evenly over time. Nationwide, the average cost of replacing the first generation of drinking water systems will total about $13,500 per household. And that's just for the drinking water system: if we were to add in the costs of replacing wastewater treatment systems, the costs would be considerably higher.

After labor and replacement parts, energy is one of the most important components of water utility budgets. Adjusted for inflation, the price of electricity in the United States was nearly constant during the twentieth century.[24] But increasing global competition for fossil fuels, expenditures associated with modernizing the electricity grid, and efforts to limit greenhouse gas emissions caused electricity rates to increase by 6 to 8 percent per year between 2000 and 2009.[25] Unless our newfound natural gas reserves result in a rapid retooling of our electricity sector, the trend is likely to continue in the future. Some utilities are insulated from increasing energy prices because they generate their own power with hydroelectric dams, but most have to purchase their electricity from the local power company. As a result, increases in electricity prices translate directly into higher water bills. Because many of the new sources of water and advanced water treatment systems that we are likely to use in the future consume more energy than their predecessors, water rates will be more sensitive to increases in energy costs in the coming decades.

According to the Electric Power Research Institute (EPRI), drinking water and sewer treatments consume about 4 percent of the nation's electricity.[26] Expressed in familiar terms, providing a day's worth of water to a family of four uses about the same amount of energy as it takes to keep a fifty-watt lightbulb burning for twenty-four hours. Treating and disposing of the family's sewage requires the operation of that fifty-watt lightbulb for another eight hours. To think of it yet another way, the electricity used to provide your family with drinking water and to treat its sewage is about equal to the amount consumed by your refrigerator.

Thinking back to the ancient Roman drinking water systems and London's early sewer system, the use of so much energy to run our modern water systems may seem puzzling. After all, the Roman aqueducts and British sewers operated entirely under the force of gravity. Sure, modern water treatment plants need some energy to keep the lights running and to generate chlorine gas, and sewage treatment plants use electricity to power pumps that bubble air into the activated sludge basins, but these processes consume a relatively small amount of electricity. Why do our modern water systems consume so much energy? The explanation can be found in the pump house: About 85 percent of the electricity consumed by modern water and wastewater systems is associated with the pumps needed to lift and move water and sewage.

But why in the world do we need to pump so much water? First, in our quest to provide water to ever-growing cities we have built a number of water systems that fight gravity rather than work with it. One of the most extreme cases can be seen as you drive out of Los Angeles on U.S. Highway 5. If you look out your window, you will see the pumps of the State Water Project that lift water about six hundred meters (two thousand feet) from the floor of California's Central Valley up to a series of reservoirs in the Tehachapi Mountains. The energy used to get the water up and over the mountains accounts for about a third of the total household electricity used in the entire region, making it one of the most energy-intensive water supplies in the world.[27] In defense of the project, the net energy picture is more reasonable when you consider the system as a whole: hydroelectric energy is generated some 400 kilometers (250 miles) to the north when the water flows down to the Central Valley from the Sierra Nevada Mountains at the start of its journey. Accounting for the energy-producing part of the system reduces the net amount of electricity used to get drinking water into Los Angeles by about 90 percent. Nonetheless, if we were to find an alternative source of water for the city, this hydroelectric power could be freed up for other uses.

As is evident in this rather extreme example, the amount of energy needed to provide a city with drinking water can vary considerably depending on the local geography. For example, New York City's massive imported water system operates almost entirely on gravity because it's a straight shot down from the Catskill Mountains to the city. Because of the limited need for pumps, the energy required to provide drinking water to residents of New York is only about 20 percent of the national average.[28] Electricity use for pumping water in those cities that obtain their water from rivers and lakes, such as St. Louis and Chicago, is a little bit higher than that of gravity-fed systems because it is necessary to lift water from its source—the water's edge at the lowest elevation in town—to the highest hills or the

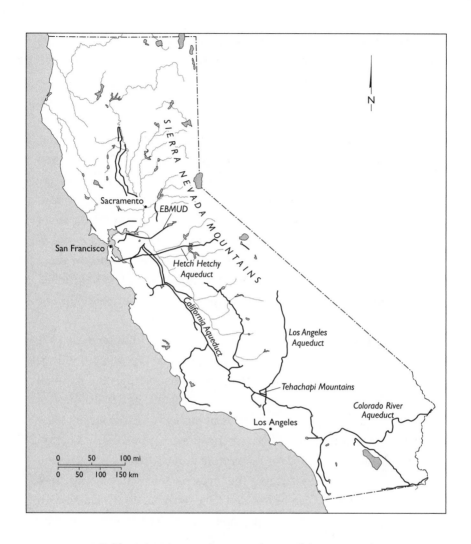

California's major aqueducts provide most of the water used
by the state's cities and farms.

farthest suburbs in the system. The story is similar in other parts of
the world. For example, in Australia, Melbourne's gravity-fed water
system uses less than 10 percent of the energy needed to transport
water over mountains in Sydney or to pump groundwater from deep
aquifers in Adelaide.[29]

Water systems that rely on gravity or local rivers and lakes often use less energy than the national average to provide water. So which cities have energy usages that pull up the national average? Los Angeles is not alone in its reliance on pumps to push water over mountains. For example, water from the Colorado River in Arizona is pumped to an elevation that is even higher than that of the Tehachapi Mountains as it climbs up to the red rocks surrounding Tucson.[30] The $5 billion Central Arizona Project is typical of the way that water projects were designed in the days when electricity was cheap and federal investments allowed arid regions to build massive systems to deliver water to cities and farms with little consideration of their long-term viability. With the low electricity prices of the twentieth century, these energy-intensive systems could be justified, but it will be hard to expand them or to build similar systems if electricity prices double or triple in the future.

The national average for energy consumption in water systems is also pulled up by cities that rely on groundwater. Overall, groundwater systems use about 30 percent more electricity than the national average for all types of water systems.[31] Although its acquisition frequently requires more electricity for pumping, groundwater is often attractive as a water source because it can usually be used as a drinking water supply with little or no treatment. It is also cost-effective if it can be obtained locally, because the investment in canals or pipelines to move it to the city can be avoided. Due to the costs associated with drilling wells and pumping water up to the surface, however, the first set of groundwater wells are usually dug to the shallowest depth at which clean water can be obtained. Therefore future exploitation of groundwater is likely to be even more energy intensive because the new wells will have to be dug to depths deeper than those that are already in use.

The second reason we consume so much electricity in modern water systems is that we need to pressurize water to get it to flow through an extensive underground pipe network and we often set the pressure for large sections of the system at values that assure that the minimum desired pressure will be experienced in the farthest faucet. To ensure that there is enough water pressure to reach the second or third floor showerhead or to fight a two-alarm fire requires relatively high water pressure. This arrangement is in contrast to the ancient Roman systems, where most of the water flowed out at street level from a relatively small number of fountains. Overall, the energy required to pump water through a modern water distribution system accounts for about a quarter of the energy consumed after the water reaches the drinking water treatment plant.[32] And when we fail to adequately maintain pipe networks, the cost of pumping increases as water pressure is lost through leaks and through friction caused by the rough interior surfaces of corroding pipes.

We even have started to rely on pumps to move sewage. Although most sewage treatment plants are located at the lowest elevations in the city, pressurized sections of sewers, known as force mains, are needed to move sewage over hills on its way to the treatment plants. Pumps are also employed to make the sewage flow fast enough to prevent it from backing up in the sewer when the topography is flat. If the sea level continues to rise, we will also need more force mains to make water flow out of our wastewater treatment plants.

The final set of challenges facing urban water systems is related to climate change and the discovery of new contaminants. At first glance, these phenomena seem quite different, but they share a common characteristic: the risks they pose to our water systems may require investments on a scale that might tip the balance toward a revolution. In other words, decisions about a future water revolution will be based on a comparison of the costs of Water 4.0 with Water 3.1 and not with the price of running the current system. The exact amount of money needed to address these issues is uncertain, but all of the available evidence points to major expenditures in the coming years.

First, let's consider climate change. Although scientists have been aware of the phenomenon for decades, most water utilities have not been very serious about planning for its effects because there was no consensus on how quickly it would occur or how it would affect their day-to-day operations. But improvements in climate models that have been made over the past ten years have led to closer agreement among scientists about the ways in which rainfall patterns are likely to change over the next three to five decades. In North America, model predictions and current observations suggest that climate change will only exacerbate the problems that are currently stretching the capabilities of water utilities in different regions.[33]

For cities in the eastern and midwestern United States, the consensus is that we can expect an overall increase in the annual amount of precipitation over the next two or three decades, with more of it falling in large storms.[34] Although more precipitation means that it will be easier to provide water to support growing cities, the extra water will pose major challenges in places where combined sewer overflows are already causing pollution problems. The predicted increase in runoff, which will be on the order of 10 to 30 percent, will lead to an increased frequency of combined sewer overflows.[35] As discussed in Chapter 7, many utilities in these regions are already struggling to come up with billions of dollars to fix their sewer overflow problems. If the amount of water and the number of big storms that the sewers have to handle increase, the improvements that they are anticipating from their billion-dollar investments may be erased by the increasing volume of runoff entering the system.

For cities in the West and the South, the most recent predictions indicate that there is going to be less water flowing into reservoirs and percolating into aquifers.[36] The expected decrease in water availability in these regions is tied to a number of factors. First, warmer air temperatures will increase the rate at which water evaporates. The warmer temperatures also will cause more of the water that comes down in the region's watersheds to evaporate before it can soak into the ground or flow to reservoirs. This means that water use for irrigation will increase. With these warmer temperatures, too, less snow will fall in the mountains. In addition to disappointing skiers, the gradual shrinking of the winter snowpack in the Rocky and Sierra Nevada Mountains will pose problems for cities and farms that rely on the spring snow-melt to refill reservoirs that have been depleted over the summer months. If more of the water falls as rain, the existing system of reservoirs will have to be greatly expanded to capture and retain the winter precipitation.

Expanding the size of reservoirs to adapt to a dryer and warmer future is likely to be expensive. For example, a 2008 study of the influence of climate change on the city of San Diego indicates that the optimal approach for coping with the expected effects of warmer temperatures will be to expand the size of the city's main drinking water reservoir by about 25 percent. This seemingly modest reservoir expansion has been projected to cost somewhere between $500 and $800 million.[37]

Of course, it might not make a lot of sense to expand the size of the reservoirs if climate change decreases the overall amount of precipitation. The latest climate models predict that the paths of winter storms that now dump much of the year's precipitation in North America's western mountain ranges will move north as ocean circulation patterns change. As a result, San Diego and other cities in the Southwest can expect decreases in precipitation of between 20 and 30 percent over the next thirty to fifty years.[38] The pattern of decreasing precipitation is being experienced in other arid places: below-average years of precipitation in the city of Perth, Australia, that started in the last decades of the twentieth century are expected to become the new normal due to the effects of climate change on local weather patterns.

Accounting for the combined effects of increased temperatures and decreased precipitation, scientists have made some pretty sobering predictions about imported water systems in the Western United States. In the Colorado River system that provides much of the water used in Los Angeles, Phoenix, and Las Vegas, the most pessimistic models indicate that there is a 50 percent chance that Lake Mead—the main reservoir on the Lower Colorado River—will no longer be able to deliver water to cities by 2017.[39] Predictions that account for the likely effects that decreasing reservoir levels will have on urban and

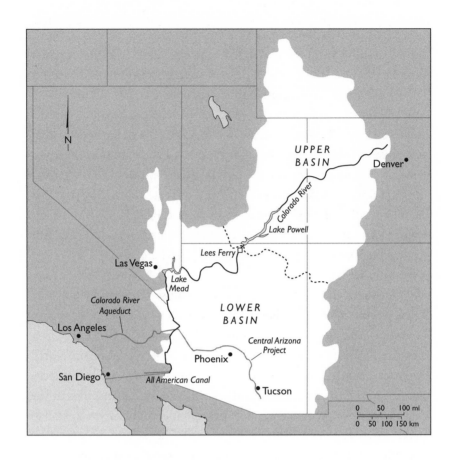

The Colorado River system supplies water to many of the
largest cities in the Southwest.

agricultural water users, by contrast, push this date back by a few
decades.[40]

No matter which prediction is exactly correct, the expected
effects of climate change should not be very comforting to the cities
that rely on the Colorado River. The drought in the region that began
in 1999 may just be part of normal variation, but it certainly has given
many cities that rely on the Colorado a glimpse of a drier future. Since
the drought started, water levels in Lake Mead and Lake Powell—the
other major reservoir on the river—have dropped as the reservoirs

have gone from being nearly full to around 40 percent of capacity.[41] As the water level receded in Lake Mead, marinas used by pleasure boaters had to be relocated to lower elevations and the city of Las Vegas spent $700 million to relocate the intake pipes of its drinking water treatment plant closer to the middle of the reservoir.[42] If the level of the lake drops a little lower, local farmers and cities will start to feel the effects of the drought more acutely as mandatory rationing comes into effect. These actions will slow the rate at which the water is consumed, but only a return to normal precipitation patterns will end the shortage.

Although hardships and uncertainties related to droughts are a way of life in the desert Southwest, the drought that started in Texas in 2010 is prompting water utility managers to reconsider the importance to the state of considering climate change when planning for the state's water future. Unlike their counterparts in the West, cities in the South are usually not located adjacent to mountain ranges or big patches of irrigated agriculture that can give up some of their water during a drought. Many of the most vulnerable cities in this region are still focused on providing ample water supplies to support rapidly increasing populations and have not put a high priority on planning for climate-change-induced droughts. Yet the droughts are already happening: over the past five years, droughts have hit Atlanta, Tampa, and Dallas. The current drought in Texas—which is the most severe in the region—has not lasted as long as the state's largest historic drought, which occurred in the 1950s. It is, however, having a major effect on the state, with reservoirs going dry and scores of small towns reaching a point where they are within a few months of running out of water.[43]

Although Governor Rick Perry has issued proclamations imploring Texans to pray for rain, unfortunately for Texans, the rain hasn't come, and water utilities are going to have to come up with a more concrete plan if the drought continues. The state's water planning agency—the Texas Water Development Board—has engaged in an extensive effort to expand the water available for industry, agriculture, and burgeoning cities, with sophisticated models that predict population and shifts in industry and agriculture, but it has not included climate change in its multi-decade planning effort.[44] For Texas, the absence of climate change in the state's water plans is not entirely due to skepticism about the existence of the phenomenon: instead, there has been considerable scientific uncertainty about whether precipitation will increase or decrease in the state in the coming decades. If in the future there are more droughts like the one that the state is currently experiencing, the Water Development Board's plans are likely to be much more expensive to implement.

Just like climate change, future regulatory requirements for improved drinking water and wastewater treatment systems add to the uncertainty surrounding the finances of urban water systems. The Clean Water Act and Safe Drinking Water Act initiated a period in which more money was spent on improving water quality. Immediately after the two laws were passed, construction activities ramped up at treatment plants as communities worked to comply with the regulations. It was natural for people to assume that the massive influx of funding and new regulations would assure clean drinking water and rivers for the foreseeable future, yet subsequent discoveries about water quality suggest that additional measures may be needed to protect public health and the environment.

For drinking water systems, the realization that additional steps would be needed to reduce the concentrations of chlorine disinfection byproducts and manage lead-contaminated water distribution systems resulted in the expenditure of about $90 billion nationwide between 1975 and 2006.[45] Depending on the outcomes of ongoing monitoring studies and health assessments, we might decide that some of the recently discovered drinking water contaminants, such as the chloramine disinfection byproduct NDMA, might have to be removed at drinking water treatment plants. Retrofitting treatment plants to remove these contaminants could be quite expensive because the most reliable treatment technologies, such as reverse-osmosis treatment and ozonation systems, have higher capital and operating costs.[46]

New scientific research is also showing that our sewage treatment plants might not be doing a good enough job. As discussed in Chapter 8, newly discovered chemical contaminants in sewage can cause endocrine disruption and other undesirable outcomes in the fish and wildlife that live in effluent-dominated waters. Because sewage treatment plants were not designed to remove the trace concentrations of chemicals that cause these problems, it is possible that additional treatment processes will be needed to protect the aquatic ecosystems downstream of the sewage discharge points. Simultaneously, regulators around the country are reconsidering their approaches for managing nutrients released by wastewater treatment plants and storm sewers as they struggle to control algae blooms and oxygen depletion in sensitive habitats. For example, a lawsuit by a local environmental group in Florida resulted in the Environmental Protection Agency setting controversial new discharge standards for nitrogen and phosphorus that are considerably more stringent than those currently in place. The new regulations are expected to require many of the state's wastewater treatment plants to upgrade to state-of-the-art nutrient removal systems and the managers of storm sewers to invest in measures to remove nutrients from urban runoff. The Environmental Protection Agency estimates that the cost will be between three to six dollars a month for a typical family, while industry groups claim it will cost the state's utilities about $21 billion to come into compliance.[47]

As we have seen, modern water systems are being pushed to the edge by costs associated with personnel, pipes, energy, and pollution, and it seems almost certain that all or most of these pressures will continue. We can be sure, then, that our water bills will continue to increase for the next few decades. According to the Organization for Economic Co-operation and Development (OECD), consumers in most developed countries already pay about twice as much as the average American for drinking water and sewer service.[48] Given the current rates at which water utility bills are increasing, it seems likely that in about fifteen years our bills will reach the current levels paid in our OECD peer countries—and there is no reason to think that they will stop there. But the knowledge that a more expensive future is coming can also be the wakeup call we need to not just patch over our aging water infrastructure, but to reinvent urban water systems in a way that ensures that they provide a more reliable source of water that will simultaneously protect our health and the environment.

10

The Toilet-to-Tap Solution

Not too long ago, we lived in a wasteful world. We tossed our aluminum cans, glass bottles, and old newspapers into the trash without a second thought. We drove gas guzzlers, turned the thermostat way up in the winter, and lit our homes with hundred-watt incandescent light bulbs. Once we were done using something, it was destined for the landfill or incinerator. Energy was what we had after a second cup of coffee and definitely not something we thought about conserving. But as the world became more crowded and we started to recognize the problems associated with our consumptive ways, we began to close the loop on materials and started to conserve energy by embracing the "Three R's" of reduce, reuse, and recycle. Now most places have instituted deposits on cans and bottles. Recycling bins are everywhere. Many of us drive fuel-efficient cars and light our homes with compact fluorescent light bulbs. As we enter an era of limited water supplies and increasing concerns about the effects of wastewater effluent on the environment, perhaps it is time to apply the same philosophy to water.

When we think about water, the first of the Three R's is reduce. Any water utility that is serious about providing an adequate quantity of water in the face of population growth and climate change has already begun to embrace water conservation by pushing its customers to grow drought-tolerant plants and to install low-flow plumbing fixtures. Beyond its potential to extend supplies, water conservation makes a lot of sense because it also saves money, conserves energy, reduces pollution, and allows cities to build smaller reservoirs and treatment plants. As a result, there is a long history of conservation in cities where water is scarce. (Chapter 12 examines the kinds of conservation programs that are already in place in water-limited cities and describes some of the up-and-coming approaches that can be used to push the practice to its limit.)

The second and third of the Three R's refer to the practice of putting treated sewage back into the water supply. Strictly speaking, "water reuse" involves finding an appropriate use for wastewater that has received little or no treatment beyond what is usually done when it is discharged to a river or the ocean. "Water recycling," by contrast, employs wastewater after it has undergone additional high-tech treatment processes for the purpose of getting the water ready to be used for a specific application. Because it is often difficult to distinguish a sewage treatment plant that has been upgraded to protect a sensitive aquatic ecosystem from one in which additional treatment processes have been added to facilitate recycling, the terms "water reuse" and "water recycling" are often used interchangeably.

Many cities around the world are considering dramatic expansions of their water reuse and recycling programs in coming decades because it is their easiest and cheapest option for coming up with more water. Unlike new sources of imported water, which require cities to obtain water rights that have already been claimed by others, wastewater is usually freely available for the taking. Reuse and recycling are also attractive, because the quantity of available wastewater does not decrease substantially during droughts, the treatment is cost-effective, and it causes less damage to the environment than many of the alternatives. But the idea of closing the loop on water is not without its detractors, who worry about the potential for disease associated with increased exposure to chemicals and waterborne pathogens that are not fully removed during treatment.

To gain a better understanding of the controversy and the potential importance of water reuse and recycling in Water 4.0, let's go to the beginning of this part of the story—shortly after sewage treatment plants were invented, when people first began reusing wastewater effluent. In the early decades of the twentieth century, farmers were still irrigating their land with untreated wastes from sewage farms in Paris, Berlin, and arid parts of the western United States. The development of septic systems and Imhoff tanks around this time made water reuse more popular on crops grown on the outskirts of cities because the simple treatment methods removed the organic-rich solids that were ultimately responsible for the noxious odors emanating from sewage farms. Given these improvements, it is perhaps not surprising that the advent of trickling filters and activated sludge treatment plants finally made the practice acceptable to city dwellers as well.

San Francisco was one of the first cities to reuse its wastewater effluent. The managers of the city's garden and playground, Golden Gate Park, started applying untreated sewage to its less-developed western section in 1919 to compensate for the city's insufficient supply of groundwater. Use of the sewage for irrigation allowed the city to save its clean groundwater for its growing population while maintaining the thirsty gardens and trees that had been planted in the park's sandy soil. As more people settled in the neighborhoods bordering the park, the city began to receive complaints about the sewage odors. In response, San Francisco built an activated sludge treatment plant in the park in 1932 that could process 4 million liters (1 million gallons) a day.[1]

The new treatment plant was indistinguishable from other activated sludge plants of its day with one exception: the plant's effluent was disinfected with chlorine prior to reuse. The disinfected effluent was used to create a chain of artificial lakes that were interconnected by a waterfall. The treated water also was used to irrigate the turf in the nearby polo stadium. The treatment plant continued to supply water to the park until 1978, when it was shut down because it was unable to meet new, stricter treatment standards.[2]

The idea of reusing effluent for landscaping and other nonpotable uses was not unique to California. In fact, an activated sludge treatment plant had already been providing water for irrigation, hot water heaters, maintenance yards, and visitor areas in the Grand Canyon National Park for three years when San Francisco built its treatment plant in Golden Gate Park.[3] The Grand Canyon Village water reuse system, which after some upgrades to improve its performance is still being used today, employed a dedicated network of distribution pipes to deliver disinfected wastewater effluent to the park's developed areas. The first-generation treatment plant consisted of an activated sludge system equipped with a sand filter and a chlorine generator. It included a network of pipes that delivered treated effluent into buildings—a practice that has come to be referred to as running a dual distribution system—which allowed the park to connect the new water source to toilets in the visitor center and hoses in the maintenance facility. Because the engineers responsible for the system worried about the potential for disease outbreak if the reused water were to be accidentally hooked up to a sink or water fountain, they color-coded the pipes with red paint and added dye to the water once a year to make sure that no drinking water was being obtained inadvertently from the reuse system.

In the intervening eight decades, the reuse of wastewater for non-potable applications has gained widespread acceptance. In most cases, wastewater is reused for irrigation and other nonpotable applications after it has been treated in a manner that is almost identical to the approach that had been used in the early systems at Golden Gate Park and Grand Canyon Village.

To minimize the risk of disease outbreak, much of today's water reuse occurs in places where there is little chance that someone will accidentally drink the water. Large industrial consumers of water are some of the biggest practitioners of water reuse for applications such as power plant cooling and the provision of water to boilers, refineries, and paper mills. Such systems are economically attractive because a dedicated pipeline can be run directly from the treatment plant to customers that consume a lot of water.[4] Landscape irrigation is another significant nonpotable water reuse application in which a single connection can be made to systems that consume large quantities of water to maintain turf and shrubs.

When effluent is used for industrial purposes, it sometimes has to undergo additional treatment to remove calcium and other ions that could deposit when the water is heated in boilers and other equipment. In contrast, no additional treatment is needed when the water is used for landscaping. In fact, the presence of nutrients and organic matter in wastewater effluent is beneficial to plants: with the exception of a few species that are damaged by the moderately high concentration of salts in wastewater effluent, plants grow better when they are irrigated with wastewater effluent than they do when they receive pristine tap water.[5]

Pipelines that deliver irrigation water from reuse systems to shrubs and grasses on highway medians and other places where public access is restricted are very common because there are no serious concerns about people coming into contact with the water. While access to fairways and greens of golf courses is not exactly restricted, the potential for exposure of people to wastewater effluent is limited to a relatively small number of adults who willingly subject themselves to other, more serious health risks, like flying golf balls and pesticide-laden grass. The use of wastewater effluent for irrigating golf courses has become so popular in water-limited regions that it sometimes seems as if the best way to find a wastewater treatment plant is to drive around the edge of the nearest golf course until you find a nondescript driveway, some low-slung cinderblock buildings, and a bunch of people without spiked shoes: more than five hundred golf courses in Florida are irrigated with water from reuse projects, and about half of Nevada's eighty-four water reuse permits were issued to projects involving golf course irrigation.[6] If you have ever wondered why there are so many golf courses in the desert surrounding the Las Vegas Strip, you need look no further for the answer than the toilets, sinks, and showers of the casinos and surrounding housing developments.

Farms, factories, highway medians, and golf courses are the low-hanging fruit of the water reuse world. These applications are attractive because each user consumes a large volume of water in a place where there is limited potential for people to come into contact with it. It is challenging to extend these kinds of systems to reuse more than a small proportion of a city's wastewater because the economics become less favorable as the reuse pipeline expands beyond the limited number of potential customers located close to the city's wastewater treatment plants. Furthermore, the construction of more golf courses does not necessarily improve the overall water picture for a city: a typical eighteen-hole course uses around half a million liters (130,000 gallons) of water per day.[7] If we assume that four hundred people use the typical course each day, a person's per capita water use would increase from around 260 liters (70 gallons) to 1,500 liters (400 gallons) on the day that he or she plays a round of golf.

Building a dedicated pipeline to deliver water from a reuse facility to an industrial user or a golf course located more than a few kilometers away quickly becomes expensive, especially in dense urban areas where new pipelines have to be fit into an underground network of sewer pipes, water pipes, and conduits for cable television and telephone lines. The long distance between the reclaimed water source and the potential users makes dual distribution systems particularly problematic in the sprawling western and southern cities of the United States that grew quickly during the second half of the twentieth century, because they frequently have a small number of large wastewater treatment plants. For example, the 1.5 million people who live in San Jose, Santa Clara, and several adjacent cities in California's Silicon Valley are all served by one massive treatment plant located on the edge of San Francisco Bay. When local water managers decided to build a nonpotable water system in the 1990s, they were able to reuse about 10 percent of the area's wastewater effluent by building a network consisting of around one hundred kilometers (sixty miles) of pipe that were used to irrigate office parks close to the treatment plant.[8] Expansion of the system to reuse the next 10 percent of the treatment plant's effluent turned out to be a greater challenge, however, because of the long distance between the treatment plant and likely users of the water, who were scattered around the 780-square-kilometer (three-hundred-square-mile) valley served by the utility. The high cost of extending the pipeline slowed the city's efforts to reuse more of its wastewater and encouraged its leaders to consider alternative approaches for enhancing the city's water supply.

The same sort of logistical problem limits the ability of cities to reuse their wastewater effluent for irrigation of agricultural crops. In water-limited areas, where wastewater treatment plants are located close to farms, irrigation of fruits and vegetables with disinfected wastewater effluent has been a great success. In Israel, water providers have enthusiastically embraced this approach, reusing about 75 percent of the country's wastewater effluent to irrigate crops. Florida and California also are active practitioners of agricultural water reuse, with 300 and 720 million liters (80 and 190 million gallons) per day of disinfected effluent being reused on farms in the two states, respectively. In fact, some of the most valuable agricultural land in California is located in the Salinas Valley, near Monterey. On farms scattered along the coastal plain, where rich soils and cool ocean air make growing conditions ideal for valuable crops such as strawberries and lettuce, a water reuse project has led to the rebirth of land that had been in decline for decades. Freshwater from the reuse project has converted land where the overpumping of irrigation wells had made the groundwater too salty to grow anything other than artichokes into plots that could once again be used to grow valuable salt-sensitive crops. After it was applied to crops, the recycled water infiltrated through the soil, the groundwater level rose, and the salt moved back toward the coast. Studies of the potential health risks associated with the application of disinfected effluent to crops indicate that the risk of illness is negligible compared to other potential sources of contamination, such as manure and wild animals.[9]

Unfortunately, farms and densely populated cities are usually located far from one another. Historically, as cities expanded, farmers were the first group to be pushed off the land to make room for suburban housing developments. Thus cities that now plan to reuse their wastewater effluent for agriculture either have to extend distribution pipelines for long distances or institute land-use controls that discourage the conversion of farms into suburban housing.

To overcome the limitations of not having enough large industrial customers, golf courses, or farms located adjacent to their wastewater treatment plants, utilities gradually began to build systems that delivered treated effluent to places where more people might come into contact with the water. Extending water reuse systems to parks, schoolyards, and playgrounds was not much of a stretch because, just like golf courses, professional groundskeepers controlled access to the plumbing systems and set irrigation schedules to times when people would not be present. Eventually, as they became more comfortable with the idea, utilities extended the reuse systems to individual homes and other places where oversight of the plumbing and water uses was less easily controlled.

St. Petersburg, Florida, was one of the first cities to build a nonpotable water reuse system in places with unrestricted access.[10] The impetus for the city's pioneering project was a 1972 state law mandating that all wastewater treatment plants that discharged their effluent to Tampa Bay had to install new treatment systems to remove nutrients. The new regulations to prevent excessive algae growth in the bay came just as the city was realizing that it did not have enough imported water to keep up with its growing needs.

To solve the problems of wastewater disposal and water shortages simultaneously, St. Petersburg built a massive nonpotable water reuse system starting in 1977. To avoid the need to make the switch from effluent discharge to full reuse all at once, the city also built a system of injection wells to dispose of any effluent that was not being reused. The wells discharged the wastewater effluent to the aquifer underneath the city, which was too salty to use as a water supply. In the first phase of the project, water from the reuse system was sent to golf courses, parks, and schools. After a few years, the city created a dual distribution network for irrigation of residential properties. Extension of the dual distribution system into a new neighborhood only occurred when more than 50 percent of the residents in the area petitioned to connect to the system. The incentive for joining was cost: water from the reuse system was substantially cheaper to a homeowner than potable water, provided that person was willing to make an initial investment of approximately $500 to $1,200 to pay for the hookup.[11]

To reduce the likelihood that someone might accidentally drink water from the reclaimed water system, the city instituted a series of measures to avoid cross-connections between the potable supply and the reuse system. They adopted the color-coding approach that had been used in Grand Canyon Village—using brown pipes instead of red to indicate water from the reuse system. (Incidentally, the International Association of Plumbing and Mechanical Officials eventually adopted light purple as the official color for nonpotable reuse systems. If you run across a purple pipe, sprinkler head, or pump, you have found a nonpotable reuse system.) The engineers in St. Petersburg also installed backflow prevention devices at the potable water meters to ensure that any inadvertent cross-connections would not spread water from the reuse system beyond the property where the unintentional connection between the two systems had been made.

By 2009, St. Petersburg's system had expanded to the point where it provided approximately 64 million liters (17 million gallons) per day of water—an amount equivalent to 40 percent of the city's average daily water use. Although some of the success of St. Petersburg's system could be chalked up to federal grants and extra care taken by engineers who knew they were doing something new, the system illustrates the possible extent of nonpotable water reuse in places where alternative sources of water are not readily available.

After nonpotable reuse systems like the one in St. Petersburg and a similar system that had been built at about the same time in Orange County, California, had operated for a decade or so without incident, utilities in other locations became more confident that landscape irrigation with disinfected effluent posed negligible risks to people who might come into contact with the irrigated grass and plants. Convinced of the safety of the practice, they began to expand water reuse to irrigate places where children might be present: by 2005, there were more than 1,600 parks, schoolyards, or playgrounds in the United States where reclaimed water was being used for irrigation. About 85 percent of these projects were located in California and Florida, two rapidly growing, water-conscious states where government agencies took an active role in encouraging water reuse by establishing regulations and promoting the benefits of the practice.[12]

Although there is little evidence that anyone has become sick from exposure to water from sprinklers at the places where nonpotable water has been used for irrigation, a handful of skeptics have argued that the risks associated with nonpotable water reuse in places where people are likely to come into contact with the water are unacceptable. While few experts on the topic are critical of the practice, concerns raised about the safety of water often resonate with members of the public who are suspicious of the idea of reusing sewage, especially when it is forced on them without their consent. Today, opposition to nonpotable reuse projects is still uncommon, because most projects still involve industrial applications or landscaping on highway medians or golf courses. But as the economic forces associated with the extension of dual distribution systems continue to grow, more homeowners will be asked to hook up their lawn sprinklers to reuse systems. When this expectation occurs, we are likely to hear more from the skeptics about the possible health effects associated with nonpotable water reuse. A preview of the ways in which opposition to the practice might develop in the future was foreshadowed in an incident that occurred in 2003, when Redwood City, California, rejected a nonpotable reuse project over health concerns.

Redwood City is a bedroom community located midway between San Francisco and San Jose. The city had relied on San Francisco's massive imported water system as its primary source of water since the 1930s. By the end of the 1990s, however, the city's population had grown to a point where it would soon be unable to provide its residents with water solely from the allocation that San Francisco had agreed to deliver when the system had first been built.[13] To solve the problem, Redwood City's consultants proposed the construction of a nonpotable water reuse system that was nearly identical to the system that had been so successful in St. Petersburg, but with one major difference: to minimize the size of the dual distribution system and to qualify for government subsidies, the consultants designed the system in a manner that required the residents to use water from the system to irrigate the land around their homes.

Alarmed by the new water source that they felt was being foisted on them by the city council, a group of residents organized to fight the project. The group was able to find a doctor from Southern California and a pharmacist from nearby Marin County who were opposed to water reuse. At a public hearing on the project, the doctor and pharmacist provided information about the potential risks from waterborne pathogens and chemicals in the water.[14] Redwood City's consultants and sympathetic state regulators assured the public that the practice was safe, but the city council, whose members would eventually stand for re-election, decided that it was best to avoid alienating their constituents. After the public meeting, the city council set up a task force composed of equal numbers of citizens who favored and opposed the project. The compromise worked out by the task force, which cost about the same amount of money as the original plan, involved the construction of a dual distribution system that delivered water from the reuse plant to areas where there was limited potential for human contact with the water. To compensate for the reuse of a smaller volume of water by the new recycled-water system, the task force recommended a number of water conservation measures— such as installing artificial turf on the city's sports fields.

Redwood City ultimately achieved its goal of reducing its reliance on imported water by a modest amount, but opposition to the project demonstrates that public acceptance of dual distribution systems like St. Petersburg's—systems that, once fully expanded, can make a dramatic difference to a city's water demand—hinges on people's trust in the safety of the practice. One major difference between the two projects is that the citizens of St. Petersburg had to petition to hook into the less expensive water reuse system, whereas Redwood City's plan did not offer citizens a choice or a discount for accepting water from the reuse system. The Redwood City controversy could presumably have been avoided if the potable water had been priced higher and those people who did not want to join were allowed to opt out.

Did the skeptics have a point? The chances of getting sick from the pathogens present in a few drops of water from a sprinkler that is hooked into a water reuse system is hundreds of times lower than other pathogen risks that we readily assume, such as visiting a petting zoo, swimming at a beach where stormwater runoff has contaminated the sand with bacteria, or eating fresh organic produce from a farm that uses animal manure for fertilizer.[15] But that does not mean that the systems are entirely safe. Disinfection and filtration of wastewater effluent remove most, but not all, waterborne pathogens. If you were to use the treated effluent as your drinking water source you could receive a dose of pathogens high enough to make you sick. Accidental cross-connections between the reuse system and the potable water supply occur infrequently, though when they do, people get stomachaches and diarrhea. Increasing the number of homes in the United States that are served by dual distribution systems a thousandfold could raise the number of cross-connections to a point where people becoming ill from exposure to reclaimed water is no longer a rare occurrence.

The designers of nonpotable water reuse systems have been aware of this issue since the Grand Canyon Village project and have gone to great lengths to minimize the likelihood of cross-connections. But no system is perfect. Over the last three decades, about a dozen reported cases of illness have been attributed to cross-connections between water reuse systems and potable water systems.[16] In most cases, the cross-connections have occurred in residential settings or on individual properties where a reuse pipe was connected to a landscape irrigation system that was still plumbed into the potable water supply.

Because pipelines for reused water are sometimes operated at higher pressures than potable water systems, water from the reuse system can force its way into the potable water system and back out at a faucet on the property where the cross-connection has been made. If a backflow prevention device is not present at the water meter, the pathogen-containing water could spread to other homes as well.

Water reuse offers a viable option for extending water supplies, but its economic viability is often tied to the operation of dual distribution networks that deliver water to homes and other places where cross-connections with drinking water systems are more likely to occur. If nonpotable reuse is going to become more prevalent in the future, we will have to establish better systems for preventing and detecting cross-connections. And if the installation of color-coded pipes and dual distribution systems is not going to be viable because of unfavorable economics or concerns over cross-connections, it might be more attractive to treat the wastewater effluent to a point where it is actually safe enough to drink. This is the idea behind potable water reuse—a form of water recycling that its critics refer to as the "toilet-to-tap" approach, and one that is becoming increasingly attractive to water-limited cities around the world. As we will see, there are many reasons why potable water recycling will be a big part of the solution to future water supply problems.

In the United States, the first potable water-recycling project was operated for two years in Chanute, Kansas, during a severe drought that began in 1956. The project involved the diversion of the town's sewage effluent into the drinking water reservoir as well as an increased application of chlorine and alum in the drinking water treatment plant. At its height, the wastewater effluent accounted for about half of the town's drinking water supply. But the Chanute experiment was only temporary. After the drought ended, the city abandoned its primitive water recycling system.[17]

The first sustained toilet-to-tap project got started a few years later with the intentional diversion of wastewater effluent to a drinking water aquifer. In 1962, the Los Angeles County Sanitation District

The Montebello Forebay Spreading Grounds in Los Angeles have been used as part of a potable water-recycling project since 1962. Photo courtesy of the Water Replenishment District of Southern California.

started routing disinfected effluent from one of its activated sludge treatment plants into a 230-hectare (570-acre) sandy strip of land at the junction of the San Gabriel and Rio Hondo rivers, east of the city. The effluent slowly percolated through the sand until it entered the shallow aquifer. The water then migrated to drinking water wells in the neighborhood next to the spreading grounds. In the early years, the sand basins referred to as the Montebello Forebay Spreading Grounds received a mixture of about 15 percent wastewater effluent with the balance consisting of stormwater runoff and water imported from the Colorado River. Over time, as imported water became more expensive, the contribution of wastewater effluent to the recharged water crept up to a point where it now accounts for about 40 percent of the water passing into the drinking water aquifer.[18]

This groundbreaking project was followed by another motivated not by water scarcity but by the recognition that suburban development had caused the wastewater effluent contribution to a water supply to increase to a point where it accounted for much of the water entering a major drinking water reservoir. The Occoquan Reservoir, which currently provides drinking water for about 1.3 million people who live just west of Washington, D.C., had been situated in a rural watershed when it was first built. The postwar boom that led to the development of the northern Virginia suburbs changed all of that. By the early 1970s, eleven wastewater treatment plants were discharging their effluent to tributaries that flowed just a few kilometers before entering the reservoir.[19]

Local health experts had expressed some concerns about the possibility that the viruses in the effluent being discharged into the reservoir could pass through the drinking water treatment plant. The utility was worried that the nutrient-rich effluent would cause excessive growth of algae in the receiving reservoir. The filters of the four drinking water treatment plants that relied on the reservoir could remove the algae. Unfortunately, the filters could not remove foul-smelling compounds that the algae sometimes produced. Certain species of cyanobacteria, or blue-green algae, produce organic compounds that impart taste and odor to water. For example, a chemical known as geosmin continuously leaks out of the cyanobacteria and is released when the organisms break apart at the end of their lives. Geosmin has a familiar earthy taste that you might recognize: it is one of the main flavor components of beets.[20] The presence in a reservoir of organisms that produce the compound can be a nightmare for a water utility because conventional drinking water treatment processes like filtration and chlorination are unable to remove the compound.

And it doesn't take a lot of geosmin to cause a problem: a sensitive person can taste geosmin at a concentration of around one part per trillion.[21]

Confronted with the problem of too much wastewater effluent being discharged into the water supply and lacking an alternative drinking water source or easy access to a different place to dump their wastewater effluent, the cities served by the Occoquan Reservoir admitted to themselves that they were operating a potable water reuse system. An analysis of the water balance made the extent of the practice clear. In a typical year, the effluent accounted for around 10 percent of the overall flow—a situation that was not much different from what happened in many other cities—but in a dry year, the wastewater effluent could account for up to 80 percent of the overall inflow of water to the reservoir. Given the relatively fast turnaround time of water in the system—less than a year—during periods of drought the people of northern Virginia were obtaining their drinking water from a source that was mainly wastewater effluent.[22]

Recognition of the importance of wastewater effluent to the drinking water supply led the local utility officials to reroute their sewers to a single state-of-the-art wastewater treatment plant that discharged about 57 million liters (15 million gallons) per day of the cleanest effluent possible to a tributary located ten kilometers (six miles) upstream of the reservoir.[23] The new Millard H. Robbins, Jr., Water Reclamation Plant employed technologies that were a water engineer's dream. The plant's designers threw everything they could come up with at the wastewater: activated sludge, filtration, activated carbon treatment, ion exchange, chlorination, and lime clarification. Lime clarification—a process that has become less popular during the past two decades—is just another process for removing particles from water. It involves the addition of a small amount of lime (that is, calcium oxide or hydroxide) to raise the pH of the water. The high pH causes the calcium to react with dissolved carbon dioxide and to precipitate as calcium carbonate. Many of the other suspended particles stick to the surfaces of the freshly formed calcium carbonate. The high pH value that occurs after lime addition also inactivates many waterborne pathogens.

When combined with activated sludge treatment, the effluent coming out of the advanced treatment plant looks more like drinking water than wastewater effluent. Because the treatment process employed at the sewage treatment plant upstream of the Occoquan Reservoir went above and beyond what had been done elsewhere, the quality of the water arriving at the drinking water treatment plants that used the reservoir was actually not all that different from that encountered at plants in other cities where effluent accounted for a smaller fraction of the water. In fact, the water in the Occoquan Reservoir was probably better than water flowing into rivers and reservoirs downstream of many cities. What distinguished the water produced by the treatment plants using Occoquan Reservoir water and the wells downstream of Los Angeles's spreading basins from other water supplies of the day was the intent of the drinking water providers. Their acknowledgment that wastewater effluent was intentionally being routed into the water supply did not alter the quality of the water. But it did increase the level of scrutiny that the plants received from government regulators, which, in some cases, motivated them to invest in state-of-the-art treatment technologies.[24]

At about the same time that the Upper Occoquan Service Authority was struggling with its water pollution problems, an upscale suburb located south of Los Angeles recognized that it would soon run out of water. In the early 1970s, Orange County had many things that its big neighbor to the north did not: Disneyland, good schools, low crime rates, planned communities, and conservative politicians. But it did not have control over its imported water supply. Instead it relied on Los Angeles to provide it with water from its massive Colorado River project. As the number of people living in the county swelled, from around 150,000 at the end of World War II to 1.5 million in 1970, the region's reliance on imported water—a source that would become more expensive and less reliable as Los Angeles's needs increased—threatened its future growth.

By the start of the 1970s, the county's only source of water that was not imported—local groundwater—could meet only about a quarter of its drinking water needs. As the density of people increased in parts of the county that relied on the aquifer, groundwater was being extracted faster than it could be recharged by infiltration of rainwater.[25]

In the 1950s, when development was first accelerating, overpumping of the county's groundwater had dropped the height of the water table below sea level in the zone adjacent to the coast. Groundwater—just like every other type of water on earth—flows downhill under the force of gravity. Once the level of the groundwater in the coastal aquifer had dropped, seawater began to flow inland, contaminating the drinking water with salt to a distance of around six kilometers (four miles) from the coast. In response, the Orange County Water District had built spreading grounds along the banks of the river that bisected the county. The artificial recharge structures on the Santa Ana River slowly raised the water level back above sea level, which reversed the inland migration of groundwater, eventually pushing the salty water back to the ocean.[26] But by the 1970s, the growing population's demand for freshwater had grown to a point where seawater was once again threatening to march inland through the overpumped aquifer.

To counteract effects of groundwater overpumping, a new source of water was needed. Lacking access to additional river water, and finding imported water to be too expensive and unreliable, the Orange County Water District turned to the local sewage treatment plant. Rather than adding the treatment plant's effluent to the aquifer through surface spreading grounds, the water utility's engineers came up with a more efficient plan for keeping the seawater at bay. By building a string of wells about two kilometers (a little more than a mile) inland and parallel to the coast, water from the wastewater treatment plant could be put into the aquifer in the exact location where seawater was threatening to spill into the aquifer. This Maginot Line of groundwater wells, which was referred to as the Talbert Barrier, con-

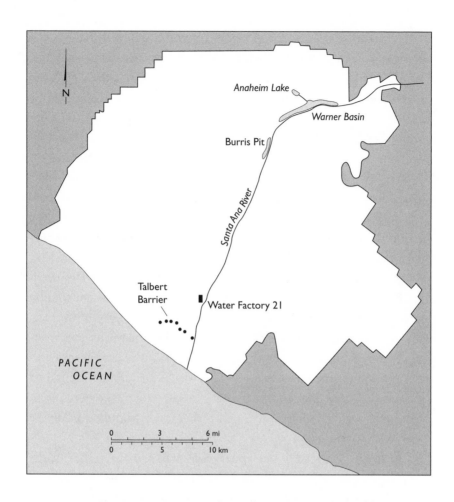

Orange County, California, and locations of features used by the local
utility to recharge groundwater. Based on an image in M. J. Hammer
and G. Elser, *Control of Ground-Water Salinity, Orange County,
California,* copyright © 2006, John Wiley and Sons.

sisted of twenty-three wells that injected about 114 million liters (30
million gallons) per day of water to the aquifer at a narrow spot where
a gap in the bedrock channeled the seawater on its inland trip. The
injected water consisted of a blend of equal volumes of wastewater
effluent and groundwater pumped from a second aquifer located deep
below the city.

In addition to raising the height of groundwater in the gap, the injected water also flowed inland where it became the drinking water supply for the homes in the area to the east. Because the water district's communication with the public maintained a focus on the role of the injected water as a seawater barrier, few members of the community recognized that the project would result in the delivery of wastewater effluent to the faucets of some of the county's residents.

The use of subsurface injection wells instead of spreading basins posed two technical challenges. First, because the wastewater effluent did not percolate through a thick layer of sand before entering the aquifer, it needed to be virtually free of suspended particles. The particles had to be removed from the water before injection because they could clog the small spaces between sand grains near the wells, eventually clogging them. Second, since the injected water was not coming into contact with a microbe-rich layer of sand at the ground surface, any organic matter that had not been removed in the wastewater treatment plant would be broken down by bacteria in the aquifer immediately adjacent to the injection well. If the wastewater effluent contained too much degradable organic matter, the bacteria in the pores adjacent to the well could grow to a point where they would also clog the well.

Following the lead of the Upper Occoquan Service Authority, the Orange County Water District built the most advanced treatment plant that they could in order to supply water to the Talbert Barrier. In addition to the suite of treatment technologies that had been used in Virginia (such as lime coagulation, activated carbon, and chlorine disinfection), the advanced treatment plant employed a brand new technology called reverse osmosis on about a third of the plant's flow.

The water district's new treatment plant, which they dubbed "Water Factory 21," was the first major water recycling project to employ the reverse-osmosis process. Before the Water Factory, the unproven nature of the technology and its high cost had discouraged its use in water treatment. But the water utility had little choice, because its effluent contained levels of dissolved ions that were so high that consumers would complain about the water's salty taste.[27] The presence of salts in the wastewater posed a bigger problem to the potable water recycling project in Orange County than it had in Virginia or Los Angeles because the local water supply was already quite salty. In fact, the mixture of imported water and local groundwater in Orange County contained salts at concentrations that were just below the threshold where consumers would start to complain about the unappealing, flat taste.[28] For the seawater barrier project to succeed, the concentration of salt in the wastewater had to be lowered.[29] While the treatment technologies that had been used at Virginia's Occoquan Reservoir could remove all of the organic chemicals and waterborne pathogens that posed concerns, only reverse osmosis could reliably remove salts from wastewater effluent.

The water utility was receptive to the idea of employing reverse osmosis to remove salt from the wastewater effluent because they already had been considering its use in a previous scheme to supply water to the Talbert Barrier. Prior to the construction of Water Factory 21, the water district had contemplated the construction of a seawater desalination plant to provide the barrier wells with low-salt water. The project was cancelled when the Department of Interior had pulled its funding due to concerns over the high price of the reverse-osmosis process.[30]

Why did the utility change its mind about reverse osmosis? Energy consumption is the Achilles' heel of reverse osmosis. Much of the daily operating expense associated with operating a reverse-osmosis plant is due to the powerful pumps that push water through the system. The amount of electricity needed is related to the initial salt content of the water undergoing treatment. Because wastewater effluent has less than 1 percent of the salt content of seawater, it is a lot less expensive to treat wastewater effluent by reverse osmosis than it is to desalinate seawater. Thus the technology that was too expensive for the Department of Interior's seawater planned desalination plant ended up being relatively cheap as a wastewater treatment strategy: in fact, it was about as expensive to run as all of the other treatment processes at Water Factory 21 combined.[31] Running only 30 percent of the wastewater effluent through the process lowered the overall cost of producing water while still making it possible for the water district to reduce the salt content of the injected water to a point where the public would not complain about the salty taste.

To separate water from salt, the reverse-osmosis process employs a thin sheet (or "membrane") composed of an organic polymer—in the case of Water Factory 21, cellulose acetate. (Cellulose acetate is the same polymer that was used to make film during the pre-digital photography era.) If you were to view the membrane at the atomic scale, you would see a network of the polymer molecules bonded together in a series of interconnected chains. The tiny gaps between the polymer molecules would be only slightly wider than the diameter of a water molecule. As a result, any molecule, ion, waterborne pathogen, or particle that is larger than a water molecule has a hard time passing through the membrane.

The selective passage of water through a manmade membrane is called reverse osmosis, because it is the opposite of the way in which osmosis normally functions in nature. You may already know that osmosis is the process through which water migrates through a membrane from an area of low salt concentration—like the water flowing in the water-conducting structures in a plant's stem—to one of high concentration, like the interior of the plant's cells. The process is driven by the natural tendency of dissolved molecules to equalize their concentrations on either side of a membrane. Reverse osmosis counteracts this natural tendency and switches the direction of flow by applying pressure to the salty-water side of the membrane. The pressure forces the water molecules through the membrane and produces water with a lower salt content.

In the process of forcing the water through the membrane, just about everything else in the wastewater effluent is left behind on the salty-water side. The liquid that remains behind is referred to as the reject stream. At Water Factory 21, the reject stream was piped back to the adjacent wastewater treatment plant, which added it to the fraction of their effluent that also was not being reused, before sending it to the Pacific Ocean. Thus, the reverse-osmosis process lowered the concentration of salts that made the water taste bad while simultaneously reducing the concentrations of chemicals, viruses, and other contaminants in the water.

Throughout the 1980s, Los Angeles's Whittier Narrows Spreading Grounds, the Occoquan Reservoir, and Water Factory 21 operated without incident. A few smaller potable water recycling projects came online without much fanfare or public attention, too, including a groundwater injection plant near El Paso that employed reverse osmosis to wastewater effluent and a project just outside of Atlanta in which highly treated wastewater entered the drinking water supply after application to soil adjacent to a reservoir.[32] The projects were considered successful because the drinking water they produced met all of the standards established by the Safe Drinking Water Act. Emboldened by their newfound ability to turn sewage into drinking water, water utilities set out to build potable water reuse projects in other communities facing imminent water shortages.

But somebody forgot to ask the public. When it came to public scrutiny, the early water recycling projects had mostly slipped under the radar. For example, some community members in the area served by the Occoquan Reservoir were undoubtedly aware that their utility was investing in a system that intentionally put wastewater effluent into the drinking water supply, but there was little point in protesting. After all, the effluent was already flowing into the reservoir and alternative approaches that would eliminate the reservoir discharge were extremely costly. In Los Angeles, Orange County, and El Paso, the connection between wastewater effluent and drinking water was clear to anyone who had been trained in the science of groundwater hydrogeology, but the public was generally unaware that the mention of an artfully named "seawater intrusion barrier" or "groundwater replenishment system" in their local water utility's annual report meant that they were receiving their water from a potable water recycling system.

In addition to being protected from public commentary by the public's lack of awareness of the connection between their sewage and their drinking water, the early water recycling projects were subject to less criticism because they had been built when public trust in government authorities was high. During this era, utilities saw little need to consult with customers when making decisions about how to provide water.[33] As long as the water kept flowing and met government safety requirements, no one questioned how it was obtained.

By the early 1990s, the relationship between consumers and their water utilities began to change. Maybe the public loss of trust in government was to blame. Or perhaps all of the talk about carcinogenic chlorine disinfection byproducts in drinking water and the accumulation of chemicals such as DDT and PCB's in the food supply had made the public more apprehensive about chemical-related health risks. Or maybe it was just poor timing. Whatever the cause, the future of potable water reuse was jeopardized when the public's awareness of the true nature of the process increased.

The more thorough scrutiny of potable water recycling began when two Southern California water utilities began to consider new projects. The first controversial reuse project involved the construction of a new spreading basin by the same Los Angeles utility that had built the Whittier Narrows Spreading Grounds three decades earlier. The basin, which was also located on the San Gabriel River just fifteen kilometers (nine miles) upriver from the original project, had a distinguishing feature: it was located adjacent to a brewery that used groundwater to make beer. After the late-night television host Jay Leno quipped that Miller beer would soon have to replace "beechwood aged" with "porcelain aged" in its motto about its beer brewing practices, the Miller Brewing Company initiated a lawsuit against the water agency and encouraged local citizens to show up at public meetings with banners emblazed with the term "toilet-to-tap."[34] The phrase resonated with the public and local news reporters. With the vivid image of toilet water in the public consciousness, it was difficult to engage in a reasoned discussion about the water cycle. After a short fight, the water utility agreed to move the project a couple of miles downstream and scale back its size.[35]

At about the same time, the city of San Diego proposed the construction of an advanced wastewater treatment plant to increase the flow of water into one of the city's drinking water reservoirs. The project was designed to help the city reduce its reliance on imported Colorado River water after the drought of 1991–1992.[36] As part of the proposal, wastewater effluent that had undergone a variety of advanced treatment processes—including reverse osmosis—was to be diluted with imported water. Compared to northern Virginia's Occoquan Reservoir project, the San Diego proposal seemed quite modest: under most conditions, the reverse-osmosis-treated wastewater effluent would account for considerably less than 20 percent of the water in the reservoir.[37]

To ensure that the community was comfortable with the massive project, the utility's managers followed recommendations from their public relations team about how to best engage the public. They enlisted the support of environmental groups, such as the local chapter of the Sierra Club, and convened focus groups to gauge public attitudes.[38] They also set up a panel of independent experts to review the project and produced glossy brochures and videos for distribution to the local news media.[39]

For the first few years everything went well, but in 1998 support for the project began to erode. The change of attitude can be traced to a combination of communication missteps and poor timing. First, the team in charge of public relations did not fully appreciate how people might interpret the affiliation of the employees who served as the public face of the project. At first members of the county water agency—an organization that had a clear interest in securing an ample drinking water supply—represented the project. But as the initiative moved into the design phase, responsibility for it transitioned to the city's wastewater department.[40] Some members of the public were already familiar with the wastewater department as a result of the department's ongoing fight with the Environmental Protection Agency over renewal of the permit that allowed the city to discharge sewage from its primary wastewater treatment plant into the Pacific Ocean. The fact that the potable water recycling plant would help satisfy the Environmental Protection Agency's concerns over ocean dumping, by reducing the volume of waste flowing to the sea, coupled with a diminution in worries about the city's water supply after the end of the drought, spelled trouble for the project: some members of the public began to wonder if the true purpose of the project was to solve the city's wastewater disposal problem.

The San Diego project's second problem was one of poor timing. Concerns about the project's motives surfaced just as a closely contested city council race began. As part of election-year politics, the council member whose district was closest to the reservoir began voicing his opposition to the project, claiming that it was being built in his ethnic-minority-dominated, low-income part of town as part of a plot to force them to drink toilet water. According to one resident, the city was becoming a place populated by "those who could afford to drink bottled water and those who could not, those who drink champagne and those who drink sewage."[41] In early 1999, San Diego's city council withdrew its support from the project.

The final blow to the prospects of potable water recycling occurred in Los Angeles, where an ambitious city councilman named Joel Wachs played the "toilet-to-tap" card as part of his mayoral campaign. Wachs tried to build support among members of his political base by presenting the city's East Valley Water Recycling Project as a push by the central city's elite to make the citizens of the suburban San Fernando Valley drink toilet water. Although the strategy did not succeed in getting Wachs elected, it did lead to the termination of a project after $55 million had already been spent on a pipeline to bring wastewater effluent to the proposed spreading grounds.[42]

The success of the toilet-to-tap critics in stopping the multi-million dollar projects jeopardized the future of potable water recycling projects throughout the country. Faced with a growing disconnect between a practice that they believed to be safe and groups of politicians and outspoken community members who viewed potable water recycling as a dangerous folly, utilities turned to the regulatory authorities. After all, protection of public health was their primary mandate and their endorsement of the practice could help assuage the fears of the community.

By this time, potable water recycling had been practiced safely for decades. But new questions were being asked that could not be answered in a definitive manner. California's regulators were hesitant to give the practice a strong endorsement because they could not state with certainty that there were no possible health effects associated with consumption of recycled water. Considering how hard it had been to prove a connection between chlorine disinfection byproducts and cancer, it is not surprising that no one in the public health community was willing to declare that there was absolutely no chance that lifetime exposure to trace amounts of pharmaceuticals and other chemicals present in wastewater could cause health problems. The regulators understood that there was no scientific basis for differentiating water produced by a water recycling systems from water that millions of people were already drinking in cities where rivers discharged wastewater upstream of a drinking water treatment plant. But in the absence of proof that water recycling was absolutely safe, regulators chose the route that would lead to the least political criticism and applied rules of thumb and an extra measure of caution when making decisions about whether or not potable water recycling was acceptable.

Robert Hultquist, one of the top regulators in California's Department of Health Services, explained to me one of the main rules of thumb for potable water reuse shortly after the San Diego water recycling project was rejected. He reasoned that existing regulations associated with the Safe Drinking Water Act were designed to protect health under conditions typically encountered in water supplies. Because wastewater effluent rarely accounts for more than 10 percent of the water entering a drinking water treatment plant, he reasoned that potable recycling projects would not need an especially high level of scrutiny if the effluent contribution was 10 percent or smaller. He went on to say that for projects where the recycled water contribution was higher, additional scrutiny and treatment would be needed. And projects at the far extreme, in which wastewater effluent accounted for more than 50 percent of the drinking water, would have to be viewed with great suspicion.

Eventually, the views of Hultquist and his colleagues were adopted by California's public health agency as a means of allocating permits for potable reuse projects.[43] The draft regulations included a stipulation that in essence required that all future water recycling projects would have to employ reverse osmosis to the entire volume of water being recycled. They also established conditions that made it difficult to increase the contribution of recycled water to greater than 50 percent of the water that would eventually reach consumers' taps. While the logic of requiring reverse-osmosis treatment and dilution of wastewater effluent with water from other sources might have sounded reasonable when explained at a public meeting, the requirements were a lot more stringent than the practices that were already being used successfully at the Whittier Narrows Spreading Basins or in the Occoquan Reservoir as well as in places where water recycling was unplanned. An advanced wastewater treatment plant without reverse osmosis could produce water that was a lot cleaner than the drinking water discharged from those standard drinking water recycling plants that receive upstream wastewater discharges. But the cautious attitudes of the regulators meant that the water recycling plants were not going to be given a chance.

After the setbacks in San Diego and Los Angeles, proponents of potable water recycling continued to advocate for their projects, despite the higher project costs associated with reverse-osmosis treatment and the potential for "toilet-to-tap" protests. The next two major potable water recycling projects in California—an expansion of Orange County's Water Factory 21 and a seawater barrier project located adjacent to Los Angeles International Airport—employed reverse osmosis to treat the entire volume of recycled water prior to diluting it with water from other sources and injecting it into coastal aquifers.

The increased public skepticism also encouraged the Orange County Water District to redouble its community outreach and public relations efforts, and to try to anticipate any concerns that might derail their project at the last minute. For example, the utility reached out to the imam of the local mosque to obtain a directive, or fatwah, establishing that recycled water is acceptable for consumption by devout Muslims. The concerns involving Muslim objections about recycled water originated with the knowledge that some of the sewage that entered Orange County's treatment plants had been used to prepare bodies for burial. According to some interpretations of the Muslim tradition, it was unacceptable to come into contact with water that had been used for such purposes. The water district's outreach efforts helped avoid any confusion about the legitimacy of the project within the local Muslim community.

In addition to public relations and community outreach, the Orange County Water District got serious about science. They funded research designed to identify potential problems with their water recycling system. When a new problem was found, they responded quickly and decisively to avoid the appearance that they were not serious about protecting public health. For example, when elevated concentrations of the carcinogen NDMA were detected in water from a well near the Talbert Gap seawater intrusion barrier, the water district recommended that the local cities take the wells out of service, even though the water still met the state's drinking water standards.[44] Working with the operators of the local sewage treatment plant, the water district managed to reduce the concentrations of NDMA entering Water Factory 21 by about 75 percent.[45] Luckily for the water district, the new upgrade to Water Factory 21 included treatment with ultraviolet light after reverse osmosis. Because NDMA is destroyed by ultraviolet light, it would not be a problem for water passing through the new treatment plant.

By being mindful of public opinion and demonstrating a cautious, professional attitude, the Orange County Water District managed to preempt the public skepticism that had killed the projects in San Diego and Los Angeles. It is an exemplary model for outreach and the building of trust in the community.

Following the success of Orange County and a less noticed, but nearly identical, project run by the West Basin Municipal Water District on land adjacent to the Los Angeles International Airport, the failed projects in San Diego and in Los Angeles's East Valley have come back to life, with reverse-osmosis-equipped advanced water recycling plants that are nearly identical to the design employed in the successful projects. The idea also has spread beyond California, with plants following the Orange County model coming on line over the last fifteen years in Arizona, Singapore, and Belgium.[46] By employing sophisticated public communication strategies and state-of-the-art treatment technologies, the forces behind potable water recycling now appear to be unstoppable. But questions linger about the high costs of the projects and the willingness of communities outside of Southern California, the desert Southwest, and a few other water-stressed locales to accept the unfamiliar practice.

11

Turning to the Sea for Drinking Water

Throughout history, cities have employed a similar set of approaches for obtaining drinking water. Those urban dwellers lucky enough to live near a river or lake have usually focused on making their local surface water safe to drink. If there is an adequate groundwater supply underneath the city, people who lack easy access to surface water have obtained their drinking water from wells. And after a city's population has grown to a point where the local water resources no longer suffice, canals and aqueducts have been built to import water from increasingly distant regions.

By the end of the twentieth century, many cities had become so populous that their drinking water needs could no longer be met easily by the normal sources. Initially, water-stressed cities adopted the Three R's of reduce, reuse, and recycle to maximize their limited water resources. That strategy worked for a while, but depending on the city's size and location, as well as the enthusiasm of its residents for low-flow showerheads and recycled water, the costs often reached a point where further water savings became difficult. Rather than raising people's water rates to encourage conservation or accepting the idea that water availability might limit their size, cities have increasingly looked to the sea as a means of breaking free of the water cycle. After all, two-thirds of the world's big cities are located along a coast.[1] If water-stressed coastal cities can find a cost-effective technology for removing the salts from seawater, they will no longer have to wait for the sun and wind to send their drinking water to them by way of the water cycle.

Seawater desalination is definitely not a modern idea. As early as the fourth century, sailors at sea were obtaining drinking water with primitive distillation systems, and early inventors like Leonardo da Vinci and Thomas Jefferson experimented with seawater desalination. But no one seriously considered using the technology to supply an entire population with drinking water prior to the Industrial Age, when steam power led to knowledge about boilers along with a need to provide large quantities of freshwater to make the steam to drive ships' engines (saltwater was too corrosive).[2] A few improvements later, and seawater desalination was being used to provide water to small communities in extremely dry places that had the means to pay for it. That's as far as desalination went for much of the twentieth century. But since the early 1990s, a series of incremental improvements has lowered the costs of desalination to a point where water-stressed cities throughout the world are starting to see the technology as an answer to their long-term water supply problems. Only time will tell if the idea will spread.

After the Industrial Revolution made massive boilers and engines possible, desalination evolved from an inefficient but intriguing scientific process that could quench the thirst of a group of sailors into a reliable means of providing large volumes of freshwater. Distillation systems were initially developed as naval ships transitioned from sail power to steam engines. Early desalination systems were then used to supply troops with drinking water during the British military's campaigns in Egypt and Sudan in the 1880s and 1890s. Just after the turn of the twentieth century, several other land-based desalination plants were built to supply fresh water to railroad depots and military garrisons in far-flung places.[3]

These early efforts proved that desalination could be a reliable source of large quantities of freshwater and paved the way for the use of the technology to provide drinking water to residents of the Caribbean island of Curaçao. The tiny island was an ideal place for a desalination plant. Curaçao lacks groundwater, gets scant rainfall, and has a flat topography that makes it tough to build a gravity-driven surface water storage and distribution system. But its oil wells and sugar plantations made it a desirable place for the Dutch to build a colony. To solve their water supply problems, the Dutch colonists built a 60,000 liter (16,000 gallon) per day desalination plant in 1928. To improve the efficiency of the process, they employed multi-effect desalination, a technology that had originally been designed for sugar refining. Using some of the island's ample supply of oil to heat the seawater, the plant passed steam through a series of chambers, each of which was held at a slightly lower pressure. The water that condensed in each successive chamber was less salty than the water in the previous chamber. After a dozen or so chambers, the water became fresh enough to drink. The success of the first plant led to the construction of eleven more desalination plants on the island over the next two decades, eventually providing around 2.65 million liters (700,000 gallons) per day of drinking water to the island's residents.[4]

With multi-effect desalination, it was possible to desalinate water with less energy than the brute-force methods in which steam from seawater was condensed on a single cold surface. For the sugar refiners, multi-effect distillation had been a worthwhile investment, because it only required about 20 percent of the energy used when syrup was boiled over open flames. It was, however, still an energy-intensive process. Even after the advent of modern equipment and technical tweaks to improve its efficiency, multi-effect distillation consumes a lot of energy, requiring about 20 to 30 kWh per thousand liters (75 to 110 kWh per thousand gallons) of freshwater produced.[5] To put that into perspective, it takes about forty to sixty times more energy to treat seawater using this form of distillation than to treat freshwater in a conventional drinking water treatment plant, and ten to fifteen times more energy than what is required to pump the same amount of water up and over the mountains that separate Los Angeles from California's Central Valley.[6]

After Curaçao's early foray into desalination, a few more multi-effect desalination plants were built in the 1930s, in water-limited places like Aruba and Saudi Arabia.[7] The substantial energy consumption associated with the technology meant that only a few locations in the world had both severe water scarcity and inhabitants who had the financial resources to justify investments in desalination plants. Further development of desalination had to be put off until there was a bigger market.

The wait wasn't long: World War II and the large numbers of submarines, ships, and thirsty soldiers and sailors needing freshwater brought new urgency to the issue of improving the efficiency of desalination. Research and development associated with the war effort led to refinements in alternative approaches to desalination that had previously been impractical. In particular, two new thermal desalination technologies—multi-stage flash distillation and vapor compression distillation—reached a point where they offered advantages over multi-effect distillation.

Multi-stage flash distillation employs a similar approach as multi-effect distillation, except that during the process the temperature and pressure in each chamber are held well above the boiling point of water. Freshwater is recovered by cooling some of the steam on the surfaces of the pipes that bring seawater into the plant. The high temperature in the chambers helps avoid the precipitation of salt—otherwise known as scale—on the heating elements. This small improvement had a dramatic effect on the efficiency of the desalination plants because it obviated the need to clean the heating elements, making the transfer of heat more efficient.

Vapor compression distillation uses boiling seawater as a source of steam, and a pump to compress the steam and recover freshwater. The heat produced upon compressing the steam is returned to the chamber where the water is boiled. Vapor compression desalination systems were particularly well suited for use on ships and submarines because they require less space than other thermal desalination methods.

Despite the technological advances, the spread of desalination during the postwar period was slow. By 1953, there were only around two hundred land-based desalination plants worldwide producing around 100 million liters (27 million gallons) per day—only about forty times the capacity of the early desalination plants on Curaçao.[8]

In an effort to translate the new developments in seawater desalination into a cost-effective technology that could provide cities with drinking water, the U.S. government established the Office of Saline Water in 1955.[9] The agency, which was housed in the Department of the Interior's Bureau of Reclamation, started funding research immediately, but the pace of research did not accelerate significantly until the Kennedy administration took an interest in the technology. Desalination was a perfect topic for the Kennedy administration: like the space race, it involved a concerted government effort to advance a technology that could provide a military advantage in the Cold War, and like the Peace Corps, its success would lead to the betterment of mankind. In a speech in 1961, President Kennedy said, "If we could ever competitively—at a cheap rate—get fresh water from salt water, that would be in the long-range interest of humanity, and would really dwarf any other scientific accomplishment."[10]

Over a period of two decades, the Office of Saline Water funded a lot of research on the practical aspects of desalination—such as the development of corrosion-resistant construction materials and more efficient means of transferring heat to water—in an effort to bring down the costs. In current dollars, the federal government's investment in desalination research during that period amounted to about $150 million per year at its peak, which is about ten times higher than its current investment in research on desalination and twenty times higher than its current investment in research on water reuse and recycling.[11]

The government's investments began to pay off just as the economies of Saudi Arabia and its oil-rich neighbors began to grow. During the 1960s, the volume of seawater being desalinated increased by almost a factor of ten, mainly through the construction of several hundred new plants in the Middle East.[12] The technology enabled a rapid transformation of the way in which drinking water was supplied throughout the region. For example, Kuwait had imported its water by boat from Iraq before the installation of its first desalination plant in 1950. The country proceeded to install a series of desalination plants in the 1960s, eventually reaching a total capacity in excess of 38 million liters (10 million gallons) per day.[13] The newly wealthy kingdoms probably had enough money to operate the less efficient multi-effect distillation plants. But instead, they jumped to the modern technologies developed with U.S. government funding. These more efficient approaches made desalination a clear choice over alternatives like the construction of pipelines to import freshwater from distant places.

The new treatment plants still consumed a lot of energy, but the Middle Eastern oil producers were not particularly troubled by the tradeoff between plentiful oil and scarce drinking water. Furthermore, the need to provide drinking water for growing populations emerged at the same time that new power plants were being built to supply electricity for the petroleum industry—which meant that many of the cities were able to locate their desalination plants adjacent to power plants. By using waste heat from the cooling systems of the power plants to preheat seawater coming into the desalination plant, the amount of energy needed for desalination was reduced by as much as 50 percent.[14]

Improvements in materials and practical experience gained from the construction of hundreds of plants in the Middle East further reduced the cost of thermal desalination. During the 1970s, thermal desalination technologies continued to spread with the construction of more plants in the Caribbean, the Middle East, and a few other places where there was enough water stress and wealth to justify building multi-stage flash distillation or vapor compression desalination plants.[15] But although global desalination capacity increased by almost a factor of five during the 1970s, it still accounted for only a tiny fraction of the world's drinking water: by 1980, seawater desalination was providing enough water to meet the daily needs of around 20 million people.

The sharp increase in oil prices that occurred in the 1970s ensured that the further spread of thermal desalination would be slow outside the oil-rich Middle East and the tourist-friendly, arid Caribbean. With the exception of these affluent, water-starved localities, the influence of seawater desalination on drinking water supplies might have been modest had it not been for the commercialization of a new, less energy-intensive approach resulting from the efforts of the Office of Saline Water. The initial discovery that led to this next phase in desalination had occurred in the late 1950s, when two scientists working at the University of Florida invented a cellulose acetate polymer that could be produced in thin sheets. By applying pressure to one side of the polymer membrane, it was possible to employ the reverse-osmosis process to separate water from salts (see Chapter 10).[16] But the early reverse-osmosis membranes were not practical for desalination, because the rate at which water passed though them was slow. In 1963, two graduate students working at the University of California at Los Angeles (UCLA)—Sidney Loeb and Srinivasa Sourirajan—developed a more porous reverse-osmosis membrane that could produce fresh-water from salty brine at a rate that was about ten times faster than any of its predecessors. By 1965, Loeb and his co-workers had built a full-size reverse-osmosis system that desalinated 19,000 liters (5,000 gallons) of groundwater per day in Coalinga—a small farming community about 320 kilometers (200 miles) northeast of Los Angeles where water from the local aquifer was too salty to drink.[17] Over the next decade, the reverse-osmosis process was employed in plants that removed salts from brackish river water as well as from the wastewater effluent that the Orange County Water District used in its pioneering water recycling system.

Finally reverse osmosis faced its toughest challenge: seawater. In 1974, a small reverse-osmosis seawater desalination plant was built in

Nagasaki, Japan.[18] This was followed by the construction of larger reverse-osmosis seawater desalination plants in the 1980s in Spain's Canary Islands and the Middle East.[19]

The new reverse-osmosis desalination systems were more energy efficient than the competing thermal approaches, but they still used a lot of electricity to pressurize the seawater enough for it to pass through the membranes. For seawater desalination to make major inroads in the provision of drinking water, reverse osmosis had to become more energy efficient. Unfortunately for the American researchers interested in taking reverse-osmosis desalination to the next level, the energy price hikes caused by the Arab oil embargo of 1973, coupled with the growing recognition that desalination was always going to be energy intensive, gave a budget-conscious Congress an excuse to trim the federal desalination research budget by around 90 percent.[20] After research funding plunged, many of the subsequent advances in seawater reverse osmosis moved into the private sector and to better-funded government and university laboratories in Europe and Asia.

During the next two decades, researchers steadily improved the efficiency of seawater reverse osmosis by developing new membrane materials, such as thin-film composite membranes that allowed water to pass through them more readily and that could be cleaned with acidic or basic cleaning solutions. Advances in materials science also resulted in a tenfold drop in the cost of membrane manufacturing.[21] In addition, high-efficiency pumps and energy recovery systems made the treatment plants more efficient. By 2006, energy consumption in seawater reverse osmosis had decreased by around 80 percent, to about 2.0 kWh per thousand liters (7.5 kWh per thousand gallons)—a value that was only about twice as high as what would be consumed if the system were perfectly efficient. For any mechanical device, achieving an efficiency of 50 percent is about as good as it gets when you consider all of the places where energy can be lost through friction and other inherent inefficiencies. (For comparison, the modern internal combustion engine is only about 30 percent efficient, and the compact fluorescent light bulb achieves an efficiency of only around 15 percent.)

Energy is consumed in a lot of other places within a desalination plant, like the pumps that pull water into the plant and the filters that remove suspended particles ahead of the reverse-osmosis membranes. Given the cumulative energy use of these other steps in the process, it is safe to assume that future improvements in the energy consumption of seawater reverse-osmosis plants will be modest. Emerging technologies for desalination, such as forward osmosis, or the development of new types of membranes made from exotic materials like carbon nanotubes, hold promise for reducing the costs of the process by decreasing bacteria growth on membrane surfaces and by lowering the costs of manufacturing membranes, but there is not a lot of room for lowering energy consumption by desalination plants.[22]

For comparison, current state-of-the-art seawater desalination plants consume about 2.9 kWh per thousand liters (11 kWh per thousand gallons) of water produced for the entire process, which is around the same amount of energy needed to pump imported water to Los Angeles, San Diego, and Tuscon.[23] If seawater desalination plants were cars, the past forty years would have witnessed an evolution from a highway full of gas-guzzling 1960s-era Lincoln Continentals to one crowded with well-engineered SUVs. Ongoing efforts might squeeze out some more efficiency, but the laws of physics make it unlikely that we will ever fill the desalination highway with a bunch of compact hybrid vehicles.

The progress made during the past few decades has encouraged water-stressed countries that had previously sat on the sidelines to enter the desalination game. Among the nations that have invested most heavily in seawater desalination, Israel is particularly noteworthy for its focus on energy efficiency and the thoughtful way in which its desalination plants have been integrated into the country's existing water infrastructure. Through a coordinated planning effort that began in 1997, Israel has been building a network of coastal desalination plants that pump water into the distribution canal—called the National

Locations of major seawater desalination plants that provide water to Israel's central-ized water system. Based on an image in Y. Dreizin, A. Tenne, and D. Hoffman, *Integrating Large-Scale Seawater Desalination Plants within Israel's Water Supply System,* copyright © 2008, Elsevier.

Water Carrier—that ties the country's major cities together. By taking advantage of economies of scale, employing a similar design in each plant, and paying attention to the places where the desalinated water is put into the canal, Israel has been able to realize significant reductions in the cost of producing desalinated seawater.[24]

The first of Israel's big desalination plants was built in 2007 in the southern city of Ashkelon. According to the Israel Water Authority, the Ashkelon desalination plant produces water for a cost of around $0.50 per thousand liters ($1.90 per thousand gallons)—which is comparable to what the Metropolitan Water District of Southern California currently charges its wholesale customers for treated drinking water.[25] Although these new desalination plants were more expensive than Israel's existing gravity-fed sources, the Ashkelon plant was probably the most cost-effective solution for a country that was already reusing 75 percent of its municipal wastewater effluent and had a household per capita water consumption of about 150 liters (40 gallons) per day—among the lowest in the developed world.[26] Currently, the network of coastal desalination plants provides around 17 percent of Israel's water supply, a proportion that is set to increase to around 30 percent by 2020.

Encouraged by the success of large, seawater reverse-osmosis desalination plants that had been built in places like Israel and Spain's Canary Islands, Australia turned to the sea in response to the worst drought in its modern history.[27] In the initial phase of its decade-long drought that began in 2003, the country's utility managers pursued the normal course of action: pushing homeowners to invest in water-conserving appliances and rainwater collection tanks. They also used the drought as an opportunity to replace leaking pipes. But by the mid-2000s, the drought had depleted Australia's reservoirs and aquifers to the point where all of the country's major cities were in danger of running out of water.[28] A more aggressive approach was needed.

After considering the different options for securing new water supplies, only two solutions seemed like they would be able to meet the pressing demand: desalination and water reuse. Desperate to prevent the cities from running out of water, the Australians pursued both paths simultaneously. Because of complications associated with project design, the expense of installing dual distribution systems, and public concerns about the safety of the unfamiliar process of potable water reuse, desalination moved ahead faster than water reuse. As time went on, desalination also came to be seen as the more viable of the two responses, because some of the water reuse projects never materialized. For example, the largest of the proposed potable water reuse projects, a plan to pump highly treated effluent into the city's main drinking water reservoir, failed in Brisbane due to public opposition.[29]

The global desalination plant-building boom ensured that there would be plenty of vendors offering their services once the Australians decided to pursue desalination. As optimistic utility managers started down the desalination path, many of the country's political leaders expressed reservations about adopting an energy-intensive technology that would make it harder for them to achieve their goal of reducing greenhouse gas emissions. The premier of New South Wales, Bob Carr, initially derided seawater desalination as "bottled electricity." But after a few years of drought and the absence of viable alternatives, he warmed to the idea, becoming a proponent of a proposed $2 billion desalination plant in Sydney in 2005.[30] To assuage concerns over increased greenhouse gas emissions, Australian politicians embraced the idea of offsetting the greenhouse gases produced by desalination through the construction of windmills and solar panels.

The first of Australia's modern desalination plants, which was built in Perth in 2007, provided the city with about 150 million liters (40 million gallons) per day of drinking water. To offset the $300 million plant's greenhouse gas production, the Water Corporation of Western Australia purchased two-thirds of the electricity generated by the Emu Downs Wind Farm located approximately 240 kilometers (150 miles) north of the desalination plant. Critics of the project suggested that the idea of offsetting the increased greenhouse gas emissions with green power was counterproductive, because energy from the windmills would have been used to meet the other needs of the rapidly growing city had the desalination plant not been built. But the existence of a reliable customer who was willing to pay a premium for renewable electricity did encourage investment in the region's fledgling alternative energy sector.[31]

In 2009 the partial completion of Perth's second desalination plant doubled the city's desalination capacity. With the completion of the second plant in 2013, about half of Perth's drinking water now comes from the sea. Throughout the process, the city's water utility has remained committed to green power, purchasing electricity for the second plant from a new solar energy plant built just outside of the city.[32]

Greenhouse gas emissions were not the only environmental issue that had to be addressed as part of Perth's desalination program. Australians are fiercely protective of their beaches, and proposals to build coastal desalination plants raised fears about damage that they might cause to the fragile coastal environment. Indeed, seawater desalination plants have the potential to affect coastal ecosystems in two ways. First, the intake pipe can suck larval fish into the plant's filters, and second, the intake pipe can kill adult fish by trapping them on the coarse screens that cover the pipe. These phenomena, which are known as entrainment and impingement, respectively, had previously been the subject of numerous debates about the environmental impacts of power plants that use seawater for cooling. The large power plants built during the second half of the twentieth century can pump up to 7.5 billion liters (2 billion gallons) of seawater through their cooling systems each day. When the power plants were initially conceived, there was little concern about pumping all of that water. But now we know better: the damage to fish populations from a single large power plant can be equivalent to the loss of thousands of hectares of marine habitat.[33] As a result, some recently constructed plants have moved away from the single pass cooling method or have invested in more expensive intake systems that do less damage to marine ecosystems.

Perth's desalination plant, which pumped a fraction as much seawater as the cooling systems of the big coastal power plants, included features intended to minimize the entrainment and impingement of marine life. First, the intake pipe was located around 300 meters (1,000 feet) offshore, where fewer marine organisms live compared with the near-shore environment. Second, the system employed a velocity cap, a design in which the flow path of the incoming seawater was shifted to the horizontal direction just as it entered the intake structure. A velocity cap decreases impingement because fish have receptors on their bodies that are sensitive to water flowing in the horizontal direction. When the change in the direction of seawater flow is coupled with the use of a lower velocity of water flowing into the pipe, only about half as many fish are sucked in for a given volume of water as were drawn in by the early generation intake structures.[34] Entrainment and impingement still occurred at Perth's desalination plant, but the local regulatory authorities were convinced by the plant's designers that the effects of pumping on marine life would be negligible.

The second concern for the coastal ecosystem is related to the extra salty water—known as reject or brine—that is returned to the sea after water is desalinated. In a typical seawater desalination plant, the water left behind after reverse osmosis is about twice as salty as seawater, and significantly denser. If the salty reject water were to be released to the sea floor without sufficient mixing, it would damage marine life—most of which is not adapted to elevated salt concentrations. In addition, a number of chemicals—such as antiscaling agents and coagulants—are added to the seawater during the desalination process.[35] Because these chemicals are unable to pass through the reverse-osmosis membranes, they end up in the reject water. After they are released, microbial breakdown of the chemicals consumes dissolved oxygen, much in the manner that oxygen was consumed downstream of the outfalls of sewers and early sewage treatment plants in the nineteenth and early twentieth centuries. Phosphate and nitrate—the two nutrients most commonly associated with algae blooms—also are released when chemicals in the reject water break down.

To minimize the potential effects of these salts and chemicals in the reject water, modern desalination plants often contain systems designed to mix it rapidly into the surrounding water. In Perth's first desalination plant, the 300-meter-long (1,000-foot) outlet system contained forty jet nozzles integrated into the last 180 meters (600 feet) of the pipe. The mixing jets ensured that by thirty-five meters (120 feet) away from the discharge point it would be nearly impossible to detect the presence of the reject water.[36]

Following Perth's lead, the other major cities in Australia—Sydney, Melbourne, Brisbane, and Adelaide—also invested in reverse-osmosis seawater desalination plants. The other cities did not increase their reliance on seawater desalination to the same extent as Perth, but after the desalination plant construction boom, Australia's big cities obtained about 15 percent of their water from the sea.

Australia's investment in seawater desalination will insulate it from its next big drought, but this insurance policy has come at a relatively high price. The approximately $9 billion spent on new desalination plants over the past five years will be passed on to consumers in the form of hefty utility bills and higher prices for goods and services.[37] And because of environmental concerns—including greenhouse gases and protection of coastal ecosystems—as well as the need for each of the country's desalination plants to be designed, permitted, and built separately, Australia's desalinated water costs about twice as much as Israel's.[38] Australians have coped with annual increases in their water bills of around 20 percent over the past five years.[39] For a typical household, this increase works out to about an extra $120 every year. Not all of the cost increases were due to desalination: water rates probably would have increased for many of the reasons discussed in Chapter 9. Nonetheless the high price for desalination, coupled with a dramatic end to the drought, has sapped the country's desire for more desalination plants.

Is there a place for reverse-osmosis seawater desalination in America's water future? It's probably too soon to tell, but trends are starting to emerge as water-stressed coastal cities have begun to turn to the sea for their next big water projects. Tampa was the first American city to make a major commitment to desalination; in 1999 it entered into a contract with a consortium of private companies to build a 94 million liter (25 million gallon) per day desalination plant. The plan was for the developers to design, build, and operate the plant for five years, then sell it to the city's water utility. The companies promised that the new plant would deliver water for about the same price as those that were being built in Israel. Tampa's new water source would be expensive, but the city was willing to make the investment due to an absence of new sources of imported water and threats to coastal wetlands posed by the depletion of local groundwater.[40]

The optimistic price projections for Tampa's desalination plant were partially attributable to its use of cooling water from an adjacent power plant. By locating the desalination plant next to the power plant, the desalination plant could tap into seawater that had already passed through the power plant's cooling system.[41] The desalination plant could also mix its reject into the much larger volume of water that the power plant's cooling system was constantly returning to the sea. By sharing the cooling system, the desalination plant would avoid the need to build and permit its own intake and discharge system. The plant's use of water from the power plant had another advantage: the water coming into the system would be three to eight degrees Celsius (five to fifteen degrees Fahrenheit) warmer than the local seawater, and because reverse-osmosis membranes become more permeable to water at higher temperatures, energy consumption by the desalination plant would be reduced by about 5 percent.[42]

Despite the strong financial incentive that the private companies had to start delivering water on schedule, shortcomings in the design for the plant's seawater pretreatment system delayed its launch by several years. Because of the delay, the consortium faced difficulties securing additional loans. Lacking the revenues from an operating desalination plant, the consortium went bankrupt.[43] After two replacement teams also went bankrupt trying to complete the job,

Tampa's water utility stepped in, hired a contractor to finish the construction, and began operating the plant in 2008.[44] The new and improved design worked, but the construction delays increased the project's cost by about 40 percent.[45] Even with subsidies from the Southwest Florida Water Management District, which were equivalent to about 15 percent of the plant's construction costs, and the relatively cheap electricity available in the regional market, Tampa's desalinated seawater costs almost twice as much as Israel's.[46]

While the fits and starts associated with Tampa's desalination plant gave utilities in the rest of the country cause for concern, they did not eliminate their interest in the technology. The only push that they needed was a good drought. In California—birthplace of modern reverse osmosis—fights over water rights among farmers, cities, and environmentalists periodically created manmade droughts. Tired of the uncertainty associated with their perpetual tug-of-war over imported water sources and anticipating future decreases in their allocations, California's coastal cities took a serious look at desalination.

Plans for big investments in seawater desalination plants had popped up at regular intervals since Sidney Loeb and his colleagues from UCLA had built their tiny system in Coalinga in the mid-1960s. Among the many ambitious plans for seawater desalination was a proposal from the Office of Saline Water and the Atomic Energy Commission to co-locate a nuclear power plant and a seawater desalination plant in Los Angeles during the 1960s. The promise of electricity that was so cheap it did not have to be metered meant that distillation could be used despite its inefficiency. Once the country got serious about the construction of nuclear power plants, however, the proponents of the plant realized that the electricity would be more expensive than they imagined.[47] Only a few desalination plants were built in California after the initial setback, including a 25-million-liter (6.7-million-gallon) per day reverse-osmosis desalination plant in the city of Santa Barbara that was built in response to a severe drought in 1991. After the drought ended and the city was offered a new connection to the state's imported water system, part of the plant was sold to Saudi Arabia. The remaining part of the decommissioned plant is being held by the city as an insurance policy against future droughts. In other words, despite its continued flirtation with tapping into the sea, no city in California has made a long-term commitment to seawater desalination. This situation, however, may soon change. Heartened by the successes of overseas desalination projects, the process of planning and permitting scores of desalination plants began up and down the coast. By 2006, a total of twenty projects had been proposed from San Diego in the south to Marin County just north of San Francisco.[48]

Among the proposed desalination plants, the project in the city of Carlsbad—a community of around 100,000 people located just north of San Diego—has moved the fastest. In 1998, Poseidon Resources Corporation LLC, the private company that had helped start the problematic plant in Tampa, teamed with Carlsbad on a proposal to build a 190-million-liter (50-million-gallon) per day reverse-osmosis desalination plant adjacent to a power plant.[49] Just like the Tampa plant, the new facility would tap into the warm water produced by the power plant and discharge its reject water into the power plant's cooling system. But unlike the Tampa project, the desalination plant in Carlsbad would not be sold back to the local utility after it was up and running. This new approach meant that the city and local utilities would not be on the hook if the project did not work out according to plans. According to Mitch Dion, general manager of one of the local water districts that had signed up to purchase water from the plant, "We've kept all the risk on Poseidon. . . . They cannot come back to us or our ratepayers."[50] But in return for accepting the risks associated with the design, financing, and permitting of the project, Poseidon gained the right to make a hefty profit if it succeeds.

According to the company's plan, there will be little profit when the price of desalinated water is still higher than that of imported water. During this period, which they estimate will last for ten to twelve years, Poseidon will charge its customers the going rate for imported water and obtain a subsidy from the Metropolitan Water District of Southern California—the regional water wholesaler—to cover its losses. After the cost of desalinated water drops to below that of imported water, the subsidies will end and the desalination plant will sell water to the local water utilities at a rate that is lower than that of imported water but higher than the cost of desalination.

Poseidon and its partners were ready to start building immediately. But the absence of an actual drought, together with strong opposition from the environmental community and the fact that it would be the state's first big coastal desalination project, slowed the plant's permitting process to a crawl.

As in Australia, environmental groups raised concerns about impacts from the salty reject water and the increase in greenhouse gas emissions associated with the process. For each of the concerns raised by the project's critics, Poseidon had an answer. Worries about the effects on the marine environment of the reject water were countered with hydraulic models showing that the salinity in the area near the power plant's outfall would be unaffected by the relatively small flow of water coming from the desalination plant.[51] Fears about increased greenhouse gas emissions were answered with rows of solar panels on the roof of the plant and other green accoutrements. After adding up the electricity produced by the solar panels, energy saved by adopting green building methods, and the purchase of carbon offsets—credits that allow people who use fossil fuels to pay for others to reduce greenhouse gas emissions through activities like the development of new renewable energy sources—Poseidon could show that its desalinated water would produce far fewer greenhouse gases per liter of water produced than the imported water that was pumped up and over the mountains outside of the city.[52]

The only aspect of the project for which Poseidon could not provide a satisfactory answer was its cost. For the project to succeed, the company's design had to include all of the special features that had been included in Australia—green power, minimal environmental impact, a site-specific design—but for Israeli prices. Many observers who had followed seawater desalination in other places were suspicious of the company's calculations. Peter Gleick, executive director of the

Pacific Institute, warned that the Carlsbad desalination plant was "a case study of how not to do desalination."[53] He criticized the deal that had been made with Poseidon, warning that the desalinated water would ultimately cost taxpayers a lot more than advertised and that the same objectives could be achieved through conservation or the purchase of imported water on the open market.

Despite legal challenges and protests from its opponents, the Carlsbad desalination project continues to move ahead. Ultimately, it will be up to Wall Street bond sellers and the local utility to make the call about financial viability of the project. Poseidon remains confident about its eventual success: in 2010, even before the final contracts were signed and the bonds were sold, the company started to prepare the site for construction. In September 2012, Poseidon reached a tentative agreement with San Diego—the neighboring city that is seeking to secure its water supply in coming years. If the construction is completed according to schedule, the plant will be up and running by 2016.[54]

The total price for California's first big coastal desalination plant is estimated to be around $800 million for a plant that will deliver about 190 million (50 million gallons) of water each day.[55] On the basis of the dollars per gallon of water delivered, that's more than twice as high as the costs for water provided by the desalination plants in Tampa and Perth. Although Poseidon has agreed to assume the financial risk if the project fails, it is still passing the cost of building the plant on to the utility's customers and the state's taxpayers. The deal has been structured so that the price tag will be less noticeable to the people in Carlsbad and its neighbors: the payments will be spread across the entire region (because the new source of water will benefit everyone who is hooked into the system). As a result, utility customers as far away as 160 kilometers (100 miles) from Carlsbad may see their annual utility rates increase by somewhere between $8.50 and $17 a month to pay for water that will be used within a short distance of Carlsbad.[56] In addition, the state's taxpayers will subsidize the project by allowing Poseidon to sell tax-exempt bonds. The Carlsbad project may eventually succeed, but it is hard to imagine many other projects securing such favorable terms.

Despite the setbacks encountered in Tampa and Carlsbad, more proposals for coastal desalination plants are moving ahead in California and Florida. From the trials and tribulations of the pioneering projects, it is evident that desalination may be part of Water 4.0, but it is not a panacea for the clean water challenges of America's coastal cities. With each new project it becomes easier to separate the reality of seawater desalination from the rhetoric on both sides. Seawater desalination is a mature, reliable technology. But if countries or regions are unable to adopt a centralized planning model similar to Israel's, and if they continue to insist on green power, carbon offsets, and lengthy environmental impact reviews, seawater desalination will remain expensive relative to other options for the foreseeable future.

12

A Different Tomorrow

ver since the Romans pioneered Water 1.0, centralization has been the big idea behind urban water systems. In fact, this original design principle has been so potent that each of the subsequent upgrades was built on this foundation. Starting with the addition of filtration and chlorine disinfection on the front end of water distribution systems (Water 2.0), and continuing to the installation of biological wastewater treatment on the sewer end (Water 3.0) and beyond, modern water infrastructure is still guided by its original blueprint of ancient Roman-style aqueducts and cloacae.

Centralized urban water systems are presently under considerable stress from a variety of forces. Increases in population density, changing precipitation patterns, competition for water resources, and recognition of the need to leave more water in streams to protect aquatic habitats are driving a movement toward formerly unusable water sources, such as seawater and wastewater effluent, for our next drinking water supply projects. Coincident with these changes, concerns about chlorine disinfection byproducts, endocrine-disrupting chemicals, and pollution of surface waters with nutrients are causing us to rethink many of our ideas about water and wastewater treatment. And a deeper awareness of the damage caused by stormwater runoff is leading to a new focus on urban drainage systems. But coming up with the money needed to expand the water supply portfolio, improve treatment efficiencies, and fix urban drainage systems at the same time that our long-neglected pipe networks and treatment plants are reaching the ends of their design lifetimes is a tall order. As a result, rapid increases in water bills and more frequent and intense controversies over water are becoming the norm in most places. In the near future, these pressures will force us to make some tough choices.

Not surprisingly, most cities appear to be on the path of least resistance, sticking with the centralized systems that have served them so well. In essence, they are doubling down on bets that their existing systems are up to the coming challenges. This approach means that utility managers will do their best to meet growing water demands by expanding imported water systems. When the conventional mode of expansion is no longer possible, they'll turn to reverse-osmosis membranes to convert sewage effluent or seawater into drinking water. To maintain the network of decaying water and sewer pipes and to reduce the frequency of combined sewer overflows, they will dig up the streets and build gigantic underground tunnels to keep excess runoff out of their treatment plants. And to pay for all of these new projects, they will turn to their customers, raising monthly bills at rates that are just low enough to avoid a serious backlash.

I am pretty confident that this approach will work in most places—at least in the short term. Money will keep the water flowing, but it won't always be pretty. Under this scenario, many of the trials and tribulations described in the previous chapters will become commonplace. The path of least resistance that is being followed means higher water bills and lots of controversy over a resource that has been taken for granted for too long. Examples of the coming problems that will be faced are evident in Indianapolis, where homeowners can expect to pay an extra hundred dollars per month to cover the construction of new stormwater-bypass tunnels; in Southern California, where more political fights and rising bills are on the way as plans to expand potable water reuse programs advance; and in Perth, where citizens are absorbing the sticker shock of new desalination plants built to compensate for the effects of climate change on local rainfall. Painful decisions about urban water systems will be further complicated by uncertainty surrounding the effects of climate change on precipitation patterns and the unlikely prospect of significant new government investments in water infrastructure. In light of all of these factors, there is no way of knowing when the cycle of crises and expenditures will end.

In recognition of the problems associated with our current approach, some people have advocated for something different. They assert that the answer to our water problems can be found in the adoption of practices that reduce the amount of water passing through urban water systems. This belief grew out of the observation that water conservation can forestall the need to develop new water supplies.[1] Conservation also saves energy and helps growing cities avoid costly investments in expanding the capacity of their sewage treatment plants.

The idea of reducing water use as a way of controlling runaway increases in water bills and simultaneously minimizing damage to the environment is intuitively appealing and often results in immediate economic benefits for utilities. Investing in efficiency should be a lot more effective than mindlessly plowing more money into the expansion of existing water systems. Unfortunately, urban water systems and the institutions that support them have evolved in ways that ultimately restrict the ability of conservation and related efficiency measures to solve our long-term problems.

The first factor that prevents conservation from being a panacea is that water utilities have a limited number of tools they can use to change the behavior of their customers. The tools they do possess— namely, raising the price of water and offering rebates to offset the costs of installing water-saving devices—are often inadequate when it comes to achieving the full potential of conservation. If a utility really wants to reduce water consumption, these approaches will only go so far; serious conservation will require a fundamental change in public attitudes about the value of water and the role that water utilities play in determining how it can be used. Unfortunately such changes tend to be unpopular with politically powerful constituencies such as real estate developers, libertarians, and members of anti-tax groups, who bristle at the idea of regulations that restrict personal liberties and increase the costs of home ownership.[2]

Talented water utility managers are sometimes able to navigate the political process to bring about the necessary policy changes, especially if there is already an awareness in the community of the consequences of impending water shortages. But water utility managers are rarely at the top of the political hierarchy. When it is time to balance the goals of water conservation against economic development, political philosophy, and the desire of elected officials to please their constituents, these managers often find themselves unable to implement the kinds of changes needed to support their desired water-saving policies. Faced with the uncertainties of the political process, utility managers find it easier to return to more politically safe solutions involving backhoes, pipes, and concrete.

The push toward water conservation has another force working against it: if a water utility succeeds in reducing the amount of water used by its customers, its overall revenues might well decrease by more than the amount it saves by treating and delivering less water. This seemingly illogical situation is associated with the decision that many utilities made to set their billing rates according to the volume of water used. Because the bulk of the costs of running urban water systems—such as payments on bonds for past water projects, employee salaries, and pipe-replacement programs—are not in fact tied to the amount of water delivered or treated, the price of water actually may have to increase as water use decreases. A situation like this one occurred during the Southern California drought of the 1990s, when the Los Angeles Department of Water and Power was forced to raise water rates to compensate for a $70 million revenue shortfall after its customers reduced their water use by about 30 percent.[3] In our current system, water utilities are in the business of selling water. As a result, any policies that substantially reduce water use are going to be less popular than investments in assets that satisfy customer demands and bring in more revenue.

Conservation becomes a much more viable option when a utility uses it to meet the expected water demands of a growing population. If a water conservation program is part of a long-term plan to provide water to accommodate population growth, it can be implemented without lowering revenues. Large expenditures on conservation can be justified for this purpose, especially if they help demonstrate the utility's commitment to environmental protection. For example, in 2009 my local water utility commissioned a study to assess conservation measures that might be used to help them meet the community's water needs over the next three decades.[4] Concentrating on approaches that have proven to be effective elsewhere, they grouped their options in order of increasing economic efficiency. The least expensive approach, which mainly involved changes in plumbing codes, expanded conservation outreach programs, and rebates for purchasing more efficient appliances, was estimated to cost the utility around $0.12 per thousand liters ($0.45 per thousand gallons) of water saved and was projected to lower daily water use by about 3 percent. The most expensive option, which consisted of an array of more extensive changes to building codes and investments in some relatively inefficient water-saving technologies, was estimated to cost around $0.69 per thousand liters ($2.60 per thousand gallons) of water saved and would reduce daily water use by around 8 percent. When the additional costs to consumers associated with installing water-saving devices and complying with new regulations were factored into the analysis, the costs jumped to approximately $1.20 and $2.60 per thousand liters ($4.60 and $10 per thousand gallons) of water saved for the least and most aggressive conservation plans, respectively. The overall cost to the utility of the most expensive of the chosen measures was about twice the price of expanding the utility's nonpotable water reuse system and four times more expensive than reservoir expansion. Nonetheless, they opted for all but the most expensive of the conservation options, because they were politically safer than some of the less popular actions, such as increasing the height of the dam on an existing reservoir in an environmentally sensitive watershed.[5]

The inclusion of water conservation measures in long-term water supply plans may well forestall the need to develop new supplies, but rarely will these measures reduce a city's overall water use. In other words, water utilities have little incentive to employ conservation to achieve savings that exceed their expected future increases in water demand. As a result, conservation measures can keep overall water use by a utility constant, but they usually do not result in a drop in total consumption.

Over the past two decades, tremendous strides have been made in water conservation. In the United States, much of this success is related to the federal government's Energy Policy Act of 1992, which mandated that plumbing fixtures become more efficient.[6] Starting in 1994, toilets had to meet a standard of 6 liters (1.6 gallons) per flush, and faucets and showerheads could deliver only 9.5 liters (2.5 gallons) of water per minute. The amount of water used by these new fixtures is typically 40 to 60 percent lower than the fixtures they replace. The result was a drop in per capita water use of about 0.5 percent annually—a move in the right direction that in the long run is probably too slow to keep up with increases in water consumption attributable to population growth.[7] The gains from water conservation have been similar in other parts of the world, with new indoor fixtures leading to reductions in per capita water use of a similar magnitude in Western Europe and Australia over the past twenty years.[8]

Water conservation, as it is currently being practiced in most places, has an important role to play, but a more powerful strategy is needed to relieve the long-term, and growing, financial pressures on our centralized water systems. Perhaps the best long-term solution to our water problems will be to abandon centralized water systems altogether. At first glance, this approach seems as if it would create more problems than it solves. But if we can figure out ways to meet our water needs with local resources, to safely treat our wastes close to where they are produced, and to drain the streets without a centralized storm sewer system, we might break free of the cycle of costly investments and environmental damage that currently plague our current water and wastewater systems.

The idea seems less farfetched if you consider that in developed countries, many people still get by without centralized water systems. Individual water supply wells, household-scale waste treatment systems, and drainage structures that handle excess runoff without storm sewers are the norm in communities with low population densities. These kinds of decentralized systems usually disappear after a community transitions from rural to suburban. But perhaps water systems don't have to work this way. To wean cities from centralized water systems and all of their associated problems, we might simply have to find a way to make decentralized water supply and treatment practical at higher population densities. It's quite likely that we'll never break free of centralized water and sewer systems in the middle of our most densely populated cities, but a society equipped with the latest innovations in information technology, biotechnology, and materials science should be able to improve on the groundwater wells, septic tanks, and unlined ditches that served our rural communities so well during the twentieth century.

Furthermore, there is no need to make a single choice among the options of conservation, improved centralized water systems (the version of Water 4.0 described in previous chapters), or decentralized systems. Instead, each city must navigate a series of decisions about which path best fits its local situation. For example, after considering energy consumption, environmental impacts, and the costs of alternatives, New Yorkers or modern-day Romans might decide that it is worthwhile to keep investing in their miraculous, gravity-fed imported water system, relying on a modest amount of conservation measures to cover future increases in water demand. In contrast, residents of Los Angeles or Sydney may decide that the economic and environmental costs of one of their city's most energy-intensive imported water sources outweigh its benefits. To compensate for the decrease in quantity of imported water, they could employ a more aggressive set of water conservation practices and invest in alternative water sources—such as decentralized water reuse and increased reliance on local groundwater—with any water deficits compensated for by centralized water recycling and seawater desalination plants. The same logic applies to sewage treatment plants and urban drainage systems. High population density, unfavorable geology, and a cold climate might push some cities to stick with centralized wastewater treatment and storm sewers, while others might find it advantageous to transition to decentralized systems that do not require sewer pipes.

In the places where decentralization makes technological, economic, and environmental sense, a gradual evolution could occur as decentralized systems start to replace the existing water infrastructure. The rate at which centralized systems evolve into hybrids of centralized and decentralized water systems would depend on how quickly the costs of several key technologies decrease; the ability of local water supply options, such as water reuse, desalination, and rainwater harvesting, to meet potable water needs; and the willingness of the public to accept a new approach for urban water. To understand these issues and the ways in which localized solutions may lead to the creation of a distributed version of Water 4.0, it makes sense to examine some of the innovations that are being embraced by cities that have already recognized the limitations of the status quo but have not yet chosen to invest in centralized water recycling and desalination.

Let's start by considering ways of achieving dramatic reductions in water use. Going beyond the gradual improvements already being achieved by garden-variety conservation programs is one of the keys to breaking our reliance on centralized water systems. After all, there are few places where there is enough water in the local rivers and aquifers to support the current water demands of a city. Even in cities where there is plenty of water, there are economic and environmental costs associated with every liter of water used. Irrespective of the amount of water available from local sources, if a city can reduce its per capita water demand by 50 to 75 percent and dramatically reduce or eliminate the need to dispose of wastewater, it may be able to abandon large parts of its network of drinking water pipes and sewers. There is no single technology or policy that can achieve such goals, but by using combinations of the approaches that are currently being pursued in a piecemeal manner in water-stressed cities, the goal of breaking free of the water grid is achievable.

The first place to look for water reduction is inside the home. Most indoor water use occurs when people use toilets, faucets, and washing machines.[9] Prior to the 1990s, these fixtures and appliances consumed lots of water. But as the need to conserve water was recognized, fixtures and appliances were redesigned to reduce water use by about half without a noticeable drop in performance. Regulations mandating the use of these low-flow devices in new construction will eventually lower per capita water use by an additional 30 percent relative to current rates.[10] Thereafter, daily indoor water use will likely level out at around 120 liters (32 gallons) per person.[11] Unfortunately, the transition to high-efficiency appliances in older homes will take several decades to achieve because the existing low-efficiency devices will be used until they wear out.

Programs that fast-track the replacement of water-hogging plumbing fixtures in older homes with low-flow alternatives and that encourage people to purchase high-efficiency appliances could accelerate the anticipated reduction in water use.[12] For example, water-conscious utilities have been offering rebates to customers who can prove that they replaced a plumbing fixture that had been installed before the adoption of water-efficient plumbing standards. Some utilities have even gone one step further in their efforts to accelerate the upgrades by paying a bounty to external parties willing to help: at the end of the 1990s, the Los Angeles Department of Water and Power provided over 750,000 low-flow toilets to community groups and paid them a twenty-five-dollar bounty for each toilet replaced.[13] With this grass-roots campaign, the city was able to reduce its daily water use by about 95 million liters (25 million gallons) over about five years while simultaneously helping fund the activities of local civic groups.

Washing machines are replaced more frequently than toilets and faucets, because they have more moving parts that wear out. When it is time to buy a new machine, however, many people pass up front-loading washers that offer daily savings of about 150 liters (40 gallons) per household because they cost around $300 more than the familiar top loaders that are still on the market.[14] Over a fifteen-year lifetime, a more efficient, front-loading washing machine will cost its owner around $2,000 less to operate.[15] It will also save around 750,000 liters (200,000 gallons) of water and cut greenhouse gas emissions by an amount that is equivalent to driving a car around 1,600 kilometers (1,000 miles).[16] To encourage people to purchase the more efficient washing machine models, many utilities are willing to provide a rebate of around a hundred dollars, funded by a pool of money provided by the local water and electric utilities.

Although rebate programs are popular and effective at reducing water use, they will only have a modest impact on overall water use because the big three indoor water uses—toilets, showers, and washing machines—typically account for less than half of a household's overall consumption of water. Utilities can realize additional water savings by working with commercial establishments such as restaurants and laundromats, but big reductions in water use will require a change in attitude about the value of water and the role that the utilities can play in determining how people use their product. If they want to realize the full benefits of conservation, water utilities will have to accept the idea that they are no longer in the business of selling water: rather, they are stewards of a limited resource that they manage for the public. For even if the resource is inexpensive relative to commodities such as gasoline, no one should have a right to waste this limited resource. The utilities that have already adopted this view are fighting entrenched attitudes and the front line of this battle is the lawn—the place where up to half of a household's water is used for a purpose that is unrelated to nourishment or hygiene.

For utilities, one of the most popular ways of pursuing the goal of reducing outdoor water use is to make it more expensive to own a lawn. To compel people who use a lot of water on their lawns to embrace conservation without penalizing everyone in the city, many utilities have adopted a targeted strategy for setting water rates in a manner that hits only the biggest water users.[17] Like taxes, water rates can be flat, progressive, or regressive. Flat rate increases that charge a fixed price for each liter of water consumed are an impractical means of discouraging excessive outdoor water use, because increasing rates also penalize the people who use most of their water indoors. That is, apartment dwellers and people who live in small homes tend to feel the effects of flat water rates at least as much as the people with big lawns do. Water rates are thus a social equity issue—a factor that greatly complicates matters for a utility that is attempting to incentivize conservation.

Between 1980 and 2000, about one-third of U.S. water utilities shifted from flat rate structures to a progressive pricing approach whereby water prices increase with the volume of water consumed.[18] When applied to residential customers, these billing systems, which are referred to as increasing block pricing, set the price that homeowners pay for each liter of water to increase after they exceed a monthly allocation, known as a block, that the utility deemed to be adequate for both indoor use and a modest amount of outdoor use. The difference in prices between the blocks can be substantial. For example, in Seattle, the price of each additional liter of water used nearly triples after a household's daily water use exceeds its first block allocation of around 1,700 liters (450 gallons) per day.[19] With increasing block pricing, only those homeowners who use exceptionally large amounts of water feel the effect of higher prices.

According to economic theory, increased block pricing should result in significant reductions in water use as the heavy water users respond to economic pressure. Unfortunately, the people with the expansive lawns don't seem to understand the economic theory: big water users often fail to change their behavior when the new billing systems are adopted.[20] In part, this change in behavior could be due to a lack of awareness of how increasing block pricing works. But the more likely explanation is that the price of water, even after adding in the penalty for excessive use, is just too low to change the behavior of the people with the big lawns. After all, those who can afford to own a large lot within an urban water utility's service area can probably toss in an extra few hundred dollars to cover the two- or three-month period when their lawns need lots of water. The invisible hand of the market just isn't very effective if the people it slaps in the face are impervious to pain.

A less common but often more effective strategy for reducing outdoor water use is to reward people for replacing their lawns with plants that consume less water. For example, in the early 2000s Las Vegas achieved a rapid, citywide reduction of water use of approximately 15 percent during a five-year drought by paying people to replace their lawns with drought-tolerant plants.[21] The "Cash for Grass" program made one-time payments of eleven dollars per square meter (a dollar per square foot) to homeowners who were willing to convert their lawns to a form of landscaping referred to as xeriscaping. Xeriscaping refers to the practice of landscaping with plants that use less water. The term was popularized (and trademarked) by Denver's water utility in the late 1970s to describe its program for establishing plants that are appropriate for the local climate. It includes a mixture of low-water-consuming perennial plants and small sections of turf.

During the five-year drought, Las Vegas spent around $60 million on its turf replacement project.[22] That may seem like a lot of money for a water conservation rebate program, but the investment in turf removal was a lot more efficient than the alternative of developing a new water supply. After factoring in typical annual savings associated with the landscaping makeovers, the program reduced water use in the city by around 38 million liters (10 million gallons) per day, assuming that xeriscapes saved around 2,300 liters per square meter (56 gallons of water per square foot) per year. "Cash for Grass" was effective, but it was not cheap. Thinking in terms of the price per volume of water saved, Las Vegas's initial investment in the turf grass removal program was on par with what other cities are spending on the construction of seawater desalination plants.[23]

Despite the high cost of buying up lawns, the conservation program may turn out to be a better long-term investment than a desalination plant. Unlike turfgrass removal, desalination requires a continued influx of money to push water through reverse-osmosis membranes and maintain the treatment plant. If homeowners continue to practice xeriscaping after the period that they agreed to when they signed up for the program, it will deliver savings well into the future without any additional investment. The CEO of Duke Energy, James Rogers, once said of the merits of energy conservation, "The most environmentally responsible plant you build is the one that you don't build."[24] A similar idea applies to water conservation: in terms of cost and environmental impact, the most efficient new water supply is the one that you avoided building through conservation.

Arguably, Las Vegas is a special case. The amount of water saved by turf replacement is higher in this desert city than it would be in cooler, more humid climates. In addition, quirks in the water rights agreements associated with the city's water allocation from its main source—the Colorado River—have created a system that awards credits to the city for returning water to the river. Thus Las Vegas has a strong incentive to decrease outdoor water use because landscape irrigation results in water that evaporates while most of the water used in homes is returned to the river through the city's sewage treatment plants—which means that the city can take more freshwater upstream.

Although cities in Texas, Colorado, and New Mexico may have less incentive to reduce outdoor water use than Las Vegas, they are also paying people to replace their lawns with plants that consume less water.[25] The desire to do away with the traditional lawn has even spread beyond the desert to places where the incongruity of a lawn is not as obvious. For example, in lawn-friendly Florida, water utilities have partnered with Florida State University to establish a program called "Florida Friendly Landscaping."[26] In this voluntary program, water agencies and state extension agents advise community members on how they can transform their lawns into attractive landscapes that consume less water. The program's reliance on public education and a sense of civic responsibility instead of a cash payout is probably preventing it from having much of an impact on the state's water use. But the real contribution of Florida's program may be psychological. In a place where water has often seemed plentiful, having a few neighbors who question the traditional lawn helps start a discussion about the value of water.

The xeriscaping movement is not without its detractors. To lawn lovers, xeriscaping is sometimes seen as a politically loaded statement that conveys a lack of respect for the community's values.[27] Defenders of the lawn tout the many benefits of turf, including its contribution to maintaining property values, its ability to hold down dust and lower temperatures around houses during summer, and its role as a community-building open space. A culture clash between the two schools of thought on landscaping threatens the future spread of xeriscaping in many places. In some developments it has even become a legal issue, with homeowner associations establishing rules that every house must have turf covering the majority of the front yard. Despite the setbacks, the xeriscapers have had some success: with the support of Florida's water utilities and environmental groups, the legislature passed a law in 2010 superseding local ordinances against xeriscaping.[28] But support from the lawn care industry and the habits of lawn owners will continue to slow the effort to rethink the traditional lawn. Without a change in attitudes, the push of a drought, or the pull of cash payments, xeriscaping may never make serious inroads beyond the arid West.

For those who prefer to keep their lawns, modern technology offers an alternative: the smart irrigation controller. The idea behind these devices is simple. Most automated lawn sprinkler systems apply too much water in most places to ensure that the driest parts of the yard will always get enough water. In addition, lawn sprinkler systems usually deliver the same amount of water to the lawn every day, although the amount of water needed by the lawn is quite variable: decreasing on cloudy days, after it rains, or when the temperature drops in spring and fall. It used to be that the only way to compensate for these variations was to manually adjust the system, which defeats the purpose of having an automatic sprinkler system. But over the past two decades, advances in electronics and microcomputing have led to the development of inexpensive controllers that continuously fine-tune the amount of water applied to different parts of the lawn.[29]

The first generation of smart irrigation controllers used historic data on rainfall and temperature to make seasonal adjustments to the amount of water applied to the lawn. They also had simple rain sensors that shut off the sprinklers for a few days after it rained. The newest smart controllers employ the Internet to take the technology one step further. Through a wireless communication device, data from the controller are sent to a website that uses the latest weather forecast along with site-specific characteristics of the yard to adjust the amount of water applied. Taking a page from the farmers who pioneered precision agriculture, some of the new smart irrigation controllers are even using inexpensive sensors placed under the turf to determine when water has reached the desired depth.

Twenty years ago, you might have only found smart irrigation controllers at golf courses or in city parks, because the devices were too expensive and complicated for the average homeowner. But as with all electronic devices, prices have decreased even as the controllers have become easier to use and have acquired more extensive features. Currently a smart controller for a household sprinkler that can be operated by a homeowner costs less than two hundred dollars. With one of these simple devices, it is possible to reduce outdoor water use at a typical home by about 40 percent.[30]

Despite the great promise of smart controllers, the jury is still out on just how much the devices can actually reduce a city's overall water use. Water savings may turn out to be much lower than expected, because the installation of smart controllers by a utility requires a visit to the home from a trained lawn care specialist to set up the irrigation program. In controlled studies on randomly selected houses in the Southwest, the installation of smart controllers reduced water use by an average of only about 10 percent because the lawn care experts recognized that some of the homes had not been applying enough water prior to the start of the study. To realize the potential of larger water savings from smart controllers, utilities might be better off targeting their efforts to water hogs, using billing records to find and provide controllers to people who are presently overwatering their lawns.

Under a best-case scenario, a program that employs some combination of the water conservation techniques described earlier for homeowners, along with similar efforts aimed at commercial and industrial water users, might eventually reduce a city's overall water use by around 30 percent. A reduction in water use of this magnitude would certainly lower the impact of urban water systems on the environment. It would also save energy and improve the utility's long-term prospects for providing a water supply. But if we really want to tip the balance away from centralized systems, we will need to find additional water savings.

One obvious place to look for these savings is water reuse. As we have seen, nonpotable water reuse systems are already being used to irrigate golf courses, highway medians, and lawns of industrial parks throughout the country. But with the exception of a handful of water-stressed cities such as St. Petersburg, Florida, and Irvine, California, nonpotable water reuse has not yet caught on in residential communities. In part, this resistance is due to the high cost of installing and maintaining a second water distribution system in a preexisting development. Even in new housing developments, where the costs of installing the extra pipes are considerably lower, attempts to hook nonpotable reuse systems to single-family homes have been hampered by concerns about accidental cross-connections between reclaimed water and potable water systems as well as a reluctance among homeowners to apply treated wastewater to their lawns. If it were possible to recycle water at the scale of an individual household or a cluster of buildings, many of the problems associated with dual distribution systems would disappear. Furthermore, it is likely that people's reluctance to use reclaimed water would be diminished if they knew that they themselves were the source of the wastewater being applied to their lawns.

There are two schools of thought on household-scale nonpotable water reuse. The first employs the same approach employed in centralized nonpotable water reuse systems, but at the scale of an individual household or a cluster of homes. The other relies on separation of wastes into different streams prior to treatment and reuse. In its simplest manifestation, source separation segregates wastes from the toilet from those produced in all of the other parts of the home. This practice makes it easier to treat and reuse water, because the wastes draining from washing machines, showers, and sinks are less contaminated with organic matter, nutrients, and pathogens than the liquid and solid matter that goes down the toilet. It also cuts down on the user's fear of being exposed to toilet water.

The approach that keeps all of the wastes together still dominates most decentralized water reuse systems being developed in North America. This mode of wastewater treatment has a lot of staying power, because it builds on a century of experience in the operation of biological wastewater treatment plants. In addition, because the pipes leaving the house already mix all wastes from different sources together, it is easier to adopt the technology without the added expense of modifying existing indoor plumbing.

In the near term, one of the most practical ways of treating wastewater from single-family dwellings would be to convert septic systems into little biological wastewater treatment plants. A small upgrade is needed, because water from most existing septic systems cannot be reused easily in their current configuration. As they are currently used, septic systems rely on a two-step treatment process beginning in a concrete tank, where solid wastes accumulate and are broken down by microbes in the absence of oxygen. The water is then sent to the leach field, where the partially treated wastewater percolates into the soil after passing through a series of perforated underground pipes that distribute it over a wide area. Microbes in the soil break down the organic matter in the wastes and the plants growing on top of the leach field take up some of the nutrients. After percolating through the soil, the water might be clean enough to reuse, but there is no easy way to recapture it—to reuse the water, the septic tank must be modified.

Luckily, necessity has already created the technology needed for septic system upgrades. Today, when the population density of a suburb increases to a point where there is too much waste being sent to septic leach fields to effectively treat the community's wastewater without contaminating the groundwater, homeowners face the expensive prospect of replacing their septic systems with sewers and centralized wastewater treatment plants. To avoid these costs, entrepreneurs have taken advantage of the latest developments in biotechnology and electronics to produce retrofit kits that improve the treatment that occurs before the water is sent to the leach field. In other words, they have adapted technologies used in centralized treatment plants, such as aeration systems and recirculating pumps, to create household-scale wastewater treatment plants.[31] In towns where the driving force behind the retrofits is the prevention of groundwater contamination, the retrofits are often a cost-effective alternative to installation of sewers and centralized wastewater treatment plants. But all of that high-quality, treated water does not have to go to the leach field: during the irrigation season, treated water produced by the upgraded septic tank can be disinfected with chlorine or ultraviolet light before being applied to the lawn and garden.

Although retrofits might make a lot of sense in a neighborhood of single-family homes that are already equipped with old-fashioned septic tanks and leach fields, this approach is incompatible with higher population densities and local geology that is not conducive to water infiltration. Under these circumstances, decentralized water re-use can be achieved by building a network of tiny wastewater treatment plants in the basements of homes and apartment buildings. Computer-controlled devices that can treat a family's wastewater in the space occupied by a washing machine and a dryer have been around for about a decade.[32] The key to these autonomous, household-scale wastewater treatment plants is the membrane bioreactor, a technology that employs materials similar to those found in reverse-osmosis membranes—only with larger pores—to separate microbes from treated wastewater. By replacing the gravity-driven solids separation systems (used in the traditional activated sludge process) with a membrane, these new systems save a lot of space while simultaneously minimizing the release of noxious odors.

Membrane bioreactors have been used by the chemical industry for about forty years, but it wasn't until the early 1990s that they started to be utilized for sewage treatment.[33] During the past two decades, technology improvements and increased manufacturing know-how have reduced the price of membrane bioreactors by approximately a factor of thirty, while research and development have improved their performance and reliability. Using sensors that constantly monitor concentrations of oxygen and nutrients in the water, these little bioreactors adjust the flow of air and the timing of membrane cleaning cycles. They even have the ability to call for help: by way of an Internet connection, the bioreactor's sensors send data back to operators at a centralized facility who come out for needed repairs. And as with the upgraded septic tanks, treated wastewater can be sent to a holding tank, where it is disinfected with an ultraviolet light or chlorine prior to reuse.

Because the technology behind these miniature, high-tech wastewater treatment systems is still young, it is estimated that about half of the cost of operating a network of membrane bioreactors would be allocated to paying the salaries of technicians who maintain and re-

A membrane bioreactor used to treat wastewater generated by a dormitory at the Colorado School of Mines. To make the system more accessible for research, it has been placed inside of a portable trailer, but it could just as easily have been placed in a basement or an unobtrusive utility shed. Photo by T. Y. Cath, 2008.

pair the devices.[34] Including labor costs, running a network of distributed membrane bioreactors would cost around $3.40 per thousand liters ($13 per thousand gallons) of water produced. That's about five times more than the current cost of water reuse or desalination.

To control labor costs, most membrane-bioreactor-based water reuse systems are currently being targeted to the scale of an apartment building or a cluster of houses. With networks of membrane bioreactors of this size, the costs associated with decentralized, nonpotable water reuse would be lower, but the smaller number of treatment systems would still require some sort of dual plumbing network to distribute the treated water back to the places where it would be reused. Just as in the area of seawater desalination, we can hope that economies of scale in the manufacturing process and further technological improvements will eventually make these systems less expensive as they become more popular.

Networks of membrane bioreactors may eventually become economically competitive with centralized water reuse systems, but their real promise lies with the prospect that they might someday eliminate the need to connect houses to sewers and centralized wastewater treatment plants. Before we can use this technology to break free of the centralized wastewater disposal system, however, membrane bioreactors have to overcome one of the problems that killed the sewage farms of nineteenth-century England: irrigation demand decreases after the growing season ends, while the production of treated water remains constant. That is, for much of the year more reclaimed water will be produced than could be reasonably used for landscaping. If these systems are going to operate without being connected to a sewer, we'll have to find a place to put the excess water.

In some situations, it may be possible to put the excess water underground, using old-fashioned leach fields or groundwater injection wells to recharge shallow groundwater supplies. If the conditions are right, it might even be possible to reuse that water when the demand for irrigation picks up again in the spring.[35] Alternatively the treated water could be put into local streams and storm sewers, from where it would flow into urban rivers. This extra water could be a welcome addition in rivers whose flow has been partially rerouted into the drinking water supply. Unfortunately, replacing the missing flow in these urban rivers with wastewater effluent would probably lead to some of the same sorts of water pollution problems that are being encountered downstream of centralized wastewater treatment plants, such as feminization of fish and excessive algal growth, unless steps were taken to further treat this extra water.

Instead of building more complicated and expensive membrane bioreactors to address these potential water quality problems, it might be feasible to take advantage of the water-purifying capabilities of natural treatment systems. Engineered treatment wetlands—shallow ponds planted with cattails, bulrush, and other wetland plants—are well suited for the task. Manmade wetlands have proven to be effective in the removal of nutrients and trace organic contaminants, such as steroid hormones and pharmaceuticals, from wastewater effluent at centralized treatment plants.[36] By integrating treatment wetlands into a network of small streams that receive wastewater from membrane bioreactors, it may be possible to achieve the necessary level of treatment while simultaneously creating or improving wildlife habitat and green spaces in a suburban development.

The idea of coupling decentralized water reuse to wetlands and then using urban streams to move this reused water out of the city may not be quite ready for broad adoption by cities. Just like with earlier water technology innovations, demonstration projects would be needed to identify any unintended consequences of the practice and to familiarize utilities and their customers with this new approach to water treatment. Like all water solutions, we need to learn how to customize the systems for local conditions. Yet it seems clear that eventually some combination of technologies will make decentralized wastewater treatment coupled with natural treatment processes a viable alternative to centralized wastewater treatment in many types of settings.

The second approach to household-scale nonpotable water reuse relies on the separation of blackwater (urine and feces) from graywater (the waste stream that contains everything else) prior to treatment. The main advantage of waste segregation is that materials with a very different composition can be treated with technologies optimized for either energy recovery or water reuse. In addition, by keeping blackwater out of the reuse system, fears associated with the prospect of coming into contact with water from the toilet are eliminated.

Treatment systems for blackwater use microbes to convert the organic matter in the solid and liquid wastes into methane gas. These energy-producing systems are a lot more efficient if the wastes are not

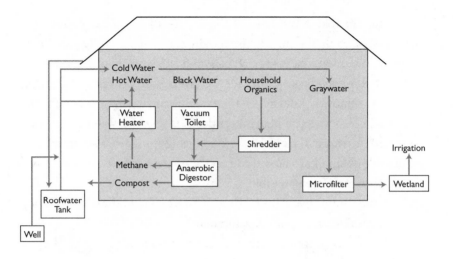

A possible configuration of an off-the-water-grid home. Separating the blackwater from the graywater may provide a more effective means of recovering energy and water from household wastes.

mixed with large volumes of water in a flush toilet prior to treatment. Keeping excess water out of the blackwater system means that a smaller bioreactor can be used and eliminates the need to treat large volumes of pathogen-contaminated water. But getting urine and feces to a bioreactor without adding a lot of water presents a new challenge: undoing nearly two centuries of habit and abandoning the gravity-flush toilet. Perhaps the idea of capturing undiluted blackwater is only exciting to environmental engineers. Anyone who has ever used a pit latrine on a camping trip knows that the average homeowner will not want one in his or her home. Luckily, the vacuum toilet provides an odorless means of moving wastes without water. These modern alternatives to the gravity-flush toilet look just like their more familiar cousins, but they include a suction system that allows the toilet to take care of business with only about a liter (0.25 gallons) of water per flush.[37] If the idea of a vacuum toilet seems far-fetched and impractical, think about the hundreds of thousands of people who already use these devices each day on commercial airplanes without incident.

Once the solids-laden blackwater leaves the vacuum toilet, microbes in the anaerobic digester convert the organic matter into methane much like Imhoff tanks did in the early years of wastewater treatment. But unlike the old days, when methane was an unwanted byproduct that was vented into the atmosphere or burned at the end of a stack, these modern treatment systems burn the methane to heat water or to power a small electrical generator. And as long as the home is equipped with a system for turning human wastes into energy, other forms of organic waste—food scraps, lawn clippings, and so on—can be turned into energy, too. In this way, a household blackwater treatment system can offset the energy used to power the vacuum toilet and run the membrane bioreactor for treating graywater.[38] It is worth noting that the same strategy of converting organic wastes to energy is already being used at centralized sewage treatment plants, where anaerobic treatment systems produce methane from the excess organic-rich solids derived from the activated sludge process.[39]

Graywater is usually less contaminated with waterborne pathogens and chemicals than blackwater, but it is still a good idea to treat it prior to reuse because it has enough waterborne pathogens to spread disease. It also contains suspended particles that could clog irrigation systems. Yet since graywater is nowhere near as dirty as blackwater or combined sewage, it can be treated with less expensive, low-tech approaches.[40] For example, in 2002 engineers in the German city of Lübeck installed a network of subsurface wetlands to treat the graywater produced by a four-hundred-person housing development.[41] This simple treatment system consists of shallow, gravel-filled trenches covered with wetland plants whose roots extend into the graywater. As the water flows slowly through the gravel bed, microbes living on the gravel and on the roots of the plants intercept waterborne pathogens and particles. The small amount of oxygen that leaks out of the roots supports microbes that speed up the breakdown of organic chemicals in the water. The plants, which are periodically harvested, also remove nutrients from the wastewater as they grow.

Subsurface wetlands are popular options for graywater treatment because they remain active when the air temperature drops below freezing. Routing the untreated graywater through the gravel also minimizes the likelihood that people will come into contact with waterborne pathogens. Subsurface wetlands can be pleasant landscaping features from a distance, but the stalks of wetland plants extending out of a gravel bed have an unnatural feel to them when viewed up close. As an alternative, surface flow wetlands—complete with little sections of open water to provide habitat for wildlife—can be used for treatment provided that the climate is warmer and provisions are made to prevent people from coming into contact with the pathogen-contaminated water.

Whether the water is treated in a low-tech treatment wetland or a state-of-the-art membrane bioreactor, there are still a number of unanswered questions about the long-term viability of graywater reuse, because the wastes contain a variety of salts and organic chemicals that could affect the health of plants.[42] For example, concerns have been raised about the effect on soil of surfactants in household cleaning products. These organic chemicals are a potential problem because they stick to the inner surfaces of the pores of soil. If the surfactant doesn't break down, an accumulation of surfactants in the soil could be detrimental to plants: after the pores are coated with surfactants, the rate at which water drains through the soil decreases, causing waterlogged soil conditions that damage plants.

In addition to problems associated with the accumulation of surfactants and other organic chemicals, soil scientists worry about the relatively high concentrations of salts present in graywater. In many of the arid regions where graywater reuse is most attractive, the buildup of salts in soil is already carefully monitored, because many ornamental plants will not grow at high salt concentrations. With the addition of more salt in graywater, soils might not be able to support the types of plants that people have become accustomed to having in their yards.

None of the unresolved issues related to graywater use appear to be intractable, but a long-term commitment to graywater use might require us to switch to more readily biodegradable soaps and other benign consumer products and to carefully regulate the amounts of different types of salts that we put down the drain.

Although graywater reuse may be technically feasible, it is not yet economically attractive in most locations. For example, the costs of installing and operating a wastewater treatment system for a new housing development in Canada with source separation, energy recovery, and graywater treatment was estimated to be about twice as much as that needed for a conventional, centralized treatment system.[43] The economics of graywater would be even less attractive for retrofits of existing neighborhoods. But circumstances might be a bit more favorable in arid regions than they are in the wet, cold places such as Canada and Central Europe that have been leading the drive toward graywater reuse, since projects designed to avoid the costs and pollution associated with centralized sewage treatment systems could be tied to a larger effort to reduce or eliminate expensive sources of imported water.

Indeed, the idea of using graywater instead of imported water, desalinated seawater, or water from centralized reuse systems is starting to resonate in water-stressed parts of the western United States and Australia.[44] In these locales, graywater reuse is becoming popular with members of the public who want to play a direct role in minimizing water consumption and the environmental impacts associated with supplying water to growing populations. Since the early 1990s, public awareness and support for graywater has intensified with each successive drought and then eased as conditions improved. But over the last few cycles, interest in graywater has even been growing between droughts.

Some of the increased interest in graywater can be traced to LEED-certified green buildings. Graywater reuse for toilet flushing or landscape irrigation in commercial buildings will probably never make much of a difference to the economics of centralized water supply and treatment if the water-saving measures are restricted to a handful of showcase buildings in the center of an existing water network. But these prototypes are still having an important influence: homeowners who see graywater reuse systems firsthand in state-of-the-art green buildings are often inspired to adopt the technology at home. Unfortunately, these new graywater enthusiasts are usually not supported by teams of green architects, engineers, and public health experts who know how to design safe graywater systems. Instead, for reasons of cost and convenience, many of the graywater reuse systems being installed in homes in many parts of the world consist simply of pipes that route untreated graywater from a sink or washing machine into a drip irrigation system in the yard. It's an expedient solution, but it is not without potential downsides.

The few available studies that have examined the health risks associated with the reuse of untreated graywater suggest that there are more than enough waterborne pathogens in graywater to spread disease. Although there are a number of places where untreated graywater has been used for subsurface irrigation for decades without incident, if the practice became more popular, it would only take a small number of households with malfunctioning or poorly designed systems to cause a public health problem.[45] In addition, a poorly designed graywater irrigation system has the potential to introduce pathogens into the potable water system if the two sources of water are connected to the same irrigation pipes without a backflow prevention device. These and other potential pitfalls associated with graywater reuse could be addressed through permits and periodic inspections as well as requirements for some type of disinfection system. But anything that increases the cost and barriers to graywater reuse is likely to limit its appeal. The current challenge for the broader adoption of graywater reuse is to direct the growing public enthusiasm for the practice into systems that are as safe and inexpensive as the established alternatives.

No matter which technology is employed, combining several of the water-conservation measures described earlier with decentralized water reuse at the scale of a single-family home or apartment building might reduce a city's potable water consumption by as much as 50 to 75 percent. Water savings of this magnitude could eliminate the need for most cities to build additional imported water systems or desalination plants for the foreseeable future. They might even allow them to abandon some of their most expensive and environmentally damaging water supplies. The biggest potential attraction is the possibility that a city might be able to break free of the water grid.

To realize the goal of eliminating their extensive centralized urban water distribution networks, most cities would have to tap into new, local water sources to make up for the decrease in imported water. One possibility for meeting these needs is to revive local water sources that were abandoned as cities grew up. For example, Los Angeles shut down a number of its drinking water supply wells when scientists detected contamination from industrial pollutants following the postwar development boom. When the wells were abandoned, it was still too expensive and difficult to clean up the groundwater and assure that it would not get contaminated again. As part of the city's new strategy for securing a future water supply, plans are now being drawn up to bring abandoned wells back into service and to better protect existing wells from contamination, with the allocation of around $970 million to treat and protect the groundwater.[46] This approach is now more feasible because engineers have gained a lot of experience from the cleanup of hazardous waste sites over the past thirty years. Switching from imported water to a network of local groundwater wells would not eliminate the city's need for a water distribution network, but its operational costs would be lower than that of the current imported water system.

Another place where cities might look in their search for local water sources is the gutter. As we learned earlier, urban drainage systems are essential to the protection of buildings and streets, but traditional approaches of using storm sewers or sewage treatment plants to move water out of the city are expensive and damaging to the environment. Newly popular alternatives discussed in Chapter 7, such as bioinfiltration systems and permeable pavement, can take the stress off of sewers by directing some of this water into the ground. This practice sometimes benefits local water supplies, but in many places the infiltrated water never reaches a drinking water aquifer. For instance, if a layer of clay blocks the path that the infiltrating water follows on its voyage to a deep aquifer, water will accumulate in the layer above the clay, known as the water table, which is rarely used as a drinking water source in modern cities. If the extra water causes the water table to rise to a point where it is close to the surface, basements and underground structures, such as tunnels and utility conduits, will leak. Whether or not the water causes damage, much of it will eventually make its way back to the surface via urban streams and rivers at lower elevations. It can also pass through cracks and leaky seals in sewer pipes, where it will increase the flow of storm sewers. Green infrastructure systems solve many of the problems associated with the existence of too many impervious surfaces by increasing the amount of time it takes for water to enter the urban drainage system, but unless the geology is conducive to aquifer recharge, these systems won't enhance the drinking water supply.

Would it make sense to build structures to capture and store precipitation above ground in places where it is impractical to try to recharge the drinking water aquifers? In part, the answer depends on the amount of water that could be captured. For a region that receives about a meter (thirty-nine inches) of precipitation per year and has a population density of around four thousand people per square kilometer (ten thousand people per square mile)—conditions typical of the Dallas–Fort Worth Metroplex or the Washington, D.C., metropolitan area—the amount of water that falls on the city is equivalent to about 640 liters (170 gallons) of water per person every day.[47] This amount of rainfall is about five to ten times more than what would be needed for a potable water supply if the city had implemented the conservation measures described here. Although it would be impossible to capture all of the water falling on an entire city, retaining just a fraction of the precipitation could go a long way toward breaking the imported water habit. And if they were designed properly, the capture and storage systems could help solve some of the problems associated with inadequate urban drainage systems.

The most practical approach for capturing precipitation in a manner that is consistent with the decentralized, local-water-supply approach would be to take advantage of the smooth surfaces and plumbing systems that already exist on the roofs of buildings. Roofwater harvesting is not a new idea. In fact, many early European civilizations obtained their drinking water from rooftop collection systems before the Romans perfected their system of reservoirs and aqueducts. Worldwide, roofwater harvesting has continued in rural communities and in places where groundwater and surface water supplies are inadequate. People living on islands with inadequate water supplies and in rural communities in Australia, Brazil, China, and India still rely on roofwater as their main drinking water source.[48] Among these places, the island of Bermuda is noteworthy because many people in this wealthy community drink roofwater.[49] In dry years, the rainwater tanks sometimes run low, and people pay for trucks to top them off. Nevertheless, the collection systems provide an average of about 130 liters (35 gallons) per day of water for each person living in single-family homes. Roofwater collection is a lot less practical in places with higher population densities, because the roof of an apartment building can only satisfy a small fraction of the water demands of the building's residents.

The decline in popularity of roofwater collection systems in developed countries was mainly attributable to the ease and low cost of hooking into piped water networks. Over the past decade, roofwater collection has seen a revival as a means of supplementing imported water supplies. But most of the new projects being built in developed countries are restricted to nonpotable applications, such as toilet flushing and landscape irrigation, because of concerns about water quality.[50] Indeed, depending on the location of the house, its proximity to trees, the diseases transmitted by local insects or animals, and the construction materials used for the roof surface and gutters, roofwater can pick up a variety of microbial pathogens as well as toxic metals and petroleum products. Failure to remove regularly the sediments that accumulate in storage tanks can exacerbate the problem, by providing places for microbes to grow and chemicals to leach into the water.

Although roofwater could provide another nonpotable water source to supplement reclaimed sewage or graywater, it would be more beneficial if it could be used as drinking water. Roofwater has survived as a potable water source in Bermuda and rural Australia because people have stuck with designs and maintenance regimens that minimize water contamination. For example, roofs in Bermuda are made of local limestone that does not leach organic chemicals or metals. In addition, homeowners are required to clean sediments from their collection tanks on a regular basis. But even in the places where people still drink roofwater, it usually contains concentrations of fecal bacteria from birds and wildlife that exceed the accepted standards.[51] The absence of major public health problems among the roofwater holdouts might thus be sheer luck—low levels of waterborne pathogens in the creatures that defecate on those roofs. Due to concerns that this good record would not continue if the practice were to expand, it is unlikely that city dwellers in developed countries could ever return to consuming untreated roofwater. Instead, for roofwater to be viable as a potable water source in developed countries, inexpensive, low-maintenance treatment systems will be needed.

Household-scale systems for treating roofwater that are equipped with ozone or ultraviolet light coupled with reverse osmosis are starting to become practical, but the prices will have to come down before the owners of single-family homes in developed countries will find it advantageous to obtain their drinking water from the roof. Perhaps in the future inexpensive and reliable treatment technologies, coupled with the prospect of breaking free of the water grid, will drive people living in single-family homes to start drinking roofwater again. If they do, they will have to accept the possibility that their tanks might need to be topped off by a water delivery truck in dry years. But unless roofwater offers a way of breaking free of imported water supplies, it is hard to see how the practice is ever going to be economically attractive.

Another factor working against roofwater consumption and any other approach to supplying water without a centralized distribution system is the need to have massive volumes of water available at short notice when a fire breaks out. The current approach to firefighting in most countries requires a reliable network of wide-diameter, pressurized water pipes capable of delivering anywhere from around 4,000 liters per minute (1,100 gallons per minute) of water to fight fires in single family homes to 20,000 liters per minute (5,200 gallons per minute) for firefighting at commercial buildings.[52] Communities that choose not to meet these standards are considered out of compliance by fire insurance companies—a condition that would likely result in high premiums for homeowners and political pressure to switch to conventional high-pressure water distribution systems.

Arguably, a lot has changed since firefighting practices were established in the first half of the twentieth century. Household wiring and appliances are safer, tobacco consumption has decreased, and cigarettes are designed to extinguish themselves if left unattended. Given the challenges associated with maintaining a network of large, underground water pipes, perhaps it's time to revisit our assumptions about firefighting. It seems as if we may always need wide-diameter, pressurized water pipes in the most densely populated parts of our cities, but the lower-density neighborhoods where distributed water systems are most attractive might be able to survive without fire hydrants and the expensive infrastructure that is required to assure that large volumes of water will be available at a moment's notice. For example, in Germany, where the water distribution system is not considered the main source of water for firefighting, fire trucks often pump water out of local ponds and streams. When natural water bodies are not available, developers and homeowners are often required to build water storage ponds or tanks for fire protection. It also may be feasible to reduce the demand for large volumes of water for firefighting by mandating home sprinkler systems or by providing firefighters with other tools, like foams that can be used to smother fires.[53]

If a decentralized drinking water supply that employs roofwater is not yet practical, perhaps it would be possible to capture the mixture of roofwater and runoff from paved surfaces and treat it to a point where it can be put into the centralized drinking water distribution system. Although this approach would not eliminate the need for an underground pipe network, it would provide an alternative to imported water.

As was the case with roofwater, most efforts to capture and store urban runoff are still focused on nonpotable applications. The hesitancy to drink urban runoff may be related to its origins: this water source was often an afterthought to efforts to prevent combined sewer overflows. According to this logic, as long as you were going through the effort to capture urban runoff, you might as well use the low-quality water for irrigation and toilet flushing. Systems that capture urban runoff and subject it to simple treatment, with wetlands or sand filtration, are becoming popular for new housing developments in Australia and parts of the United States, but the economic benefits of this form of urban runoff reuse are usually small relative to the overall cost of the projects.[54]

Larger projects that capture and reuse urban runoff from an entire neighborhood, while still uncommon, have been built in recent decades. For example, Santa Monica, California, invested $12 million to capture and reuse urban runoff that was contaminating its beloved beaches with waterborne pathogens.[55] The Santa Monica Urban Runoff Recycling Facility (SMURRF) uses microfiltration membranes and ultraviolet disinfection to treat dry weather runoff. Dry weather runoff may seem like an oxymoron, but when it is not raining the water that flows through the city's storm sewers from sprinkler systems, people washing their cars in the streets, and other activities is a lot more polluted than the water that flows into the sewers on rainy days. After treatment, the facility provides approximately 1.1 million liters (300,000 gallons) per day of water for landscape irrigation and toilet flushing in the neighborhood along the beach. Although the name is no longer recognized as cute now that the little blue cartoon characters called Smurfs have largely been forgotten, the increased visibility of the beach protection project that provides a new source of water is probably enough to justify the extra expense associated with the storage and distribution of the water. But that does not mean that other communities are rushing to replicate the project.

If urban runoff is ever going to help cities eliminate the need for imported water, we will have to find a way to put the water from urban runoff back into the local drinking water system. This essential next step in the development of local water supplies could follow two possible paths. The first would be to use advanced treatment technologies such as reverse osmosis and disinfection with ultraviolet light to make urban runoff safe to drink. As we have seen, these technologies can turn sewage effluent or seawater into drinking water. They could also purify urban runoff, but the cost of such projects would be five to ten times higher than it would be for treating wastewater effluent or seawater, because the reuse of urban runoff would require the construction of new storage and capture systems.[56] The treatment plant would also have to deal with water of highly variable quality, which complicates treatment and drives up costs. A runoff recycling facility would have the added benefit of addressing urban drainage and might be more acceptable to the public than potable water reuse or seawater desalination, but the economic reality is that it is unlikely to be chosen over less expensive water-supply options.

The other approach would be to keep urban runoff from getting too polluted in the first place and sending the water to urban drinking water reservoirs. This idea is not as out of reach as it might seem. After all, there are plenty of cities that draw their drinking water downstream of the discharges of storm sewers. In essence, they already have urban runoff reservoirs—only they are located outside of the city. For those cities, urban runoff is converted into drinking water through a combination of dilution with water from more pristine sources and conventional drinking water treatment.

Some cities have already built systems to route urban runoff to reservoirs located within the city. In Singapore, urban runoff is piped directly into drinking water reservoirs with little or no dilution with pristine water.[57] Through an elaborate system of stormwater interception basins, nearly all of the rain that falls on the streets and buildings of the city's populated residential neighborhoods is captured by a network of urban reservoirs. In part, Singapore has been able to achieve this goal because the city and surrounding region receive monsoon rains that dump large quantities of water over a short period of time. The high quality of the city's runoff is also attributable to the vigilance of the national water utility and city planning agencies in preventing sewer leaks and the rigorous enforcement of laws related to land use, automobile maintenance, and the application of chemicals on buildings and gardens.

Because of differences in climate and political systems, this approach probably would not translate easily to many other developed countries. But contamination of urban runoff could be reduced by a combination of low-impact development and policies designed to minimize further contamination of runoff after it leaves an individual property. With some investment in clean streets and functioning sewer systems, coupled with vigilance about land development and chemical use, urban runoff might someday become an important part of our drinking water supply.

13

Reflections

Modern urban water systems are unobtrusive by design. The pipes that bring water to our homes, drain our streets, and transport our wastes are hidden underground. Treatment plants are tucked away on the water's edge or are located on a side street in an obscure part of the city that almost nobody visits. Even the huge reservoirs that hold our drinking water are usually locked behind fences in protected watersheds. By handing the management of water over to the professionals, we have reduced our daily encounters with the water cycle to the turning of a faucet and the flushing of a toilet. That's exactly the way we have wanted it since the days of the first Roman aqueduct.

When we absentmindedly pay the monthly water bill, we are not only buying water, pipes, and treatment plants, but also hiring someone to sweat the details for us. There is nothing unique about this behavior. We act the same way when it comes to many other elements of modern life—food, electricity, cell phone, and cable television bills—as well as toward the countless day-to-day decisions that need to be made about the infrastructure that supports our daily lives and lifestyles. As long as our bills are paid and the service continues, we assume that the people who provide the service and the government officials responsible for overseeing their activities will make sure that we are safe. For people in a complex, modern world, it's difficult to imagine living any other way.

But there is something special about water. In most situations, it's probably reasonable to delegate decisions about infrastructure to others and to form our opinions about the quality of service on the basis of price, convenience, and personal tastes. These three attributes are certainly an important means of assessing the adequacy of urban water systems. But they are not enough: after all, decisions about how we obtain and dispose of water have important implications for our health, the environment, and the long-term viability of society. Putting a little effort into becoming better informed about urban water systems is a necessary first step in navigating the water challenges that society will face in the coming decades.

Looking back at the development of urban water, it is evident that we have inherited a complex system that evolved to meet a variety of needs. After the two thousand years of trial and error that went into developing an approach for managing the urban water cycle, it would be a mistake to simply throw it all away and start over. Imported water, centralized treatment and distribution systems, storm sewers, biological wastewater treatment processes, and many other inventions have made it possible for people living in the developed world to put aside their worries about whether or not there will be enough water to drink, if the water they use will make them sick, or if their streets and homes will flood after the next rainstorm. As people living in rapidly growing cities of the developing world acquire the economic means to upgrade their inadequate water systems, they will seek the safety and reliability that are taken for granted in wealthy countries. Any attempt to alter the designs of these complex systems will have to be made in a way that does not interfere with their ability to deliver these essential functions.

Studying the history of urban water also provides us with an understanding of the difficulties faced by those who have tried to change the system. Urban water infrastructure is one of the biggest investments that we make in our cities, so it's built to last. Extreme durability makes it possible to borrow money to finance massive water infrastructure projects, but it also means that there is little incentive for the operators of the systems to adopt unproven technologies prematurely. Absent a few modest improvements, most cities are still managing to survive with Water 3.0, often delivering drinking water, disposing of sewage, and draining streets with pipes and treatment plants that were built fifty to a hundred years ago.

Before the twentieth century, major technological advances occurred over the span of multiple decades. This slow rate of change was not much of a problem, unless a major crisis arose that could only be solved with a new approach. For urban water systems, incremental improvements resulting from better designs and construction materials could wait until the parts were so worn out that they could no longer be repaired. But the rate of technological change is accelerating in the modern world. A state-of-the-art computer is obsolete after five years. High-performance plastics and composite materials make it possible to achieve dramatic improvements in the fuel efficiency of cars and airplanes with each new model. And exponential progress is being made in the development of tools to manipulate biological systems. With the benefits of technology resulting in rapid improvement to so many facets of modern life, the failure of urban water systems to more quickly adopt innovative new technologies is a missed opportunity.

Although no physical limitation keeps the latest innovations in computing, materials science, and biotechnology out of urban water systems, our assumption that continued investment in water is unnecessary removes many of the normal incentives for innovation. It's a lot easier to justify substantial research and development budgets for an electronic device that has a global market and will be replaced within five years than it is to lay down money for research on a bunch of custom-made pipe and concrete water networks that are supposed to last for a century. The meager budgets for research and development that follow from this mindset are unfortunate, because technological innovations can make a dramatic difference for water, too. As we saw, the Kennedy administration's desire to provide the world with an inexpensive means of obtaining drinking water from the sea ultimately led to the development of the reverse osmosis membranes that are now essential parts of modern seawater desalination plants and water recycling systems. An entrepreneur tinkering away in a garage in Silicon Valley did not invent reverse osmosis membranes; they came from a sustained, government-funded effort that supported fundamental research, built demonstration projects, and subsidized first-generation treatment systems.

History also teaches us the importance of crisis as a catalyst for change. Although shortcomings in outdated or underperforming urban water systems become evident as people complain that the water smells bad or that there are too many dead fish washing up on the shore, there is generally not enough political will or funding to bring about improvements until an exceptional event catches the public's attention. London's Great Stink; a typhoid fever outbreak in Lawrence, Massachusetts; a fire on the Cuyahoga River; a television program about cancer in New Orleans; lead in Washington, D.C.'s drinking water; and a decade-long drought in Australia are all examples of well-publicized failures that galvanized the public's desire for change. Once a desire for action has been established, the search for a technological fix begins. Quite often the solution is developed on the front lines of the battle—the cities facing the toughest problems—and from there the solutions spread to the rest of the world.

That's not to say that the cycle of failure, publicity, innovation, and investment is the only way that urban water systems can change. Sometimes necessity provides an economic incentive for creative and persistent people to develop new technologies. Rapid sand filters, low-flow household appliances, and biological-nutrient-removal wastewater treatment plants are examples of now commonplace technologies that were motivated by the monetary payoff that would accompany innovations that made urban water systems more efficient. Today the rising cost of energy and concerns about future taxes on greenhouse gas emissions are sparking innovations in centralized water and waste-water treatment systems. Entrepreneurs are seeking ways to reduce energy consumption with more efficient pump designs and are forming startup companies to install miniature hydroelectric generators and heat exchangers in water and sewer systems to capture excess energy that is currently being wasted. The operators of centralized water systems are joining the movement by developing approaches for generating all of the electricity needed to operate their wastewater treatment plants by turning the organic matter in sewage into electricity.

This pathway to the evolution of urban water systems may take the edge off some of our future crises, especially if it is coupled to economic incentives and flexible policies that lower some of the risks inherent in experimentation. Along with increased energy efficiency, I am hopeful that this form of innovation will lead to improvements in urban drainage systems, like the low-impact development projects that are being installed to reduce the frequency of combined sewer overflows in Philadelphia. The prospect of saving money has already led to improvements in smart irrigation systems and water-saving home appliances, efforts that hopefully will continue.

But although these types of activities may free up money for investments in maintenance and system upgrades, they will not solve all of our future problems. Reflecting on the current state of affairs and the ways that urban water systems evolve, I predict that over the next two decades cities will be pushed to start building the next generation of urban water solutions—Water 4.0—as their water supplies and urban drainage systems fail to keep up with the effects of climate change and population growth, and as public opinion and new scientific data clarify the need to address previously underappreciated forms of pollution. I anticipate that change will arrive first in cities where extreme weather patterns create situations that cannot be easily remedied with water rationing or the construction of a few more storm sewers. By necessity, these places will serve as the laboratories where the rest of the owner's manual for Water 4.0 will be written. Through this crisis-driven process, I predict we will develop two distinct types of blueprints for the next generation of urban water systems.

In terms of water supply, the first version of Water 4.0 will look a lot like the upgraded, centralized systems that are emerging in Singapore and the water-stressed cities of Southern California, Australia, and Israel. As part of this approach, imported water will be supplemented or replaced by desalination and potable water recycling employed in conjunction with a full arsenal of policies designed to incentivize water conservation. Waste treatment will also look a lot different in this version of Water 4.0: centralized sewage treatment plants will evolve from a means of protecting surface waters from pollution to systems that recover water, energy, and nutrients from sewage. In this future, there will no longer be separate divisions within cities or utilities dedicated exclusively to water supply, sewage treatment, or urban drainage. Instead, we will manage water holistically and will integrate the natural environment into water conveyance and treatment systems.

The other version of Water 4.0 takes a more radical approach to urban water by pushing the responsibility for acquisition, treatment, and management of water back to the individual household or neighborhood. In the distributed version of Water 4.0, a shift in public attitudes will make it possible to reduce consumptive water use by around 75 percent through the installation of ultraefficient appliances and elimination of wasteful forms of outdoor water use. In the distributed water future, landscape irrigation with drinking water will be unthinkable, and rooftop rainwater collection tanks, rain gardens, and household wells will be common features of housing developments. In areas where conditions are right, housing developments will operate without help from the expensive and difficult-to-maintain centralized water infrastructure. By necessity, the distributed version of Water 4.0 will have to exist in conjunction with some sort of centralized system because it won't be possible to abandon the underground pipes and treatment plants that serve the most densely populated parts of our cities. Even so, a future that includes the distributed version of Water 4.0 would feature the disappearance of the water grid from many less-populated urban and suburban areas.

The operating manual for the distributed version of Water 4.0 is a lot further from completion than that of its centralized counterpart. Nonetheless, I am confident that we can figure out the technical details of these seemingly radical changes. A key barrier to adoption of the distributed version of Water 4.0 will be the public's continuing desire to ignore water management. Unless activities like graywater recycling and rain gardens are embraced beyond a core group of enthusiasts, I doubt that we'll ever move off the centralized water path.

If we are serious about building the distributed version of Water 4.0 or its centralized counterpart, a large fraction of the population will have to be involved. Where should we start? Due to the complex nature of urban water systems and the importance of site-specific conditions like climate, topography, geology, and population density there is no simple, one-size-fits-all answer. But there are some actions that we can all take without radically changing our lifestyles. These small steps can help minimize the impacts of our existing system on the environment while simultaneously saving money. They also are the first stage of a longer-term effort to remake public attitudes about water.

To reduce your water use, install water-saving appliances and change your landscaping habits. Purchasing a front-loading washing machine and installing modern, low-flow fixtures can result in a substantial decrease in your indoor water use while simultaneously saving money on water and heating bills. Replacing parts of your lawn with plants that consume less water and installing drip irrigation systems can be an effective tool in reducing outdoor water use. But it's not the only viable approach. A modest investment in a smart irrigation controller or a tune-up of an existing landscape irrigation system can often result in significant water savings.

Modest behavioral changes also can protect aquatic ecosystems and downstream water supplies from pollution. If you are concerned about the effects of organic compounds in sewage effluent on rivers and drinking water aquifers you can make a difference by paying attention to the household products that you use and ultimately put down the drain. Reduce the impacts of pesticides and nutrients in urban runoff by using only what is needed to maintain your property or by changing your expectations about the urban landscape. If it makes sense for your location, rethink the ways that rainwater moves across your property by directing water away from impervious surfaces. Think about the storm sewer as if it were connected to your faucet (which in a way, it is): don't wash your car in the street and don't pour used oil, unwanted coffee, and rinse water from dirty paint brushes into the gutter.

Most importantly from the standpoint of bringing about lasting change, raise awareness within your community about the importance of figuring out the right path for a local version of Water 4.0. Your water utility and the government that regulates its actions pay attention to public opinion. Until now, members of the public who worry about excessive spending on water projects have often dominated the dialogue. Make sure your opinions are heard: when decisions are being made about water infrastructure investments, speak up about the need to consider both climate change and chemicals that pose risks to human health and the environment.

Ultimately, no one person or small group of people will determine the path that urban water systems will follow. The map to our future will be drawn collectively by the thousands of small decisions made in our homes, at community meetings, and in the voting booth. We all have a role to play in determining when Water 4.0 will become a reality and what it will look like when we build it. Once we better understand the costs and benefits of different approaches, we can make informed choices about supporting or opposing investments in desalination plants, potable reuse systems, graywater recycling sys-

tems, and other new forms of infrastructure. We need to start learning and working on Water 4.0 now because the simple and inexpensive
responses that have helped us in the past are not going to be enough to
get us through future challenges. The time has come to secure the
water future we want before a crisis forces it upon us.

Notes

Chapter 1. Water Supply in Rome

1. C. E. N. Bromehead, "The Early History of Water-Supply," *Geographical Journal* 99, no. 3 (1942).
2. P. W. English, "The Origin and Spread of Qanats in the Old World," *Proceedings of the American Philosophical Society* 112, no. 3 (1968).
3. Bromehead, "Early History of Water-Supply."
4. S. J. Burian et al., "Historical Development of Wet-Weather Flow Management," *Journal of Water Resources Planning and Management (ASCE)* 125, no. 1 (1999).
5. G. R. Storey, "The Population of Ancient Rome," *Antiquity* 71, no. 274 (1997); A. T. Hodge, *Roman Aqueducts and Water Supply,* 2d ed. (London: Duckworth, 2002).
6. Anon., "The Water Supply of Ancient Roman Cities," in *Scientific American Supplement* (New York: Scientific American, 1886).
7. H. Chanson, "The Hydraulics of Roman Aqueducts: What Do We Know? Why Should We Learn?," in *World Environmental and Water Resources Congress, 2008 Ahupua'a* (Reston, VA: American Society of Civil Engineers, 2008).
8. R. D. Hansen, "Water and Wastewater in Imperial Rome," *Water Resources Bulletin* 19, no. 2 (1983).
9. N. Smith, "Roman Hydraulic Technology," *Scientific American* 238, no. 5 (1978).
10. J. Salzman, "Thirst: A Short History of Drinking Water," *Duke Law School Legal Studies Research Paper Series* 92 (2005).
11. Ibid.; D. Karmon, "Restoring the Ancient Water Supply System in Renaissance Rome: The Popes, the Civic Administration, and the Acqua Vergine," *Waters of Rome* 3, no. 1 (2005).
12. Smith, "Roman Hydraulic Technology."
13. Chanson, "Hydraulics of Roman Aqueducts."
14. Hansen, "Water and Wastewater in Imperial Rome."
15. Smith, "Roman Hydraulic Technology."
16. Anon., "Water Supply of Ancient Roman Cities"; Hansen, "Water and Wastewater in Imperial Rome."

17. Hansen, "Water and Wastewater in Imperial Rome"; Hodge, *Roman Aqueducts and Water Supply.*
18. Chanson, "Hydraulics of Roman Aqueducts."
19. Hodge, *Roman Aqueducts and Water Supply.*
20. Hansen, "Water and Wastewater in Imperial Rome."
21. A. T. Hodge, "Vitruvius, Lead Pipes and Lead-Poisoning," *American Journal of Archaeology* 85, no. 4 (1981).
22. J. O. Nriagu, "Saturnine Gout among Roman Aristocrats—Did Lead-Poisoning Contribute to the Fall of the Empire?," *New England Journal of Medicine* 308, no. 11 (1983).
23. J. Scarborough, "Lead and Lead-Poisoning in Antiquity—Nriagu, J. O.," *Journal of the History of Medicine and Allied Sciences* 39, no. 4 (1984).
24. Hodge, "Vitruvius, Lead Pipes and Lead-Poisoning."
25. Ibid.
26. C. E. Spencer, *Revised Guidance Manual for Selecting Lead and Copper Control Technologies* (Washington, D.C.: U.S. Environmental Protection Agency, 2003).
27. Anon., "Water Supply of Ancient Roman Cities"; Hansen, "Water and Wastewater in Imperial Rome."
28. Hansen, "Water and Wastewater in Imperial Rome"; Bromehead, "Early History of Water-Supply."
29. A. T. Hodge, "In Vitruvium Pompeianum: Urban Water Distribution Reappraised," *American Journal of Archaeology* 100, no. 2 (1996); Hodge, *Roman Aqueducts and Water Supply.* Vitruvius, in his treatise on Roman water supplies, had suggested a means of completely cutting off the flow of water to baths and private homes during droughts, but his advice was never followed.
30. Hansen, "Water and Wastewater in Imperial Rome."
31. Hodge, "Vitruvius, Lead Pipes and Lead-Poisoning."
32. J. N. N. Hopkins, "The Cloaca Maxima and the Monumental Manipulation of Water in Archaic Rome," *Waters of Rome* 4, no. 1 (2007).
33. J. C. Schladweiler, "Cloacina: Goddess of the Sewers," *sewerhistory.org* (2010), available at http://www.sewerhistory.org/articles/wh_era/cloacina/cloacina.pdf.
34. J. R. Stone, *The Routledge Book of Latin Quotations* (New York: Routledge, 2005).
35. T. A. Larsen et al., "Nutrient Cycles and Resource Management: Implications for the Choice of Wastewater Treatment Technology," *Water Science and Technology* 56, no. 5 (2007).

36. Karmon, "Restoring the Ancient Water Supply System in Renaissance Rome."

Chapter 2. The Bucket Era

1. L. Mumford, *The Culture of Cities* (New York: Harcourt, Brace, 1938).
2. R. Johnson, *All Things Medieval: An Encyclopedia of the Medieval World* (Westport, CT: ABC-CLIO, 2011).
3. R. J. Magnusson, *Water Technology in the Middle Ages* (Baltimore: Johns Hopkins University Press, 2001).
4. Ibid.; B. Krekic, "Notes on Provision of Water to the City of Dubrovnik in the Fifteenth and Sixteenth Centuries," in *Central and Eastern Europe in the Middle Ages: A Cultural History,* ed. N. Deusen and P. S. Van Gorecki (London: I. B. Tauris, 2009).
5. Magnusson, *Water Technology in the Middle Ages.*
6. M. Illi, *Von der Schîssgruob zur modernen Stadtentwässerung* (Zurich: Neue Zürcher Zeitung, 1987).
7. Magnusson, *Water Technology in the Middle Ages.*
8. C. S. Sterner, "Waste and City Form: Reconsidering the Medieval Strategy," *Journal of Green Building* 3, no. 3 (2008).
9. Magnusson, *Water Technology in the Middle Ages.*
10. Ibid.
11. C. E. N. Bromehead, "The Early History of Water-Supply," *Geographical Journal* 99, no. 4 (1942).
12. Anon., "The Diana Association," available at http://faculty.washington.edu /kucher/diana/english/index.html.
13. Ibid.
14. Ibid.
15. Magnusson, *Water Technology in the Middle Ages.*
16. F. Schevill, *Siena: The History of a Mediaeval Commune* (New York: Harper and Row, 1909).
17. Magnusson, *Water Technology in the Middle Ages.*
18. Mumford, *The Culture of Cities.*
19. A. D. Brown, *Feed or Feedback: Agriculture, Population Dynamics and the State of the Planet* (Utrecht, Neth.: International Books, 2003).
20. W. Laqueur, *The Changing Face of Anti-Semitism: From Ancient Times to the Present Day* (New York: Oxford University Press, 2006).
21. Brown, *Feed or Feedback.*
22. S. Johnson, *The Ghost Map* (New York: Riverhead Books, 2006).
23. Sterner, "Waste and City Form."

24. C. Pedretti, *Leonardo da Vinci: The Royal Palace at Romorantin* (Cambridge, MA: Harvard University Press, 1972).

25. Brown, *Feed or Feedback.*

26. Illi, *Von der Schissgruob zur modernen Stadtentwässerung.*

27. A. Macfarlane, "The Non-Use of Night Soil in England" (2002), available at http://www.alanmacfarlane.com/savage/A-NIGHT.PDF.

28. S. B. Hanley, "Urban Sanitation in Preindustrial Japan," *Journal of Interdisciplinary History* 18, no. 1 (1987).

29. C. De Decker, "Recycling Animal and Human Dung Is the Key to Sustainable Farming," *Low-Tech Magazine,* Sept. 15, 2010.

Chapter 3. Europe's Sewage Crisis

1. R. D. Hansen, "Water-Related Infrastructure in Medieval London," available at http://www.waterhistory.org/histories/london; C. E. N. Bromehead, "The Early History of Water-Supply," *Geographical Journal* 99, no. 4 (1942).

2. Hansen, "Water-Related Infrastructure in Medieval London."

3. T. G. Smollett, *The Expedition of Humphry Clinker* (N.p., 1857), p. 96.

4. T. M. Walski, "A History of Water Distribution," *Journal of the American Water Works Association* 98, no. 3 (2006).

5. Anon., "Description for London Bridge Waterworks Company Purchase Records," ed. London Metropolitan Archives (London, 1822), available at the National Archives, http://www.nationalarchives.gov.uk//a2a/records.aspx?cat=074-acc2558_3&cid=10&kw=kent%20river%20board#10.

6. P. F. Cooper, "Historical Aspects of Wastewater Treatment," in *Decentralised Sanitation and Reuse,* ed. G. Zeeman, P. Lens, and G. Lettinga (London: International Water Association, 2001).

7. R. M. McHiggins, "The 1832 Cholera Epidemic in East London," *East London Record* 2 (1979).

8. Cooper, "Historical Aspects of Wastewater Treatment."

9. S. Johnson, *The Ghost Map* (New York: Riverhead Books, 2006).

10. W. T. Sedgwick, *Principles of Sanitary Science and the Public Health* (London: Macmillan, 1914).

11. Cooper, "Historical Aspects of Wastewater Treatment."

12. R. R. Frerichs, "John Snow Web Site," available at http://www.ph.ucla.edu/epi/snow.html.

13. M. N. Baker, *The Quest for Pure Water,* vol. 1, 2d ed. (Denver: American Water Works Association, 1981).

14. Cooper, "Historical Aspects of Wastewater Treatment."

15. J. von Liebig and J. J. Mechi, "The Sewage of Towns," *Farmer's Magazine* (1860).

16. N. Goddard, " 'A Mine of Wealth'? The Victorians and the Agricultural Value of Sewage," *Journal of Historical Geography* 22, no. 3 (1996).

17. J. D. Thompson, "The Great Stench or the Fool's Argument," *Yale Journal of Biology and Medicine* 64, no. 5 (1991); S. Halliday, *The Great Stink of London: Sir Joseph Bazalgette and the Cleansing of the Victorian Capital* (Charleston, SC: History Press, 1999).

18. S. Barles, "Urban Metabolism and River Systems: An Historical Perspective—Paris and the Seine, 1790–1970," *Hydrology and Earth System Sciences* 11, no. 6 (2007).

19. D. Reid, *Paris Sewers and Sewermen: Realities and Representations* (Cambridge, MA: Harvard University Press, 1991); Cooper, "Historical Aspects of Wastewater Treatment."

20. Reid, *Paris Sewers and Sewermen.*

21. Cooper, "Historical Aspects of Wastewater Treatment."

22. Ibid.

23. Reid, *Paris Sewers and Sewermen.*

24. Barles, "Urban Metabolism and River Systems."

25. Reid, *Paris Sewers and Sewermen.*

26. Barles, "Urban Metabolism and River Systems."

27. Reid, *Paris Sewers and Sewermen.*

28. Ibid.

29. Anon., "Sewage Utilization near Paris," *Scientific American* (1877).

30. V. Hugo, *Les Misérables,* vol. 5 (Fairfield, IA: 1st World Library, 2007).

31. P. Burkett, *Marx and Nature: A Red and Green Perspective* (New York: St. Martin's, 1999).

32. Reid, *Paris Sewers and Sewermen.*

33. C. Hamlin, "Sewage—Waste or Resource?," *Environment* 22, no. 8 (1980).

34. Barles, "Urban Metabolism and River Systems."

35. Reid, *Paris Sewers and Sewermen.*

36. Goddard, " 'A Mine of Wealth'?"

37. Hamlin, "Sewage—Waste or Resource?"

38. Barles, "Urban Metabolism and River Systems."

39. Goddard, " 'A Mine of Wealth'?"

Chapter 4. Growing Old Thanks to Water Treatment

1. C. E. Rosenberg, *The Cholera Years* (Chicago: University of Chicago Press, 1962); M. V. Melosi, *The Sanitary City: Urban Infrastructure in America*

from Colonial Times to the Present (Baltimore: Johns Hopkins University Press, 2000).

2. L. P. Cain, "Unfouling the Public's Nest—Chicago's Sanitary Diversion of Lake Michigan Water," *Technology and Culture* 15, no. 4 (1974).

3. W. T. Sedgwick, *Principles of Sanitary Science and the Public Health* (London: Macmillan, 1914).

4. Anon., "History of Lowell, Massachusetts," available at http://www.lowell .com/city-of-lowell/lowell-history.

5. M. N. Baker, *The Quest for Pure Water,* vol. 1, 2d ed. (Denver, CO: American Water Works Association, 1981).

6. Sedgwick, *Principles of Sanitary Science and the Public Health.*

7. D. Schoenen, "Role of Disinfection in Suppressing the Spread of Pathogens with Drinking Water: Possibilities and Limitations," *Water Research* 36, no. 15 (2002).

8. T. E. Bell, "Designing against Disease," *The Bent of Tau Beta Pi* (2010), quoting the *Annual Report of the Cambridge, MA Water Company* (Cambridge, MA: Harvard Printing Company, 1891), p. 63.

9. Sedgwick, *Principles of Sanitary Science and the Public Health.*

10. Baker, *Quest for Pure Water.*

11. Melosi, *Sanitary City,* quotation on p. 57.

12. Anon., "Pollution of Streams; Self-Purification," *The Independent* (1889).

13. Sedgwick, *Principles of Sanitary Science and the Public Health.*

14. B. G. Rosenkrantz, *Public Health and the State: Changing Views in Massachusetts, 1842–1936* (Cambridge, MA: Harvard University Press, 1972).

15. *Background Document: The Diagnosis, Treatment and Prevention of Typhoid Fever* (Geneva: World Health Organization, 2003).

16. Baker, *Quest for Pure Water.*

17. Ibid.; A. Hazen, *Clean Water and How to Get It* (New York: John Wiley and Sons, 1909).

18. Quoted in Baker, *Quest for Pure Water.*

19. H. W. Clark, "An Outline of Sewage Purification Studies at the Lawrence Experiment Station," *Industrial and Engineering Chemistry* 19, no. 1 (1927).

20. C. Hamlin, "Sewage—Waste or Resource?" *Environment* 22, no. 8 (1980).

21. P. F. Cooper, "Historical Aspects of Wastewater Treatment," in *Decentralised Sanitation and Reuse,* ed. G. Zeeman, P. Lens, and G. Lettinga (London: International Water Association, 2001).

22. Clark, "Outline of Sewage Purification Studies at the Lawrence Experiment Station."

23. Baker, *Quest for Pure Water.*

24. Sedgwick, *Principles of Sanitary Science and the Public Health*; G. E. Waring, "Out of Sight, Out of Mind," *Century Illustrated Magazine* (1894); Anon., "Purification of Drinking Water by Means of Filtration," *Scientific American* (1896).

25. G. A. Johnson, "Hypochlorite Treatment of Public Water Supplies: Its Adaptability and Limitations," *Journal of the American Public Health Association* 1, no. 8 (1911).

26. Hazen, *Clean Water and How to Get It.*

27. Baker, *Quest for Pure Water.*

28. Hazen, *Clean Water and How to Get It.*

29. W. T. Sedgwick and J. S. MacNutt, "On the Mills-Reincke Phenomenon and Hazen's Theorem Concerning the Decrease in Mortality from Diseases Other Than Typhoid Fever Following the Purification of Public Water-Supplies," *Journal of Infectious Diseases* 7, no. 4 (1910), quotation on p. 490.

30. D. Cutler and G. Miller, "The Role of Public Health Improvements in Health Advances: The Twentieth-Century United States," *Demography* 42, no. 1 (2005).

31. Baker, *Quest for Pure Water.*

32. M. W. H., *Water Treatment: Principles and Design,* 2d ed., ed. J. C. Crittenden et al. (New York: John Wiley and Sons, 2005).

33. Baker, *Quest for Pure Water.*

34. G. C. White, *Handbook of Chlorination* (New York: Van Nostrand, 1972).

35. Ibid.

36. Baker, *Quest for Pure Water.*

37. White, *Handbook of Chlorination.*

38. L. Szinicz, "History of Chemical and Biological Warfare Agents," *Toxicology* 214, no. 3 (2005).

39. Baker, *Quest for Pure Water.*

40. Ibid.; Melosi, *Sanitary City.*

41. Johnson, "Hypochlorite Treatment of Public Water Supplies," p. 574.

42. Baker, *Quest for Pure Water.*

43. Anon., "Greatest Engineering Achievements of the 20th Century," National Academy of Engineering, available at http://www.greatachievements.org.

Chapter 5. Burning Rivers, Fading Paint

1. Anon., "Sewage and Its Disposal in Great Britain," *The Independent,* Oct. 16, 1884.

2. "How London Is to Be Drained," *The Albion: A Journal of News, Politics and Literature* (1859); P. F. Cooper, "Historical Aspects of Wastewater

Treatment," in *Decentralised Sanitation and Reuse,* ed. G. Zeeman, P. Lens, and G. Lettinga (London: International Water Association, 2001).

3. S. S. Elkind, *Bay Cities and Water Politics* (Lawrence: University of Kansas Press, 1998).

4. R. Marshall, ed., *Waterfronts and Post-Industrial Cities* (London: Spon Press, 2001).

5. M. Kurlansky, *The Big Oyster: History on the Half Shell* (New York: Ballantine, 2006).

6. Anon., "What Shall Be Done with the Sewage?," *Los Angeles Times,* Feb. 12, 1921; "The City of Los Angeles Hyperion Treatment Plant," City of Los Angeles Public Works Department, available at http://www.san.lacity.org /wpd/Siteorg/general/hyprnhist.htm; S. A. Greeley, C. G. Hyde, and F. Thomas, "Report of the Board of Consulting Engineers upon a Program of Sewerage and Sewage Treatment and Disposal for the City of Los Angeles, California and Certain Environs" (1939).

7. L. Hill, *The Chicago River: A Natural and Unnatural History* (Chicago: Lake Claremont Press, 2000).

8. Report from *Water and Sewage Works Record* (1903), p. 32, quoted in ibid., p. 134.

9. D. G. Laing, A. Eddy, and D. J. Best, "Perceptual Characteristics of Binary, Trinary, and Quaternary Odor Mixtures Consisting of Unpleasant Constituents," *Physiology and Behavior* 56, no. 1 (1994); P. Gostelow, S. A. Parsons, and R. M. Stuetz, "Odour Measurements for Sewage Treatment Works," *Water Research* 35, no. 3 (2001).

10. Anon., "Chronic Toxicity Profile: Hydrogen Sulfide," California Office of Health Hazards Assessment, available at http://oehha.ca.gov/air/chronic _rels/pdf/7783064.pdf.

11. H. W. Streeter, "Comparative Rates of Stream Purification under Natural and Controlled Conditions," *Industrial and Engineering Chemistry* 22 (1930).

12. "Comparative Rates of Stream Purification under Natural and Controlled Conditions: A Nomographic Solution of the Oxygen Sag Equation," *Sewage Works Journal* 21, no. 5 (1949).

13. Hill, *Chicago River.*

14. Quoted in R. J. Glennon, *Unquenchable: America's Water Crisis and What to Do about It* (Washington, DC: Island Press, 2009).

15. Y. J. Shao et al., "Advanced Primary Treatment: An Alternative to Biological Secondary Treatment; the City of Los Angeles Hyperion Treatment Plant Experience," *Water Science and Technology* 34, nos. 3–4 (1996).

16. S. Hoy, "The Garbage Disposer, the Public-Health, and the Good Life," *Technology and Culture* 26, no. 4 (1985).

17. J. Benidickson, *The Culture of Flushing* (Vancouver: University of British Columbia Press, 2007).

18. R. Hering, "Sewage Treatment," *Journal of the Franklin Institute* 178 (1914).

19. C. G. Hyde, "Gas Collection and Utilization," *Sewage Works Journal* 16, no. 6 (1944).

20. Hering, "Sewage Treatment."

21. C. G. Hyde, "Developments in Sewerage and Sewage Treatment," in *Convention of the American Concrete Pipe Association* (1939).

22. G. E. Waring, "Out of Sight, Out of Mind," *Century Illustrated Magazine* (1894).

23. H. W. Clark, "An Outline of Sewage Purification Studies at the Lawrence Experiment Station," *Industrial and Engineering Chemistry* 19, no. 1 (1927).

24. Waring, "Out of Sight, Out of Mind."

25. M. V. Melosi, *The Sanitary City: Urban Infrastructure in America from Colonial Times to the Present* (Baltimore: Johns Hopkins University Press, 2000).

26. P. F. Cooper, "Historical Aspects of Wastewater Treatment," in *Decentralised Sanitation and Reuse: Concepts, Systems and Implementation*, ed. P. Lens, G. Lettinga, and G. Zeeman (London: International Water Association, 2001).

27. Ibid.

28. Melosi, *The Sanitary City*; H. W. Clark, "Development of the Purification of Sewage by Aeration and Growths at Lawrence Massachusetts," *Journal of Industrial and Engineering Chemistry* 8, no. 7 (1916).

29. C. G. Hyde, "Some Comments on Sewage Disposal Practice in Europe" (1929), available at Water Resources Collections and Archives, University of California, Riverside.

30. U.S. Environmental Protectional Agency, *Clean Water Needs Survey: 2004 Report to Congress* (Washington, DC: U.S. Environmental Protection Agency, 2008).

31. Cooper, "Historical Aspects of Wastewater Treatment."

32. A. Hazen, *Clean Water and How to Get It* (New York: John Wiley and Sons, 1909), quotation on p. 36.

33. A. Leopold, *A Sand County Almanac* (1949; New York: Oxford University Press, 2001), p. 171.

34. Melosi, *Sanitary City*.

35. *Economic Report of the President* (Washington, DC: U.S. Bureau of Economic Analysis, 1951).

36. Page Mosier, "A Brief History of Population Growth in the Greater San Francisco Bay Region," in *Geology and Natural History of the San Francisco Bay Area* (Menlo Park, CA: U.S. Geological Survey, 2001).

37. C. G. Hyde, "Stream Pollution and Present Status of Controlling Legislation in California," *American Journal of Public Health* 4, no. 10 (1914).

38. T. J. Conomos, R. E. Smith, and J. W. Gartner, "Environmental Setting of San Francisco Bay," *Hydrobiologia* 129 (Oct. 1985).

39. A. Fonseca and P. Prange, "The History of the San Jose/Santa Clara Water Pollution Control Plant: Celebrating over 50 Years of Service" (San Jose, CA: City of San Jose Environmental Services, 2008).

40. G. Chanin, J. R. Elwood, and E. H. Chow, "A Simplified Technique for Atmospheric Hydrogen Sulfide Studies," *Sewage and Industrial Wastes* 26, no. 10 (1954).

41. C. G. Hyde, H. F. Gray, and A. M. Rawn, "East Bay Cities Sewage Disposal Survey: Report upon the Collection, Treatment and Disposal of Sewage and Industrial Wastes of the East Bay Cities, California" (N.p.: Board of Consulting Engineers, June 30, 1941).

42. M. G. Wolman, "The Nation's Rivers," *Science* 174, no. 4012 (1971).

43. C. E. Schwob, "Federal Water Pollution Control Act—Objectives and Policies," *Industrial and Engineering Chemistry* 45, no. 12 (1953).

44. Melosi, *Sanitary City.*

45. "California's Water Pollution Problem," *Stanford Law Review* 3 (1951).

46. Fonseca and Prange, "History of the San Jose/Santa Clara Water Pollution Control Plant."

47. D. Haydel, "Regional Control of Air and Water Pollution in San Francisco Bay Area," *California Law Review* 55, no. 3 (1967).

48. G. Matthews, "'The Los Angeles of the North'—San Jose's Transition from Fruit Capital to High-Tech Metropolis," *Journal of Urban History* 25, no. 4 (1999).

49. P. Garfield, "The Control of Ohio River Pollution," *Land Economics* 30, no. 2 (1954).

50. C. M. Everts and A. H. Dahl, "The Federal Water-Pollution Control Act of 1956," *American Journal of Public Health and the Nation's Health* 47, no. 3 (1957).

51. Melosi, *Sanitary City.*

52. U.S. Environmental Protection Agency, "Clean Water Needs Survey."

53. Everts and Dahl, "Federal Water-Pollution Control Act of 1956."

54. F. E. Moss, *The Water Crisis* (New York: Praeger, 1967).

55. D. Stradling and R. Stradling, "Perceptions of the Burning River: Deindustrialization and Cleveland's Cuyahoga River," *Environmental History* 13, no. 3 (2008).

56. K. M. Mackenthun, "Environmental Controls—Are They Swords of Damocles?," *Journal (Water Pollution Control Federation)* 54, no. 7 (1982), quotation on p. 1064.

57. Ibid.

58. A. Wolman, "Clean Water Act—The View from Here," *Journal (Water Pollution Control Federation)* 55, no. 1 (1983); U.S. Environmental Protection Agency, *Progress in Water Quality: An Evaluation of the National Investment in Municipal Wastewater Treatment* (Washington, DC: U.S. Environmental Protection Agency, Office of Wastewater Management, 2000).

59. Stradling and Stradling, "Perceptions of the Burning River."

Chapter 6. The Chlorine Dilemma

1. "Environmental Defense Fund—Yannacone Out as Ringmaster," *Science* 166, no. 3913 (1969).

2. L. J. Carter, "Environmental Pollution—Scientists Go to Court," *Science* 158, no. 3808 (1967).

3. J. Firor, "Institutions—Environmental-Defense-Fund," *Environment* 26, no. 8 (1984).

4. T. Page, R. H. Harris, and S. S. Epstein, "Drinking-Water and Cancer Mortality in Louisiana," *Science* 193, no. 4247 (1976); J. L. Marx, "Drinking-Water—Another Source of Carcinogens," *Science* 186, no. 4166 (1974).

5. U.S. Environmental Protection Agency, *Identification of Organic Compounds in Effluents from Industrial Sources* (Washington, DC: Office of Toxic Substances, 1975).

6. F. W. Pontius, "History of the Safe Drinking Water Act," in *Drinking Water Regulation and Health*, ed. F. W. Pontius (New York: John Wiley and Sons, 2003).

7. Ibid.

8. J. E. Lovelock and L. Margulis, "Atmospheric Homeostasis by and for Biosphere—Gaia Hypothesis," *Tellus* 26, nos. 1–2 (1974).

9. J. E. Lovelock, "Atmospheric Fluorine Compounds as Indicators of Air Movements," *Nature* 230, no. 5293 (1971); J. E. Lovelock and R. J. Maggs, "Halogenated Hydrocarbons in and over Atlantic," *Nature* 241, no. 5386 (1973).

10. M. J. Molina and F. S. Rowland, "Stratospheric Sink for Chlorofluoromethanes—Chlorine Atomic-Catalysed Destruction of Ozone," *Nature* 249, no. 5460 (1974).

11. S. D. Richardson, "The Role of GC-MS and LC-MS in the Discovery of Drinking Water Disinfection By-Products," *Journal of Environmental Monitoring* 4, no. 1 (2002).

12. National Research Council, *Drinking Water and Health,* vol. 2 (Washington, DC: National Academy Press, 1980).

13. National Research Council, *Drinking Water and Health,* vol. 1 (Washington, DC: National Academy Press, 1977).

14. Pontius, "History of the Safe Drinking Water Act."

15. P. C. Singer, "Control of Disinfection By-Products in Drinking-Water," *Journal of Environmental Engineering (ASCE)* 120, no. 4 (1994).

16. J. M. Symons et al., *Treatment Techniques for Controlling Trihalomethanes in Drinking Water* (Washington, DC: U.S. Environmental Protection Agency, 1981).

17. National Research Council, *Drinking Water Distribution Systems: Assessing and Reducing Risks* (Washington, DC: National Academies Press, 2006).

18. B. L. Pihlstrom, B. S. Michalowicz, and N. W. Johnson, "Periodontal Diseases," *Lancet* 366, no. 9499 (2005).

19. Singer, "Control of Disinfection By-Products in Drinking-Water," quotation on p. 728.

20. National Research Council, *Drinking Water and Health,* vol. 2.

21. H. Marsh and F. Rodriguez, *Activated Carbon* (Oxford, Eng.: Elsevier, 2006).

22. R. D. Morris et al., "Chlorination, Chlorination By-Products, and Cancer— A Meta-analysis," *American Journal of Public Health* 82, no. 7 (1992).

23. B. N. Ames et al., "Carcinogens Are Mutagens—Simple Test System Combining Liver Homogenates for Activation and Bacteria for Detection," *Proceedings of the National Academy of Sciences of the United States of America* 70, no. 8 (1973).

24. B. N. Ames, H. O. Kammen, and E. Yamasaki, "Hair Dyes Are Mutagenic—Identification of a Variety of Mutagenic Ingredients," *Proceedings of the National Academy of Sciences of the United States of America* 72, no. 6 (1975).

25. A. M. Cheh et al., "Non-Volatile Mutagens in Drinking-Water—Production by Chlorination and Destruction by Sulfite," *Science* 207, no. 4426 (1980); H. J. Kool et al., "Presence, Introduction and Removal of Mutagenic

Activity during the Preparation of Drinking-Water in the Netherlands," *Environmental Health Perspectives* 46 (Dec. 1982).

26. J. Hemming et al., "Determination of the Strong Mutagen 3-Chloro-4-(Dichloromethyl)-5-Hydroxy-2(5h)-Furanone in Chlorinated Drinking and Humic Waters," *Chemosphere* 15, no. 5 (1986); L. Kronberg et al., "Identification and Quantification of the Ames Mutagenic Compound 3-Chloro-4-(Dichloromethyl)-5-Hydroxy-2(5h)-Furanone and of Its Geometric Isomer (E)-2-Chloro-3-(Dichloromethyl)-4-Oxobutenoic Acid in Chlorine-Treated Humic Water and Drinking-Water Extracts," *Environmental Science and Technology* 22, no. 9 (1988).

27. Kronberg et al., "Identification and Quantification."

28. Singer, "Control of Disinfection By-Products in Drinking-Water"; U.S. Environmental Protection Agency, *National Primary Drinking Water Regulations: Disinfectants and Disinfection Byproducts; Final Rule* (Washington, DC: Code of Federal Regulations, 1998).

29. P. Roccaro, G. Mancini, and F. G. A. Vagliasindi, "Water Intended for Human Consumption—Part I: Compliance with European Water Quality Standards," *Desalination* 176, nos. 1–3 (2005); N. F. Gray, *Water Technology: An Introduction for Environmental Scientists and Engineers* (Oxford, Eng.: Butterworth-Heinemann, 2010).

30. R. Renner, "Plumbing the Depths of DC's Drinking Water Crisis," *Environmental Science and Technology* 38, no. 12 (2004).

31. R. A. Ward, "Water Processing for Hemodialysis—Part I: A Historical Perspective," *Seminars in Dialysis* 10, no. 1 (1997); N. A. Junglee et al., "When Pure Is Not So Pure: Chloramine-Related Hemolytic Anemia in Home Hemodialysis Patients," *Hemodialysis International* 14, no. 3 (2010).

32. Vermont Department of Health, "CDC Experts to Hear Concerns about Chloramine," available at http://healthvermont.gov/news/2007/092507 chloramine.aspx.

33. H. L. Needleman et al., "Deficits in Psychologic and Classroom Performance of Children with Elevated Dentin Lead Levels," *New England Journal of Medicine* 300, no. 13 (1979).

34. W. Troesken, *The Great Lead Water Pipe Disaster* (Cambridge, MA: MIT Press, 2006).

35. A. T. Hodge, "Vitruvius, Lead Pipes and Lead-Poisoning," *American Journal of Archaeology* 85, no. 4 (1981).

36. Troesken, *Great Lead Water Pipe Disaster.*

37. J. A. Switzer et al., "Evidence That Monochloramine Disinfectant Could Lead to Elevated Pb Levels in Drinking Water," *Environmental Science and Technology* 40, no. 10 (2006).

38. M. Edwards and A. Dudi, "Role of Chlorine and Chloramine in Corrosion of Lead-Bearing Plumbing Materials," *Journal of the American Water Works Association* 96, no. 10 (2004); M. L. Miranda et al., "Changes in Blood Lead Levels Associated with Use of Chloramines in Water Treatment Systems," *Environmental Health Perspectives* 115, no. 2 (2007).

39. M. Edwards, S. Triantafyllidou, and D. Best, "Elevated Blood Lead in Young Children Due to Lead-Contaminated Drinking Water: Washington, DC, 2001–2004," *Environmental Science and Technology* 43, no. 5 (2009).

40. D. Nakamura, "WASA to Replace 2,800 Lead Pipes over Next Year," *Washington Post,* Nov. 13, 2004.

41. L. S. McNeill and M. Edwards, "Phosphate Inhibitor Use at US Utilities," *Journal of the American Water Works Association* 94, no. 7 (2002).

42. J. D. B. Featherstone, "The Science and Practice of Caries Prevention," *Journal of the American Dental Association* 131, no. 7 (2000).

43. W. A. Mitch et al., "N-Nitrosodimethylamine (NDMA) as a Drinking Water Contaminant: A Review," *Environmental Engineering Science* 20, no. 5 (2003).

44. W. A. Mitch and D. L. Sedlak, "Characterization and Fate of N-Nitrosodimethylamine Precursors in Municipal Wastewater Treatment Plants," *Environmental Science and Technology* 38, no. 5 (2004); S. H. Park et al., "Degradation of Amine-Based Water Treatment Polymers during Chloramination as N-Nitrosodimethylamine (NDMA) Precursors," *Environmental Science and Technology* 43 (2009).

45. R. G. Rice, "Ozone in the United States of America—State-of-the-Art," *Ozone-Science and Engineering* 21, no. 2 (1999).

46. W. R. Haag and J. Hoigne, "Ozonation of Bromide-Containing Waters— Kinetics of Formation of Hypobromous Acid and Bromate," *Environmental Science and Technology* 17, no. 5 (1983).

Chapter 7. "Drains to Bay"

1. U.S. Environmental Protection Agency, *Report to Congress: Impacts and Controls of CSOs and SSOs* (Washington, DC: U.S. Environmental Protection Agency, 2004).

2. S. J. Burian et al., "Historical Development of Wet-Weather Flow Management," *Journal of Water Resources Planning and Management (ASCE)* 125, no. 1 (1999).

3. D. Hill, *A History of Engineering in Classical and Modern Times* (Beckenham, Eng.: Croom Helm, 1984).

4. "Tracking Down the Roots of Our Sanitary Sewers," available at http://www.sewerhistory.org/chronos/convey.htm.

5. R. S. Kirby and P. G. Laursen, *The Early Years of Modern Civil Engineering* (New Haven: Yale University Press, 1932).

6. G. B. Thomas and D. Crawford, "London Tideway Tunnels: Tackling London's Victorian Legacy of Combined Sewer Overflows," *Water Science and Technology* 63, no. 1; PlanNYC, *NYC Green Infrastructure Plan* (New York: New York City Department of Environmental Protection, 2010).

7. J. A. Tarr, "Separate vs. Combined Sewer Problem—Case-Study in Urban Technology Design Choice," *Journal of Urban History* 5, no. 3 (1979).

8. U.S. Environmental Protection Agency, *Report to Congress: Impacts and Controls of CSOs and SSOs.*

9. Ibid.

10. Ibid.; T. T. Fong et al., "Quantitative Detection of Human Adenoviruses in Wastewater and Combined Sewer Overflows Influencing a Michigan River," *Applied and Environmental Microbiology* 76, no. 3.

11. T. J. Wade et al., "High Sensitivity of Children to Swimming-Associated Gastrointestinal Illness—Results Using a Rapid Assay of Recreational Water Quality," *Epidemiology* 19, no. 3 (2008).

12. U.S. Environmental Protection Agency, *Report to Congress: Impacts and Controls of CSOs and SSOs.*

13. D. I. Taylor, "The Boston Harbor Project, and Large Decreases in Loadings of Eutrophication-Related Materials to Boston Harbor," *Marine Pollution Bulletin* 60, no. 4 (2010).

14. M. V. Melosi, *The Sanitary City: Urban Infrastructure in America from Colonial Times to the Present* (Baltimore: Johns Hopkins University Press, 2000).

15. P. C. Anderson, "The CSO Sleeping Giant: Combined Sewer Overflow or Congressional Stalling Objective," *Virginia Environmental Law Journal* 10, no. 371 (1991).

16. Ibid.

17. Congressional Budget Office, *Future Investment in Drinking Water and Wastewater Infrastructure* (Washington, DC: U.S. Congressional Budget Office, 2002).

18. Taylor, "Boston Harbor Project"; M. Hawthorne, "Feds Probe Chronic Sewage Overflows into Lakes, Streams," *Chicago Tribune*, Mar. 19, 2011.

19. L. A. Roesner and P. Traina, "Overview of Federal-Law and USEPA Regulations for Urban Runoff," *Water Science and Technology* 29, nos. 1–2 (1994).

20. J. Tibbetts, "Down, Dirty, and Out of Date," *Environmental Health Perspectives* 113, no. 7 (2005).

21. C. Copeland, *Water Quality: Implementing the Clean Water Act* (Washington, DC: U.S. Congressional Research Service, 2006).

22. Evan West, "Pipe Dreams," *Indianapolis Monthly* (June 2006).

23. P. Freund, "Mayor Details Largest Infrastructure Investment in City's History," publication by the Office of the Mayor of Indianapolis, Indiana, May 2011.

24. T. Cook, "Citizens Asks for Sewer Rate Hike of Nearly 50%," *Indystar,* Feb. 22, 2013.

25. S. Nielsen and M. C. Jacob, *Sanitary Sewer Rates Now and in the Future* (Indianapolis, IN: Department of Public Works, 2008).

26. Hawthorne, "Feds Probe Chronic Sewage Overflows"; L. Baker, "New Strategies for Controlling Stormwater Overflows," *Governing* (Feb. 2011); Anon., "City of Portland—Willamette River CSO Project," *Energy and Infrastructure* (Nov. 16, 2009).

27. M. J. Paul and J. L. Meyer, "Streams in the Urban Landscape," *Annual Review of Ecology and Systematics* 32 (2001).

28. D. B. Booth and C. R. Jackson, "Urbanization of Aquatic Systems: Degradation Thresholds, Stormwater Detection, and the Limits of Mitigation," *Journal of the American Water Resources Association* 33, no. 5 (1997).

29. Paul and Meyer, "Streams in the Urban Landscape."

30. Metcalf and Eddy, *Wastewater Engineering* (Boston: McGraw Hill, 2003).

31. M. S. Hogan, "Problems Caused by Roots in Sewers," available at http://www.waterworldce.com.

32. A. B. Boehm et al., "Tiered Approach for Identification of a Human Fecal Pollution Source at a Recreational Beach: Case Study at Avalon Cay, Catalina Island, California," *Environmental Science and Technology* 37, no. 4 (2003).

33. J. D. McGregor, "The Case for Cleaning," *Civil Engineering* 73, no. 1 (2003).

34. U.S. Environmental Protection Agency, *Report to Congress: Impacts and Controls of CSOs and SSOs.*

35. B. O'Keefe et al., "Urban Diffuse Sources of Faecal Indicators," *Water Science and Technology* 51, nos. 3–4 (2005).

36. R. M. Hopkins et al., "Ribosomal RNA Sequencing Reveals Differences between the Genotypes of Giardia Isolates Recovered from Humans and

Dogs Living in the Same Locality," *Journal of Parasitology* 83, no. 1 (1997); U. M. Morgan et al., "Cryptosporidium Spp. in Domestic Dogs: The 'Dog' Genotype," *Applied and Environmental Microbiology* 66, no. 5 (2000).

37. H. Takada et al., "Distribution and Sources of Polycyclic Aromatic-Hydrocarbons (PAHs) in Street Dust from the Tokyo Metropolitan Area," *Science of the Total Environment* 107 (1991).

38. U.S. Environmental Protection Agency, *Urban Runoff Pollution Prevention and Control Planning Handbook* (Cincinnati: Office of Research and Development, 1993).

39. "Maryland Developer Grows 'Rain Gardens' to Control Residential Runoff," *Non-Point News-Notes* (Aug.–Sept. 1995).

40. Anon., *Low-Impact Development Design Strategies: An Integrated Design Approach* (Largo, MD: Prince Georges County Department of Environmental Resources, 1999).

41. F. Montalto et al., "Rapid Assessment of the Cost-Effectiveness of Low Impact Development for CSO Control," *Landscape and Urban Planning* 82, no. 3 (2007).

42. L. M. Ahiablame, B. A. Engel, and I. Chaubey, "Effectiveness of Low Impact Development Practices: Literature Review and Suggestions for Future Research," *Water Air and Soil Pollution* 223, no. 7 (2012).

43. T. Carter and A. Keeler, "Life-Cycle Cost-Benefit Analysis of Extensive Vegetated Roof Systems," *Journal of Environmental Management* 87, no. 3 (2008).

44. M. Quigley, C. Brown, and R. Stack, "Transforming Our Cities: High Performance Green Infrastructure; Internet-of-Things Based; Highly Distributed Real-Time Control (DTRC)," paper presented at the 2012 Chesapeake Bay Stormwater Retreat, Shepherdstown, WV, 2012.

45. M. Scholz and P. Grabowlecki, "Review of Permeable Pavement Systems," *Building and Environment* 42, no. 11 (2007).

46. R. B. McKinstry et al., "Unpave a Parking Lot and Put up a Paradise: Using Green Infrastructure and Ecosystem Services to Achieve Cost-Effective Compliance," *Environmental Law Reporter* 42 (Sept. 2012).

47. U.S. Environmental Protection Agency, "EPA Administrator Jackson and Philadelphia Mayor Nutter Sign Landmark Green City, Clean Waters Partnership Agreement," *EPA Newsroom*, Apr. 10, 2012.

Chapter 8. Traces of Trouble

1. J. P. Sumpter and A. C. Johnson, "10th Anniversary Perspective: Reflections on Endocrine Disruption in the Aquatic Environment: From Known

Knowns to Unknown Unknowns (and Many Things in between)," *Journal of Environmental Monitoring* 10, no. 12 (2008).

2. C. E. Purdom et al., "Estrogenic Effects of Effluents from Sewage Treatment Works," *Chemistry and Ecology* 8 (1994).

3. D. G. J. Larsson et al., "Ethinyloestradiol—An Undesired Fish Contraceptive?," *Aquatic Toxicology* 45, nos. 2–3 (1999); L. C. Folmar et al., "Vitellogenin Induction and Reduced Serum Testosterone Concentrations in Feral Male Carp (*Cyprinus carpio*) Captured Near a Major Metropolitan Sewage Treatment Plant," *Environmental Health Perspectives* 104, no. 10 (1996).

4. A. K. Hotchkiss et al., "Fifteen Years after 'Wingspread'—Environmental Endocrine Disrupters and Human and Wildlife Health: Where We Are Today and Where We Need to Go," *Toxicological Sciences* 105, no. 2 (2008).

5. D. V. Henley et al., "Brief Report—Prepubertal Gynecomastia Linked to Lavender and Tea Tree Oils," *New England Journal of Medicine* 356, no. 5 (2007).

6. T. Colborn, D. Dumanoski, and J. P. Meyers, *Our Stolen Future: Are We Threatening Our Fertility, Intelligence, and Survival?* (New York: Plume Press, 1997); R. Carson, *Silent Spring* (Boston: Houghton Mifflin, 1962).

7. J. J. Hickey and D. W. Anderson, "Chlorinated Hydrocarbons and Eggshell Changes in Raptorial and Fish-Eating Birds," *Science* 162, no. 3850 (1968).

8. L. Holm et al., "Embryonic Exposure to o,p'-DDT Causes Eggshell Thinning and Altered Shell Gland Carbonic Anhydrase Expression in the Domestic Hen," *Environmental Toxicology and Chemistry* 25, no. 10 (2006).

9. S. Jobling and J. P. Sumpter, "Detergent Components in Sewage Effluent Are Weakly Estrogenic to Fish—An in-Vitro Study Using Rainbow-Trout (Oncorhynchus-Mykiss) Hepatocytes," *Aquatic Toxicology* 27, nos. 3–4 (1993); S. Jobling et al., "A Variety of Environmentally Persistent Chemicals, Including Some Phthalate Plasticizers, Are Weakly Estrogenic," *Environmental Health Perspectives* 103, no. 6 (1995).

10. A. C. Johnson, A. Belfroid, and A. Di Corcia, "Estimating Steroid Oestrogen Inputs into Activated Sludge Treatment Works and Observations on Their Removal from the Effluent," *Science of the Total Environment* 256, nos. 2–3 (2000).

11. F. Piferrer et al., "Induction of Sterility in Coho Salmon (Oncorhynchus-Kisutch) by Androgen Immersion before First Feeding," *Aquaculture* 119, no. 4 (1994).

12. C. Desbrow et al., "Identification of Estrogenic Chemicals in STW Effluent. 1. Chemical Fractionation and in Vitro Biological Screening," *Environmental Science and Technology* 32, no. 11 (1998); S. A. Snyder et al., "Analytical

Methods for Detection of Selected Estrogenic Compounds in Aqueous Mixtures," *Environmental Science and Technology* 33, no. 16 (1999); C. H. Huang and D. L. Sedlak, "Analysis of Estrogenic Hormones in Municipal Wastewater Effluent and Surface Water Using Enzyme-Linked Immunosorbent Assay and Gas Chromatography/Tandem Mass Spectrometry," *Environmental Toxicology and Chemistry* 20, no. 1 (2001).

13. M. Y. Gross-Sorokin, S. D. Roast, and G. C. Brighty, "Assessment of Feminization of Male Fish in English Rivers by the Environment Agency of England and Wales," *Environmental Health Perspectives* 114 (Apr. 2006).

14. K. A. Kidd et al., "Collapse of a Fish Population after Exposure to a Synthetic Estrogen," *Proceedings of the National Academy of Sciences of the United States of America* 104, no. 21 (2007).

15. N. Yamashita et al., "Fate Estimation of Estrogenic Substances in an Urban River by Flux Calculation," *Water Environment Research* 78, no. 12 (2006).

16. A. C. Johnson et al., "Predicting National Exposure to a Point Source Chemical: Japan and Endocrine Disruption as an Example," *Environmental Science and Technology* 45, no. 3 (2011); N. Jonkers et al., "Mass Flows of Endocrine Disruptors in the Glatt River during Varying Weather Conditions," *Environmental Pollution* 157, no. 3 (2009).

17. Folmar et al., "Vitellogenin Induction and Reduced Serum Testosterone Concentrations."

18. L. J. Fono, E. P. Kolodziej, and D. L. Sedlak, "Attenuation of Wastewater-Derived Contaminants in an Effluent-Dominated River," *Environmental Science and Technology* 40, no. 23 (2006).

19. Trinity River Authority of Texas, *Trinity River Basin Master Plan* (Arlington: Trinity River Authority of Texas, 2010).

20. C. Hoppe-Jones, G. Oldham, and J. E. Drewes, "Attenuation of Total Organic Carbon and Unregulated Trace Organic Chemicals in U.S. Riverbank Filtration Systems," *Water Research* 44, no. 15 (2010); L. Lauver and L. A. Baker, "Mass Balance for Wastewater Nitrogen in the Central Arizona-Phoenix Ecosystem," *Water Research* 34, no. 10 (2000); L. J. Fono and D. L. Sedlak, "Use of the Chiral Pharmaceutical Propranolol to Identify Sewage Discharges into Surface Waters," *Environmental Science and Technology* 39, no. 23 (2005).

21. S. Rose, "The Effects of Urbanization on the Hydrochemistry of Base Flow within the Chattahoochee River Basin (Georgia, USA)," *Journal of Hydrology* 341, nos. 1–2 (2007); A. J. Ramirez et al., "Occurrence of Pharmaceuticals and Personal Care Products in Fish: Results of a National Pilot Study

in the United States," *Environmental Toxicology and Chemistry* 28, no. 12 (2009).

22. C. G. Daughton and T. A. Ternes, "Pharmaceuticals and Personal Care Products in the Environment: Agents of Subtle Change?," *Environmental Health Perspectives* 107 (1999).

23. Ramirez et al., "Occurrence of Pharmaceuticals and Personal Care Products in Fish."

24. D. W. Kolpin et al., "Pharmaceuticals, Hormones, and Other Organic Wastewater Contaminants in U.S. Streams, 1999–2000: A National Reconnaissance," *Environmental Science and Technology* 36, no. 6 (2002); M. J. Focazio et al., "A National Reconnaissance for Pharmaceuticals and Other Organic Wastewater Contaminants in the United States—(II) Untreated Drinking Water Sources," *Science of the Total Environment* 402, nos. 2–3 (2008); F. Sacher et al., "Pharmaceutical Residues in the River Rhine—Results of a One-Decade Monitoring Programme," *Journal of Environmental Monitoring* 10, no. 5 (2008).

25. T. Brodin et al., "Dilute Concentrations of a Psychiatric Drug Alter Behavior of Fish from Natural Populations," *Science* 339, no. 6121 (2013).

26. K. Fent, A. A. Weston, and D. Caminada, "Ecotoxicology of Human Pharmaceuticals," *Aquatic Toxicology* 76, no. 2 (2006).

27. D. Martinovic et al., "Environmental Estrogens Suppress Hormones, Behavior, and Reproductive Fitness in Male Fathead Minnows," *Environmental Toxicology and Chemistry* 26, no. 2 (2007).

28. A. Joss et al., "Removal of Estrogens in Municipal Wastewater Treatment under Aerobic and Anaerobic Conditions: Consequences for Plant Optimization," *Environmental Science and Technology* 38, no. 11 (2004); M. Clara et al., "Removal of Selected Pharmaceuticals, Fragrances and Endocrine Disrupting Compounds in a Membrane Bioreactor and Conventional Wastewater Treatment Plants," *Water Research* 39, no. 19 (2005); A. Joss et al., "Biological Degradation of Pharmaceuticals in Municipal Wastewater Treatment: Proposing a Classification Scheme," *Water Research* 40, no. 8 (2006).

29. S. S. Schiffman et al., "Molecular Mechanism of Sweet Taste—Relationship of Hydrogen-Bonding to Taste Sensitivity for Both Young and Elderly," *Neurobiology of Aging* 2, no. 3 (1981); M. Scheurer et al., "Performance of Conventional Multi-Barrier Drinking Water Treatment Plants for the Removal of Four Artificial Sweeteners," *Water Research* 44, no. 12 (2010).

30. A. Putschew, S. Wischnack, and M. Jekel, "Occurrence of Triiodinated X-Ray Contrast Agents in the Aquatic Environment," *Science of the Total*

Environment 255, no. 1–3 (2000); J. E. Drewes, P. Fox, and M. Jekel, "Occurrence of Iodinated X-Ray Contrast Media in Domestic Effluents and Their Fate during Indirect Potable Reuse," *Journal of Environmental Science and Health, Part A—Toxic/Hazardous Substances and Environmental Engineering* 36, no. 9 (2001); T. A. Ternes et al., "Ozonation: A Tool for Removal of Pharmaceuticals, Contrast Media and Musk Fragrances from Wastewater?," *Water Research* 37, no. 8 (2003); J. L. Kormos et al., "Biotransformation of Selected Iodinated X-Ray Contrast Media and Characterization of Microbial Transformation Pathways," *Environmental Science and Technology* 44, no. 13 (2010).

31. L. J. Fono and D. L. Sedlak, "A Simple Method for the Measurement of Organic Iodine in Wastewater and Surface Water," *Water Research* 41, no. 7 (2007); Drewes, Fox, and Jekel, "Occurrence of Iodinated X-Ray Contrast Media in Domestic Effluents."

32. J. Oppenheimer et al., "Occurrence and Suitability of Sucralose as an Indicator Compound of Wastewater Loading to Surface Waters in Urbanized Regions," *Water Research* 45, no. 13 (2011); I. J. Buerge et al., "Ubiquitous Occurrence of the Artificial Sweetener Acesulfame in the Aquatic Environment: An Ideal Chemical Marker of Domestic Wastewater in Groundwater," *Environmental Science and Technology* 43, no. 12 (2009); Fono and Sedlak, "A Simple Method for the Measurement of Organic Iodine."

33. Fono, Kolodziej, and Sedlak, "Attenuation of Wastewater-Derived Contaminants in an Effluent-Dominated River."

34. P. Westerhoff et al., "Fate of Endocrine-Disruptor, Pharmaceutical, and Personal Care Product Chemicals during Simulated Drinking Water Treatment Processes," *Environmental Science and Technology* 39, no. 17 (2005).

35. Ibid.; K. E. Pinkston and D. L. Sedlak, "Transformation of Aromatic Ether- and Amine-Containing Pharmaceuticals during Chlorine Disinfection," *Environmental Science and Technology* 38, no. 14 (2004); M. C. Dodd and C. H. Huang, "Transformation of the Antibacterial Agent Sulfamethoxazole in Reactions with Chlorine: Kinetics, Mechanisms, and Pathways," *Environmental Science and Technology* 38, no. 21 (2004); M. C. Dodd et al., "Interactions of Fluoroquinolone Antibacterial Agents with Aqueous Chlorine: Reaction Kinetics, Mechanisms, and Transformation Pathways," *Environmental Science and Technology* 39, no. 18 (2005).

36. B. C. Lee et al., "Effects of Chlorine on the Decrease of Estrogenic Chemicals," *Water Research* 38, no. 3 (2004).

37. E. M. Fiss, K. L. Rule, and P. J. Vikesland, "Formation of Chloroform and Other Chlorinated Byproducts by Chlorination of Triclosan-Containing Antibacterial Products," *Environmental Science and Technology* 41, no. 7 (2007); K. L. Rule, V. R. Ebbett, and P. J. Vikesland, "Formation of Chloroform and Chlorinated Organics by Free-Chlorine-Mediated Oxidation of Triclosan," *Environmental Science and Technology* 39, no. 9 (2005); M. Deborde and U. von Gunten, "Reactions of Chlorine with Inorganic and Organic Compounds during Water Treatment—Kinetics and Mechanisms: A Critical Review," *Water Research* 42, nos. 1–2 (2008).

38. S. W. Krasner et al., "Occurrence of a New Generation of Disinfection Byproducts," *Environmental Science and Technology* 40, no. 23 (2006).

39. S. E. Duirk et al., "Formation of Toxic Iodinated Disinfection By-Products from Compounds Used in Medical Imaging," *Environmental Science and Technology* 45, no. 16 (2011).

40. U.S. Environmental Protection Agency, *2006 Community Water System Survey* (Washington, DC: Office of Ground and Drinking Water, 2009).

41. Westerhoff et al., "Fate of Endocrine-Disruptor, Pharmaceutical, and Personal Care Product Chemicals during Simulated Drinking Water Treatment Processes"; Scheurer et al., "Performance of Conventional Multi-Barrier Drinking Water Treatment Plants for the Removal of Four Artificial Sweeteners."

42. Scheurer et al., "Performance of Conventional Multi-Barrier Drinking Water Treatment Plants for the Removal of Four Artificial Sweeteners"; J. Reungoat et al., "Biofiltration of Wastewater Treatment Plant Effluent: Effective Removal of Pharmaceuticals and Personal Care Products and Reduction of Toxicity," *Water Research* 45, no. 9 (2011).

43. C. K. Schmidt and H. J. Brauch, "N,N-Dimethosulfamide as Precursor for N-Nitrosodimethylamine (NDMA) Formation upon Ozonation and Its Fate during Drinking Water Treatment," *Environmental Science and Technology* 42, no. 17 (2008).

44. W. A. Mitch et al., "N-Nitrosodimethylamine (NDMA) as a Drinking Water Contaminant: A Review," *Environmental Engineering Science* 20, no. 5 (2003).

Chapter 9. Paying for the Fourth Revolution

1. U.S. Environmental Protection Agency, *Progress in Water Quality: An Evaluation of the National Investment in Municipal Wastewater Treatment* (Washington, DC: U.S. Environmental Protection Agency, Office of Wastewater Management, 2000).

2. A. Wolman, "Clean Water Act—The View from Here," *Journal of the Water Pollution Control Federation* 55, no. 1 (1983).

3. U.S. Environmental Protection Agency, *Progress in Water Quality.*

4. *Clean Water State Revolving Fund Programs: 2007 Annual Report* (Washington, DC: U.S. Environmental Protection Agency, 2008).

5. *Drinking Water State Revolving Fund: 2009 Annual Report* (Washington, DC: U.S. Environmental Protection Agency, 2010).

6. G. T. Means, "The Business of Water: It Is Time to Embrace a New Model for Water Services," *Daily Environment Report*, Oct. 19, 2011; National Utility Service Consulting Group, *2007–2008 International Water Report and Cost Survey* (New York: National Utility Service, 2008).

7. D. Misczynski, *Proposition 218 after Two Years* (Sacramento: California Research Bureau, California State Library, 1998).

8. R. Anderson, *Who Pays for the Water Pipes, Pumps and Treatment Works?—Local Government Expenditures on Sewer and Water, 1991 to 2005* (Washington, DC: U.S. Conference of Mayors, 2007).

9. U.S. Environmental Protection Agency, *The Clean Water and Drinking Water Infrastructure Gap Analysis* (Washington, DC: U.S. Environmental Protection Agency, Office of Water, 2002).

10. This estimate is a national average assuming that all cost increases are directly translated into higher customer bills with no offsets from government grants or contributions by industrial water users. The estimate uses the U.S. Census average household size of 2.6 people.

11. Water Infrastructure Network, *Clean and Safe Water for the 21st Century: A Renewed National Commitment to Water and Wastewater Infrastructure* (Washington, DC: Water Infrastructure Network, 2000); U.S. General Accounting Office, *Water Infrastructure: Information on Financing, Capital Planning, and Privatization* (Washington, DC: General Accounting Office, 2002); C. Copeland and M. Tiemann, *Water Infrastructure Needs and Investment: Review and Analysis of Key Issues* (Washington, DC: Congressional Research Service, 2010).

12. U.S. General Accounting Office, *Water Infrastructure.*

13. D. Morse and K. Shaver, "Water Main Break Forces Dramatic Rescue of Nine,"*Washington Post,* Dec. 24, 2008.

14. C. Cunningham, "Main Events: Water Main Break Causes, Costs and a Case in Point," *Water and Wastes Digest* (Feb. 2009).

15. K. Shaver, "As Inspections Dwindled, Water Main Breaks Rose," *Washington Post,* May 7, 2009.

16. U.S. Congressional Budget Office, *Future Investment in Drinking Water and Wastewater Infrastructure* (Washington, DC: Congressional Budget Office, 2002).

17. *Biennial Budget Fiscal Year, 2012–2013*, vol. 1: *Overview and Operating Budget* (Oakland, CA: East Bay Municipal Utility District, 2011).

18. B. Kingdom, R. Liemberger, and P. Marin, "The Challenge of Reducing Non-Revenue Water (NRW) in Developing Countries. How the Private Sector Can Help: A Look at Performance-Based Service Contracting," in *Water Supply and Sanitation Sector Board Discussion Paper Series* (Washington, DC: World Bank, 2006); A. F. Colombo and B. W. Karney, "Energy and Costs of Leaky Pipes: Toward a Comprehensive Picture," *Journal of Water Resources Planning and Management (ASCE)* 128, no. 6 (2002).

19. A. B. Boehm et al., "Tiered Approach for Identification of a Human Fecal Pollution Source at a Recreational Beach: Case Study at Avalon Cay, Catalina Island, California," *Environmental Science and Technology* 37, no. 4 (2003).

20. U.S. Environmental Protection Agency, *Deteriorating Buried Infrastructure: Management Challenges and Strategies* (Washington, DC: U.S. Environmental Protection Agency, Office of Water, 2002).

21. American Water Works Association, *Reinvesting in Drinking Water Infrastructure: Dawn of the Replacement Era* (Denver: American Water Works Association, 2001).

22. U.S. Environmental Protection Agency, *Clean Water and Drinking Water Infrastructure Gap Analysis.*

23. American Water Works Association, *Reinvesting in Drinking Water Infrastructure.*

24. G. Basheda et al., *Why Are Electricity Prices Increasing?* (Washington, DC: The Brattle Group, 2006).

25. Bloom Energy, *Understanding California's Electricity Prices* (Sunnyvale, CA: Bloom Energy, 2009).

26. Electric Power Research Institute, *Water and Sustainability*, vol. 4: *U.S. Electricity Consumption for Water Supply and Treatment—The Next Half Century* (Palo Alto, CA: Electric Power Research Institute, 2002).

27. R. Cohen, G. Wolff, and B. Nelson, *Energy down the Drain: The Hidden Costs of California's Water Supply* (Washington, DC: Natural Resources Defense Council, 2004).

28. M. Yonkin, K. Clubine, and K. O'Connor, "Importance of Energy Efficiency to the Water and Wastewater Sector," *Clearwaters* (Spring 2008).

29. S. J. Kenway et al., *Energy Use in the Provision and Consumption of Urban Water in Australia and New Zealand* (Canberra, Australia: Commonwealth Scientific and Industrial Research Organisation [CSIRO], 2008).

30. W. M. Hanemann, "The Central Arizona Project," working paper no. 937 (Davis: California Agricultural Experiment Station and Giannini Foundation of Agricultural Economics, 2002).

31. Electric Power Research Institute, *Water and Sustainability*.

32. Ibid.

33. National Climate Assessment and Development Advisory Committee, *Draft Climate Assessment Report* (Washington, DC: National Climate Assessment and Development Advisory Committee, 2013).

34. Intergovernmental Panel on Climate Change, "Climate Change and Water," IPCC technical paper no. 6, ed. B. Bates et al. (Geneva: Intergovernmental Panel on Climate Change, 2008).

35. National Research Council, "Adapting to the Impacts of Climate Change," in *America's Climate Choices: Panel on Adapting to the Impacts of Climate Change* (Washington, DC: National Research Council, 2010).

36. Ibid.

37. J. K. O'Hara and K. R. Georgakakos, "Quantifying the Urban Water Supply Impacts of Climate Change," *Water Resources Management* 22, no. 10 (2008).

38. Intergovernmental Panel on Climate Change, "Climate Change and Water."

39. T. P. Barnett and D. W. Pierce, "When Will Lake Mead Go Dry?," *Water Resources Research* 44, no. 3 (2008).

40. B. Rajagopalan et al., "Water Supply Risk on the Colorado River: Can Management Mitigate?," *Water Resources Research* 45, no. 8 (2009).

41. J. Overpeck and B. Udall, "Dry Times Ahead," *Science* 328, no. 5986 (2010).

42. H. Brean, "Drought-Stricken Lake Mead Falls to a Level Not Seen since 1937," *Las Vegas Review-Journal*, Oct. 19, 2010.

43. S. Jacob, "A Small Town, Almost Waterless, Takes a Big Gamble," *New York Times*, Nov. 12, 2011.

44. Texas Water Development Board, *Water for Texas: 2012 State Water Plan—Draft* (Austin: Texas Water Development Board, 2011).

45. S. J. Reiling, J. A. Roberson, and J. E. Cromwell, "Drinking Water Regulations: Estimated Cumulative Energy Use and Costs," *Journal of the American Water Works Association* 101, no. 3 (2009).

46. P. Westerhoff et al., "Fate of Endocrine-Disruptor, Pharmaceutical, and Personal Care Product Chemicals during Simulated Drinking Water

Treatment Processes," *Environmental Science and Technology* 39, no. 17 (2005); W. A. Mitch et al., "N-Nitrosodimethylamine (NDMA) as a Drinking Water Contaminant: A Review," *Environmental Engineering Science* 20, no. 5 (2003).

47. P. Quinlan, "Industry to Congress—EPA Fight with Fla. Coming to a State Near You," *New York Times,* Feb. 16, 2011.

48. Organization for Economic Co-operation and Development, *Household Water Pricing in OECD Countries* (Paris: Organization for Economic Co-Operation and Development, 1999).

Chapter 10. The Toilet-to-Tap Solution

1. C. G. Hyde, "The Beautification and Irrigation of Golden Gate Park with Activated Sludge Effluent," *Sewage Works Journal* 9, no. 6 (1937).

2. San Francisco Public Utilities Commission, "Recycled Water," available at http://sfwater.org/index.aspx?page=141.

3. H. B. Hommon, "Treatment and Disposal of Sewage in the National Parks," *American Journal of Public Health and the Nation's Health* 25, no. 2 (1935).

4. National Research Council, *Water Reuse: Expanding the Nation's Water Supply through Reuse of Municipal Wastewater* (Washington, DC: National Research Council, 2012).

5. B. Sheikh et al., "Monterey Waste-Water Reclamation Study for Agriculture," *Research Journal of the Water Pollution Control Federation* 62, no. 3 (1990); E. Castro, M. P. Manas, and J. De Las Heras, "Effects of Wastewater Irrigation on Soil Properties and Turfgrass Growth," *Water Science and Technology* 63, no. 8 (2011).

6. On Nevada, see National Research Council, *Water Reuse;* on Florida, see N. S. Bracken, *Water Reuse in the West: State Programs and Institutional Issues* (Murray, UT: Western States Water Council, 2011).

7. Golf Course Superintendents Association of America, *Golf Course Environmental Profile,* vol. 2: *Water Use and Conservation Practices on U.S. Golf Courses* (Lawrence, KS: Golf Course Superintendents Association of America, 2009).

8. E. Rosenblum, "Selection and Implementation of Nonpotable Water Recycling in 'Silicon Valley' (San Jose Area) California," *Water Science and Technology* 40, nos. 4–5 (1999).

9. Sheikh et al., "Monterey Waste-Water Reclamation Study for Agriculture."

10. National Research Council, *Water Reuse.*

11. Committee on U.S.-Iranian Workshop on Water Conservation, Reuse, and Recycling, the Office for Central Europe and Eurasia Development,

Security, and Cooperation, and National Research Council, *Water Conservation, Reuse, and Recycling: Proceedings of an Iranian-American Workshop* (Washington, DC: National Academies Press, 2005).

12. J. Crook, *Irrigation of Parks, Playgrounds, and Schoolyards with Reclaimed Water: Extent and Safety* (Alexandria, VA: WateReuse Foundation, 2005).

13. P. C. Ingram et al., "From Controversy to Consensus: The Redwood City Recycled Water Experience," *Desalination* 187, nos. 1–3 (2006).

14. CH2M Hill, "Response to Comments on the Addendum to the Mitigated Negative Declaration for the Redwood City Recycled Water Project," prepared for the City of Redwood City, 2003, available at http://www.redwoodcity.org/publicworks/pdf/Reg_030728-8B.pdf.

15. H. Tanaka et al., "Estimating the Safety of Wastewater Reclamation and Reuse Using Enteric Virus Monitoring Data," *Water Environment Research* 70, no. 1 (1998).

16. National Research Council, *Water Reuse*.

17. D. F. Metzler et al., "Emergency Use of Reclaimed Water for Potable Supply at Chanute, Kan.," *Journal of the American Water Works Association* 50, no. 8 (1958).

18. National Research Council, *Ground Water Recharge Using Waters of Impaired Quality* (Washington, DC: National Academies Press, 1994); T. Johnson, *Groundwater Replenishment at the Montebello Forebay Spreading Grounds* (Lakewood, CA: Water Replenishment District of Southern California, 2008).

19. F. L. Burton et al., *Water Reuse* (New York: McGraw Hill, 2006).

20. G. Izaguirre et al., "Geosmin and 2-Methylisoborneol from Cyanobacteria in 3 Water-Supply Systems," *Applied and Environmental Microbiology* 43, no. 3 (1982).

21. W. F. Young et al., "Taste and Odour Threshold Concentrations of Potential Potable Water Contaminants," *Water Research* 30, no. 2 (1996).

22. National Research Council, *Water Reuse*; T. E. Acree et al., "Geosmin: Earthy Component of Table Beet Odor," *Journal of Agricultural and Food Chemistry* 24, no. 2 (1976): 430–431.

23. Burton, *Water Reuse*.

24. National Research Council, *Water Reuse*.

25. D. G. Argo, "Energy and Water-Supply, Orange County, California," *Desalination* 25, no. 2 (1978).

26. M. J. Hammer and G. Elser, "Control of Groundwater Salinity, Orange-County, California," *Ground Water* 18, no. 6 (1980).

27. W. H. Bruvold, A. A. Rosen, and R. M. Pangborn, "Human Perception and Evaluation of Water Quality," *Critical Reviews in Environmental Science and Technology* 5, no. 2 (1975).

28. A. J. Whelton et al., "Minerals in Drinking Water: Impacts on Taste and Importance to Consumer Health," *Water Science and Technology* 55, no. 5 (2007).

29. O. K. Buros, "Role of Desalination in Water Reuse," *Desalination* 32, nos. 1–3 (1980).

30. D. G. Argo and J. G. Moutes, "Wastewater Reclamation by Reverse-Osmosis," *Journal of the Water Pollution Control Federation* 51, no. 3 (1979).

31. Argo, "Energy and Water-Supply, Orange County."

32. National Research Council, *Water Reuse.*

33. M. Po, J. D. Kaercher, and B. E. Nancarrow, *Literature Review of Factors Influencing Public Perceptions on Water Reuse* (Canberra, Australia: Commonwealth Scientific and Industrial Research Organisation [CSIRO], 2003); J. S. Marks, "Taking the Public Seriously: The Case of Potable and Non Potable Reuse," *Desalination* 187, nos. 1–3 (2006).

34. H. Dellios, "Brewer Fights to 'Stand Clear' of Recycled Water," *Chicago Tribune*, Nov. 23, 1994.

35. Marks, "Taking the Public Seriously."

36. "City of San Diego Water Reuse Study 2005: Water Reuse Opportunities, Goals and Values," paper presented at the American Assembly Workshop I, San Diego, Oct. 6–7, 2004.

37. CH2M Hill, "Successful Public Information and Education Strategies: Technical Memorandum," in *Southern California Water Recycling Projects Initiative* (Washington, DC: U.S. Department of the Interior, 2004).

38. Ibid.

39. Po, Kaercher, and Nancarrow, *Literature Review.*

40. "City of San Diego Water Reuse Study 2005."

41. T. W. Hartley, "Public Perception and Participation in Water Reuse," *Desalination* 187, nos. 1–3 (2006): 121.

42. J. Krist, "Consumers Gag on L.A.'s Toilet-to-Tap Program," *California Planning and Development Report* (June 2000).

43. P. Anderson et al., *Monitoring Strategies for Chemicals of Emerging Concern (CECs) in Recycled Water* (Sacramento: California Water Resources Control Board, 2010); California Department of Public Health, *Draft Regulations for Groundwater Replenishment with Recycled Water* (Sacramento: California Department of Public Health, 2011).

44. "Orange County Water District Takes a Proactive Stance on Newly Regulated Compound—N-Nitrosodimethylamine," press release from Orange County Water District, Fountain Valley, CA, June 6, 2000.

45. D. L. Sedlak and M. Kavanaugh, *Removal and Destruction of NDMA and NDMA Precursors during Wastewater Treatment* (Washington, DC: WateReuse Foundation, 2006).

46. National Research Council, *Water Reuse*; E. Van Houtte and J. Verbau-whede, "Operational Experience with Indirect Potable Reuse at the Flemish Coast," *Desalination* 218, nos. 1–3 (2008).

Chapter 11. Turning to the Sea for Drinking Water

1. Here "big cities" means those with populations greater than five million. See G. McGranahan, D. Balk, and B. Anderson, "The Rising Tide: Assessing the Risks of Climate Change and Human Settlements in Low Elevation Coastal Zones," *Environment and Urbanization* 19, no. 1 (2007).

2. J. D. Birkett, "A Brief Illustrated History of Desalination—From the Bible to 1940," *Desalination* 50 (1984).

3. Ibid.

4. A. Ophir and S. Manor, "The Curaçao KAE-LT-MED and Auxiliary Steam-Turbine Project—A Model for Dual Purpose MSF Plants Replacement," *Desalination* 66 (Dec. 1987).

5. M. A. Darwish, F. Al-Juwayhel, and H. K. Abdulraheim, "Multi-Effect Boiling Systems from an Energy Viewpoint," *Desalination* 194, nos. 1–3 (2006); J. E. Miller, *Review of Water Resources and Desalination Technologies* (Albuquerque, NM: Sandia National Laboratory, 2003).

6. S. G. S. A. Rothausen and D. Conway, "Greenhouse-Gas Emissions from Energy Use in the Water Sector," *Nature Climate Change* 1, no. 4 (2011).

7. R. Bakish, "The Caribbean, the Other Area of Concentration of Desalination Plants," *Desalination* 39, nos. 1–3 (1981); H. Cooley, P. H. Gleick, and G. Wolff, *Desalination with a Grain of Salt: A California Perspective* (Oakland, CA: Pacific Institute, 2006).

8. U.S. Congress, Office of Technology Assessment, *Using Desalination Technologies for Water Treatment* (Washington, DC: Office of Technology Assessment, 1988).

9. Cooley, Gleick, and Wolff, *Desalination with a Grain of Salt*.

10. "Tapping the Oceans: Environmental Technology; Desalination Turns Salty Water into Fresh Water," *The Economist*, June 5, 2008.

11. National Research Council, *Desalination: A National Perspective* (Washington, DC: National Academies Press, 2008); National Research Council,

Water Reuse: Expanding the Nation's Water Supply through Reuse of Municipal Wastewater (Washington, DC: National Research Council, 2012).

12. Worldwater.org, "The World's Water," in *Supplement to the World's Water,* ed. Global Water Intelligence (Oakland, CA: Pacific Institute, 2012).

13. M. H. I. El-Saie, "History, Experience and Economics of Water Production in Kuwait," *Desalination* 1, no. 1 (1966).

14. I. Kamal, "Integration of Seawater Desalination with Power Generation," *Desalination* 180, nos. 1–3 (2005).

15. R. Bakish, "The Caribbean, the Other Area of Concentration of Desalination Plants," *Desalination* 39 (1981).

16. K. P. Lee, T. C. Arnot, and D. Mattia, "A Review of Reverse Osmosis Membrane Materials for Desalination—Development to Date and Future Potential," *Journal of Membrane Science* 370, nos. 1–2 (2011).

17. S. Loeb, "Circumstances Leading to the First Municipal Reverse-Osmosis Desalination Plant," *Desalination* 50 (1984).

18. Y. Magara et al., "Development of Reverse Osmosis Membrane Seawater Desalination in Japan," *Water Science and Technology* 41, nos. 10–11 (2000).

19. J. J. Sadhwani and J. A. Veza, "Desalination and Energy Consumption in Canary Islands," *Desalination* 221, nos. 1–3 (2008).

20. U.S. Congress, Office of Technology Assessment, *Using Desalination Technologies for Water Treatment.*

21. Lee, Arnot, and Mattia, "Review of Reverse Osmosis Membrane Materials for Desalination."

22. M. Elimelech and W. A. Phillip, "The Future of Seawater Desalination: Energy, Technology, and the Environment," *Science* 333, no. 6043 (2011).

23. R. Cohen, G. Wolff, and B. Nelson, "Energy down the Drain: The Hidden Costs of California's Water Supply" (Washington, DC: Natural Resources Defense Council, 2004).

24. Y. Dreizin, A. Tenne, and D. Hoffman, "Integrating Large Scale Seawater Desalination Plants within Israel's Water Supply System," *Desalination* 220, nos. 1–3 (2008).

25. For the Israel Water Authority figure, see A. Tal, "The Desalination Debate—Lessons Learned Thus Far," *Environment* 53, no. 5 (2011); for the Metropolitan Water District of Southern California figure see Metropolitan Water District of Southern California, "Water Rates and Charges," available at http://www.mwdh2o.com/mwdh2o/pages/finance/finance_03 .html#Anchor-Treatment-24935.

26. B. A. Portnou and I. Meir, "Urban Water Consumption in Israel: Convergence or Divergence?," *Environmental Science and Policy* 11, no. 4 (2008).

27. G. S. McGrath et al., "Tropical Cyclones and the Ecohydrology of Australia's Recent Continental-Scale Drought," *Geophysical Research Letters* 39 (2012).

28. I. El Saliby et al., "Desalination Plants in Australia: Review and Facts," *Desalination* 247, nos. 1–3 (2009).

29. A. Chanan et al., "A Gradualist Approach to Address Australia's Urban Water Challenge," *Desalination* 249, no. 3 (2009); J. C. Radcliffe, "Evolution of Water Recycling in Australian Cities since 2003," *Water Science and Technology* 62, no. 4 (2010).

30. A. Mitchell, "Carr Backs Desalination Project," *Sydney Morning Herald,* July 10, 2005.

31. D. Knights, I. Macgill, and R. Passey, "The Sustainability of Desalination Plants in Australia: Is Renewable Energy the Answer?," paper presented at the OzWater Conference, Mar. 5, 2007, Sydney.

32. "West Australia Farms for Solar Power," Eco-Business.com, available at http://www.eco-business.com/news/west-australia-farms-for-solar-power.

33. California Energy Commission, *Issues and Environmental Impacts Associated with Once-through Cooling at California's Coastal Power Plants* (Sacramento: California Energy Commission, 2005).

34. Water Reuse Association, Desalination Plant Intakes—Impingement and Entrainment Impacts and Solutions (Washington, DC: Water Reuse Association, 2011).

35. S. Lattemann and T. Hopner, "Environmental Impact and Impact Assessment of Seawater Desalination," *Desalination* 220, nos. 1–3 (2008).

36. G. Crisp, "Australia's First Big Plant Thinks 'Green,'" *International Desalination and Water Reuse Quarterly* 16, no. 3 (2006).

37. N. Bita, "Water's Quick Fix a Long-Term Drain," *The Australian,* Jan. 23, 2010.

38. Cooley, Gleick, and Wolff, *Desalination with a Grain of Salt.*

39. NUS Consulting Group, *2007–2008 International Water Report and Cost Survey* (New York: National Utility Service, 2008).

40. Cooley, Gleick, and Wolff, *Desalination with a Grain of Salt.*

41. B. Alspach and I. Watson, "Sea Change," *Civil Engineering* 74, no. 2 (2004).

42. National Research Council, *Desalination.*

43. Ibid.

44. Anon., "Tampa Bay Seawater Desalination Plant, United States of America," water-technology.net, available at http://www.water-technology.net/projects/tampa.

45. P. Hatfield, "As Plans for Coquina Coast Desal Plant Go Forward, Lessons Come from Tampa Bay: An Interview with Tampa Bay Water Operations Manager Chuck Carden," *West Volusia Beacon,* Mar. 4, 2010.

46. Ibid.; K. Kranhold, "Water, Water, Everywhere . . . Seeking Fresh Sources, California Turns to the Salty Pacific, but Desalination Plants Face Criticism on Environment, Costs," *Wall Street Journal,* Jan. 17, 2008; National Research Council, *Desalination.*

47. C. R. Boehlert, *Legislative History: Saline Water Conversion Act,* vol. 5, pt. 2, ed. U.S. Department of the Interior, Office of Saline Water (Washington, DC: U.S. Government Printing Office, 1965).

48. Cooley, Gleick, and Wolff, *Desalination with a Grain of Salt.*

49. "Carlsbad Desalination Project, United States of America," water-technology.net, available at http://www.water-technology.net/projects/carlsbaddesalination.

50. J. Wilson, "Poseidon's Desalinization Plant: Dream Water Supply or Draining the Pacific and Taxpayers?," Public Education Center, available at http://www.dcbureau.org/20100511749.

51. N. Voutchkov, "Overview of Seawater Concentrate Disposal Alternatives," *Desalination* 273, no. 1 (2011).

52. "Carlsbad Desalination Plan to Feature Green Solutions," *Water World* 24, no. 12 (2008).

53. Wilson, "Poseidon's Desalinization Plant."

54. E. Spagat, "Deal Reached for Massive Calif. Desalination Plant," Associated Press, available at http://abcnews.go.com/US/wireStory/deal-reached-huge-desalination-plant-calif-17343036#.UGWoyxgyEyI; Deborah Sullivan Brennan, "Desalination Comes of Age with Poseidon Plant," *San Diego Union Tribune,* Mar. 31, 2013, available at http://www.utsandiego.com/news/2013/Mar/31/Poseidon-carlsbad-desalination-water.

55. P. H. Gleick, "Zombie Water Projects (Just When You Thought They Were Really Dead . . .)," *Forbes,* Dec. 7, 2011.

56. Wilson, "Poseidon's Desalinization Plant."

Chapter 12. A Different Tomorrow

1. P. H. Gleick, "Global Freshwater Resources: Soft-Path Solutions for the 21st Century," *Science* 302, no. 5650 (2003); G. T. Daigger, "Evolving Urban Water and Residuals Management Paradigms: Water Reclamation and Reuse, Decentralization, and Resource Recovery," *Water Environment Research* 81, no. 8 (2009).

2. S. M. Olmstead, W. M. Hanemann, and R. N. Stavins, "Water Demand under Alternative Price Structures," *Journal of Environmental Economics and Management* 54, no. 2 (2007).

3. J. Ferraro, "A Conservation Boomerang: We Must Pay More: Water: Frugal L.A. Users Put Less Money in DWP Coffers, Imperiling Maintenance Budget," *Los Angeles Times,* Dec. 4, 1991.

4. W. Maddaus, "Conservation Program Evaluation—Summary of Data Inputs, Assumptions and Results," in *Report to the East Bay Municipal Water District* (Alamo, CA: Maddaus Water Management, 2009).

5. East Bay Municipal Water District, *Water Supply Management Program, 2040 Plan* (Oakland, CA: East Bay Municipal Water District, 2012).

6. A. Vickers, "The Energy-Policy Act—Assessing Its Impact on Utilities," *Journal of the American Water Works Association* 85, no. 8 (1993).

7. T. D. Rockaway et al., "Residential Water Use Trends in North America," *Journal of the American Water Works Association* 103, no. 2 (2011).

8. Aquaterra, *International Comparisons of Domestic Per Capita Consumption* (Bristol: UK Environment Agency, 2008); R. Cahill and J. Lund, "Residential Water Conservation in Australia and California," *Journal of Water Resources Planning and Management (ASCE)* 139, no. 1 (2013).

9. M. Lee, B. Tansel, and M. Balbin, "Influence of Residential Water Use Efficiency Measures on Household Water Demand: A Four Year Longitudinal Study," *Resources Conservation and Recycling* 56, no. 1 (2011); Cahill and Lund, "Residential Water Conservation in Australia and California."

10. Lee, Tansel, and Balbin, "Influence of Residential Water Use Efficiency Measures."

11. H. Cooley et al., *Hidden Oasis: Water Conservation and Efficiency in Las Vegas* (Oakland, CA: Pacific Institute, 2007); Aquaterra, *International Comparisons of Domestic per Capita Consumption.*

12. P. H. Gleick et al., *Waste Not, Want Not: The Potential for Urban Water Conservation in California* (Oakland, CA: Pacific Institute, 2003); Cooley et al., *Hidden Oasis.*

13. M. Dickinson, "Water Conservation in the United States: A Decade of Progress," University of Colorado at Boulder, 2001, available at the website for the California Urban Water Conservation Council, http://www.cuwcc.org/docDetail.aspx?id=1892.

14. Lee, Tansel, and Balbin, "Influence of Residential Water Use Efficiency Measures."

15. "Washers and Dryers," *Consumer Reports* (Feb. 2010).

16. M. S. Lee and B. Tansel, "Life Cycle Based Analysis of Demands and Emissions for Residential Water-Using Appliances," *Journal of Environmental Management* 101 (2012).

17. S. M. Olmstead and R. N. Stavins, "Comparing Price and Nonprice Approaches to Urban Water Conservation," *Water Resources Research* 45 (2009).

18. Olmstead, Hanemann, and Stavins, "Water Demand under Alternative Price Structures."

19. Cooley et al., *Hidden Oasis*.

20. S. Nataraj and W. M. Hanemann, "Does Marginal Price Matter? A Regression Discontinuity Approach to Estimating Water Demand," *Journal of Environmental Economics and Management* 61, no. 2 (2011).

21. K. A. Sovocool, M. Morgan, and D. Bennett, "An In-Depth Investigation of Xeriscape as a Water Conservation Measure," *Journal of the American Water Works Association* 98, no. 2 (2006).

22. Cooley et al., *Hidden Oasis*.

23. Due to various financial incentives it is tough to make accurate estimates of the true construction costs of seawater desalination plants, but a value of around $1.30 to $2.50 for every liter of water per day that a plant can deliver is consistent with reported costs for the desalination plants built in Tampa and Perth. In Las Vegas, turf replacement rebates cost around $1.60 for each liter per day of water saved.

24. J. Rogers, "Building a Bridge to a Low-Carbon World," Duke Energy, available at http://www.duke-energy.com/about-us/low-carbon-world-112907.asp.

25. G. Bounds, "Turf Battle Heats up over Limits on Water-Guzzling Landscapes," *Wall Street Journal,* Sept. 18, 2009.

26. Florida Department of Environmental Protection, "Florida-Friendly Landscaping," available at http://floridayards.org.

27. D. Mustafa et al., "Xeriscape People and the Cultural Politics of Turfgrass Transformation," *Environment and Planning D-Society and Space* 28, no. 4 (2010).

28. M. FitzRoy, "New Florida Landscaping Law Supersedes Homeowner Association Rules," *Florida Times-Union,* Jan. 30, 2010.

29. R. S. Hilaire et al., "Efficient Water Use in Residential Urban Landscapes," *HortScience* 43, no. 7 (2008).

30. M. D. Dukes, "Water Conservation Potential of Landscape Irrigation Smart Controllers," *Transactions of the ASABE* 55, no. 2 (2012).

31. H. Leverenz, G. Tchobanoglous, and J. L. Darby, *Review of Technologies for the Onsite Treatment of Wastewater in California* (Davis: University of California at Davis, 2002).

32. C. Abegglen, M. Ospelt, and H. Siegrist, "Biological Nutrient Removal in a Small-Scale MBR Treating Household Wastewater," *Water Research* 42, nos. 1–2 (2008).

33. A. G. Fane and S. A. Fane, "The Role of Membrane Technology in Sustainable Decentralized Wastewater Systems," *Water Science and Technology* 51, no. 10 (2005).

34. B. Verrecht et al., "Economical Evaluation and Operating Experiences of a Small-Scale MBR for Nonpotable Reuse," *Journal of Environmental Engineering (ASCE)* 138, no. 5. (2012).

35. Daigger, "Evolving Urban Water and Residuals Management Paradigms."

36. For the removal of nutrients, see R. L. Knight and R. H. Kadlec, *Treatment Wetlands* (Boca Raton, FL: CRC Press, 1996); for the removal of trace organic contaminants, see J. Jasper et al., "Unit Process Wetlands for Treatment of Municipal Wastewater Effluent," *Environmental Engineering Science* (forthcoming 2013).

37. C. Remy and M. Jekel, "Energy Analysis of Conventional and Source-Separation Systems for Urban Wastewater Management Using Life Cycle Assessment," *Water Science and Technology* 65, no. 1 (2012).

38. Ibid.

39. East Bay Municipal Utility District, *Biosolids Performance Report* (Oakland, CA: East Bay Municipal Utility District, 2011).

40. F. Y. Li, K. Wichmann, and R. Otterpohl, "Review of the Technological Approaches for Grey Water Treatment and Reuses," *Science of the Total Environment* 407, no. 11 (2009).

41. R. Otterpohl, "Options for Alternative Types of Sewerage and Treatment Systems Directed to Improvement of the Overall Performance," *Water Science and Technology* 45, no. 3 (2002).

42. A. Maimon et al., "Safe On-Site Reuse of Greywater for Irrigation—A Critical Review of Current Guidelines," *Environmental Science and Technology* 44, no. 9 (2010).

43. C. Thibodeau et al., "Economic Viability and Critical Influencing Factors Assessment of Black Water and Grey Water Source-Separation Sanitation System," *Water Science and Technology* 64, no. 12 (2010).

44. B. Sheikh, *White Paper on Graywater* (Washington, DC: WateReuse Association, 2010).

45. Maimon et al., "Safe on-Site Reuse of Greywater for Irrigation."

46. A. R. Villaraigosa, *Securing L.A.'s Water Supply: City of Los Angeles Water Supply Action Plan* (Los Angeles: City of Los Angeles Department of Water and Power, May 2008); Los Angeles Department of Water and Power,

Water System Ten-Year Capital Improvement Program (Los Angeles: Los Angeles Department of Water and Power, 2010).

47. Daigger, "Evolving Urban Water and Residuals Management Paradigms."

48. J. Dean and P. R. Hunter, "Risk of Gastrointestinal Illness Associated with the Consumption of Rainwater: A Systematic Review," *Environmental Science and Technology* 46, no. 5 (2012).

49. M. P. Rowe, "Rain Water Harvesting in Bermuda," *Journal of the American Water Resources Association* 47, no. 6 (2011).

50. D. J. Lye, "Rooftop Runoff as a Source of Contamination: A Review," *Science of the Total Environment* 407, no. 21 (2009).

51. A. J. Peters, K. L. Weidner, and C. L. Howley, "The Chemical Water Quality in Roof-Harvested Water Cisterns in Bermuda," *Journal of Water Supply Research and Technology-Aqua* 57, no. 3 (2008).

52. National Research Council, *Drinking Water Distribution Systems: Assessing and Reducing Risks* (Washington, DC: National Academies Press, 2006).

53. J. K. Snyder et al., *Impacts of Fire Flow on Distribution System Water Quality, Design and Operation* (Denver: American Water Works Association Research Foundation, 2002).

54. T. D. Fletcher et al., "Reuse of Urban Runoff in Australia: A Review of Recent Advances and Remaining Challenges," *Journal of Environmental Quality* 37, no. 5 (2008); M. Quigley, C. Brown, and R. Stack, "Transforming Our Cities: High Performance Green Infrastructure; Internet-of-Things Based; Highly Distributed Real-Time Control (DTRC)," paper presented at the 2012 Chesapeake Bay Stormwater Retreat, Shepherdstown, WV, 2012.

55. California Department of Water Resources, *California Water Plan* (Sacramento: California Department of Water Resources, 2009).

56. P. McArdle et al., "Centralised Urban Stormwater Harvesting for Potable Reuse," *Water Science and Technology* 63, no. 1 (2011).

57. T. Y. Soon, *Clean, Green and Blue: Singapore's Journey towards Environmental and Water Sustainability* (Singapore: Institute for Southeast Asian Studies, 2009).

Index

Page numbers in *italics* refer to illustrations.

Australia, 76, 278; conservation in, 243; desalination in, 228–30, 231, 235, 239; drought in, 166, 227, 231, 276; graywater reuse in, 263; riverborne effluent in, 145; roofwater in, 267, 268; urban runoff reuse in, 270; utility rates in, 166, 231; water-sensitive design in, 132

bald eagle, 142
bathing, 8–9, 34–35
Bavaria, 16
beaches, 64, 65, 120, 129, 229
beer, 16
Beijing, 24
Belgium, 216
Bellar, Thomas, 96
benzene, 92
Bermuda, 267, 268
Biochemical oxygen demand (BOD), 69
biodegradation, 154, 157–58, 162, 263
biofilm, 52, 78; composition of, 51; electric charge of, 53; on teeth, 99, 108; water flow slowed by, 54, 55, 57; water temperature and, 109–10
bioinfiltration systems, 134, 135, 266
biotechnology, 244, 255, 275
birds, 87, 112, 128, 142, 152
birth control pills, 143, 145, 153
bisphenol A, 142
blackwater, 259–61
bleach, 95
blending, 124
Block pricing, 248–49
boilers, 190, 191, 218
boiling, 57–58
Boonton Reservoir, 60

Boston, 42, 63, 65, 73, 120–21, 123
bottini, 18
Brazil, 267
breweries, 72, 93, 210
brine (reject stream), 208–9, 230–31, 235
Brisbane, Australia, 228, 231
Brita (filter company), 57
Brockton, Mass., 49
bromate, 110
bromine, 93, 96, 100, 102
Brooks, Bryan, 150
Bubbly Creek Water Treatment Plant, 59–60, 61
bubonic plague, 21
bulrush, 259
butanethiol, 66
butanone, 66

calcite, 8, 106, 107
calcium, 191
calcium carbonate, 202
calcium hydroxide, 202
calcium hypochlorite, 58, 59, 61
calcium oxide, 202
California, 84, 150, 176, 177, 237; anti-tax movement in, 167; desalination in, 227, 233–37; drought in, 211, 212, 233, 241–42; effluent used in, 190, 192, 193, 195, 196, 210, 213–14, 239; NDMA reported in, 108–9; reverse osmosis in, 206, 211, 214–15, 216, 233, 234; upgrading and centralization in, 288; utility rates in, 227, 236
Canada, 263
Canal de l'Ourcq, 34
canals, 3, 148, 178, 217
Canary Islands, 224, 227

cancer: Ames test and, 101; disinfection byproducts linked to, 95, 100,
103, 110–11, 210, 213; MX linked to,
103, 160; NDMA linked to, 162; in
New Orleans, 91–92, 97, 100, 154,
276; trihalomethanes linked to, 97
canneries, 72, 83
carbon offsets, 234
carbon tetrachloride, 92
Caribbean, 222, 223
Carlsbad, Calif., 234–37
Carr, Bob, 228
Carson, Rachel, 86, 141
castellum divisorium, 9, 117
cast iron, 99, 113
Catskill Mountains, 176
cattails, 259
cellulose acetate, 208, 223
Central Arizona Project, 178
centralized water systems, 254–56,
259, 261, 273, 274; annexation and,
85; breaking free of, 243–44, 245,
253, 258, 265; decentralized systems
combined with, 245, 270; as durable
design principle, 238–39, 254;
economics of, 243, 263, 264, 278;
innovations in, 277; in Israel, 226,
237; reformers' advocacy of, 63.
See also decentralized water
systems
Central Valley, Calif., 176
cesspools, 11, 23, 24, 25, 31, 35, 39, 80
Chadwick, Edwin, 32–33, 34, 37, 63
chamber pots, 16, 21
Chandler, Charles F., 45–46
Chanute, Kan., 199
charge repulsion, 53
Chattahoochee River, 150
Chelsea Waterworks, 32

Chicago, 92, 147, 176; growth of,
41–42, 70, 75; sewage re-routed by,
65, 66, 70; sewers upgraded in, 123,
126; stockyards in, 42, 59–60
Chicago Sanitary and Ship Canal, 65
Chile, 40
China, 24–25, 267
chloramines, 104–5, 107, 108, 109,
169, 184
chlorination, 93, 95, 97, 105, 189, 190,
199, 202, 206; in blending process,
124; bromines linked to, 96;
byproducts of, 158–61, 184, 210, 213,
238; early use of, 58–59; filtration
combined with, 60–61, 63, 153, 158,
198, 238; geosmin impervious to,
201; incomplete knowledge of,
61–62; lead concentrations and, 107,
110; low cost of, 59, 61; microbial
growth checked by, 98–99, 104, 109;
mutagenicity linked to, 100–101,
102–3; ozonation and, 109–10, 111;
in septic systems, 255; taste affected
by, 100, 109, 161; trihalomethanes
increased by, 98
chlorofluorocarbons, 94
chloroform, 92, 93, 95, 96
cholera, x, 22, 91; in American cities,
41, 72; in London, 30–32, 44, 48, 56,
58; prevention of, 52, 56, 62
chromatography, 93
cigarette smoke, 101
Cincinnati, 42, 55, 147
cisterns, 2, 15, 135
class actions, 91
clay, 53, 54, 134, 266
cleaning products, 262
Clean Water Act (1972), 88, 121,
122–23, 165, 184

distilleries, 65

drip irrigation, 264, 279

drought, vii, 15; in ancient Rome, 9, 13; in Australia, 166, 227, 231, 276; in California, 211, 212, 233, 241–42; climate change and, 170, 180–84; effluent used during, 199, 202; in Las Vegas, 249; in London, 33; plants resistant to, 133, 188; in Texas, 150

dual distribution systems, 190, 192, 194–99, 228, 254

Dublin, 18

East Bay Municipal Utility District (EBMUD), 171

East Jersey Water Company, 60

eggshells, 142, 152

Ehgraben, 22

electricity, 174–75, 176, 178, 179

electron capture detector, 93–94

El Paso, Texas, 209

Emu Downs Wind Farm, 228

endocrine disruption, 141–42, 151, 185, 238

energy consumption: activated sludge and, 175; of boiling, 57–58; conservation vs., 240–50; cost to utilities of, 174–75, 185; of desalination, 207, 219, 220, 222, 224, 225; of green roofs, 133; of pumps, 175–76, 179, 225, 277; of reverse osmosis, 207; variability of, 176–78

Energy Policy Act (1992), 243

England, 23, 78

entrainment, 229–30

Environmental Defense Fund, 91, 96–97, 100

environmental movement, 86, 90

Environmental Protection Agency: lead exposure regulated by, 105; New Orleans problems detected by, 91, 92, 93; nitrogen and phosphorus regulated by, 185; ocean dumping regulated by, 211–12; sewer systems regulated by, 122, 123–25, 130, 132, 137; trihalomethanes regulated by, 96–98, 99, 103, 104

Erbil, Iraq, 1

erosion, 128, 131

estradiol, 140–41, 143, 158, 159

estrogen: conversion of, 158–59; degradability of, 154; fish exposed to, 141–42, 143, 144, 145, 151, 152

ethinyl estradiol, 143–44, 145, 158, 159

Etruscans, 114

European Union, 104

Expedition of Humphrey Clinker, The (Smollett), 29

fathead minnow, 145

faucets, 243, 246, 247

feces, 30–31, 48, 71–72, 259–60, 268; as fertilizer, 16, 21, 23, 24, 25, 27, 35, 39, 79

ferric chloride, 54

fertilizer: animal waste as, 23; human waste as, 16, 21, 24, 25, 27, 35, 39, 79; mineral, 33, 40; synthetic, 33, 63; urine as, 12, 24

filtration, 32, 48–49, 62, 99, 104, 202; chlorination combined with, 60–61, 63, 153, 158, 198, 238; geosmin impervious to, 201; intermittent, 50, 77; sand, 50–55, 56–57, 59, 190, 270; trickling, 77–78, 80, 115, 189; ultra-, 111

Finland, 102

173; in London, 29; in reverse-
osmosis plants, 207; for sewage,
25, 33, 179; in water treatment
plants, 55

qanats, 1

rain gardens, 134, 137, 278, 279
rainbow trout, 144
rainwater, 15, 34, 60, 145, 227; in
    drainage systems, 112–18, 131–35;
    groundwater recharged by, 113,
    127; sewage diluted by, 115–16,
    147, 158
rapid sand filtration, 54, 55, 158, 276
rationing, 9, 183, 277
rebate programs, 240, 242, 246, 247
recontamination, 98
recycling, 13, 187–88, 217, 221, 223, 245,
    276, 278
Redwood City, Calif., 196–98
refineries, 190
reject stream (brine), 208–9, 230–31,
    235
religious objections, 215
Resources for the Future, 91
reuse, 187–99, 221, 227–28, 253–54, 259,
    261–65, 280
reverse osmosis: in California, 206,
    211, 214–15, 216, 233, 234; cost of, 184,
    207, 214, 250; in desalination, 207,
    208, 209, 223–25, 227, 230–31, 276;
    outlook for, 231–32, 239; roofwater
    treated by, 268; urban runoff
    treated by, 271
revolving funds, 165–66
Rhine River, 145, *146*
Rio Hondo, 200
River Lee, 28

River Thames, 26, 27, 30, 31, 32, 33,
    40, 140
Rocky Mountains, 180
Rogers, James, 250
Rome, 244; ancient, x, 1–13, 114, 179,
    238, 267
roofs, 133–34
roofwater, 267–70, 278
Rook, Johannes, 93, 94, 96, 102, 159
Roosevelt, Theodore, 71
Rotterdam, 93, 94, 159
Rowland, Sherwood, 94
runoff, 114, 117, 127, 128, 158, 172, 185; in
    American cities, 53, 119, 200;
    climate change and, 180; from
    farms, 87, 92; in London, 28–29;
    new approaches to, 132–36, 138, 238,
    239, 244, 270, 271; in Paris, 34, 37;
    pollutants in, 28–29, 53, 87, 92, 119,
    130, 131, 198, 271; in Singapore, 272.
    See also storm sewers

saccharin, 154
Safe Drinking Water Act (1974), 92,
    96, 97, 111, 184, 209, 213
St. Louis, 48–49, 53, 65, 92, 147, 176
St. Petersburg, Fla., 194–95, 197–98,
    253
Salinas Valley, Calif., 193
salmon, 152
Salmonella typhi, 44, 45, 48, 51
salt, 8, 218; marine life sensitive to, 72,
    230; plants sensitive to, 191, 193, 262;
    in reject water, 230–31, 235; in River
    Thames, 27; taste of, 207–8, 209,
    223. *See also* desalination; seawater
Salt River, 150
Sand County Almanac, A
    (Leopold), 81